.CCH

a Wolters Kluwer business

P9-CQB-448

Introduction to Federal Income Taxation in Canada: Fundamentals

Study Guide

CCH Canadian Limited
300-90 Sheppard Avenue East
Toronto Ontario
M2N 6X1
1 800 268 4522
www.cch.ca

2009-2010

By
Robert E. Beam, F.C.A.
Professor Emeritus, University of Waterloo
Stanley N. Laiken, Ph.D.
Deloitte Professor, University of Waterloo
James J. Barnett, F.C.A.
Director of the School of Accounting and Finance,
University of Waterloo

Contributing Editors
Lisa M. Feil, CGA
Shirley Lamarre, CGA

Contributors
Ling Chu, M.Tax
Wilfrid Laurier University
Julie Robson, M.Acc., C.A.
University of Waterloo
Barbara Rockx, M.Acc., C.A.
University of Toronto and University of Waterloo
Michael Zender, B.Comm., LLB
Ernst & Young, Chartered Accountants, Toronto

Published by CCH Canadian Limited

ISBN: 978-1-55496-050-7

Typeset by CCH Canadian Limited.
Printed in Canada.

About This Study Guide

The purpose of this study guide is to provide you with an effective tool for finding problem material related to the topic you are studying. The Learning Chart found in each chapter aligns the topics covered in that chapter with example problems, review questions, multiple choice questions, exercises, and assignment problems (which are found in the textbook) so that you can easily find either the commentary or problem material related to a particular tax issue. For example, for the Chapter 1 topic "Determination of Income and Taxable Income" (¶1,260), there are three items related to this topic: an Example Problem, Exercise 2, and Assignment Problem 2.

This study guide also contains the solutions to the following problem material:

- Review Questions
- Multiple Choice Questions
- Exercises

The solutions to the Assignment Problems are not provided, as many instructors use them for hand-in assignments for grading.

Study Tips: Throughout the Study Guide, you will find a number of tips to help you get the most out of your study time.

Study Notes: Space has been provided in the Study Guide for you to write your own notes.

How the Text is Organized

The study of Canadian federal income taxation is made more complex, particularly at the introductory level, not because of the lack of good interpretive materials to guide the student, but, in the authors' opinion, because of the lack of organization in the presentation of these materials for systematic study. While the *Income Tax Act* (the Act), the statute governing the federal taxation of income in Canada, is organized generally by source of income, interpretive material available to students at the introductory level is often organized by topics which may cover elements of several sources.

Since the authors of these materials feel that it is important to the understanding of the Act that the student generally studies the major provisions of the statute in sequence, the chapters of this book generally follow the organization of the Act. The purpose of these materials is to guide the student in the study at the introductory level of the major provisions of the Act and some of the related provisions in the *Excise Tax Act* (the ETA) pertaining to the Goods and Services Tax. A copy of the Act plus the Canada Revenue Agency's (CRA's) Interpretation Bulletins, Information Circulars, and Advance Tax Rulings are considered to be important materials for the course. The purpose is to organize the student's reference to interpretive material in the order of presentation in the Act. This book is designed to encourage students to refer to the Act, case law, and the CRA's publications. CRA publications are available at no charge on the CRA website: www.cra-arc.gc.ca.

The Importance of Problem Material

The commentary presented in this book highlights key areas of the Act. The textbook provides additional interpretation of particularly difficult provisions of the Act or elements of the common law or case law in the area. The basic concepts and principles underlying the rules of the legislation are emphasized throughout these materials. Most important for the study of income taxation, it provides fact situations or example problems which demonstrate the application of the provisions of the Act to realistic situations. In fact, the primary teaching approach used in this commentary is the presentation of example problems and exercises with solutions. These solutions demonstrate various methods of approaching actual problems in income taxation. The solutions also provide explanatory and interpretive notes, which are an important component of these materials, often expanding a topic beyond the confines of the particular facts under discussion.

These materials are designed to present situations which will help students to focus their attention on the reading and understanding of a particular provision or set of provisions with the objective of developing more generalized skills to be used in the interpretation of the Act.

References

References are provided in the outer margin of the text beside the paragraphs to which they pertain. These references are to the following sources:

1. ITA refers to the sections of the *Income Tax Act* to be discussed in the chapter;
2. ITAR refers to the *Income Tax Application Rules, 1971,* which are found in the volume containing the Act immediately following the provisions of the Act;
3. ITR refers to the Income Tax Regulations which are also found in the volume containing the Act;
4. ETA refers to sections of the *Excise Tax Act* in which provisions of the Goods and Services Tax (GST) can be found;
5. IT, IC, TR, and ATR refer, respectively, to Interpretation Bulletins, Information Circulars, Tax Rulings, and Advance Tax Rulings — Second Series, and are available in a one-volume softcover edition published by CCH Canadian Limited;
6. Cda-U.S. TT refers to the *Canada-United States Income Tax Convention (1980)*; and
7. Doc refers to documents released by the federal government under *Access to Information* legislation and contained in the Tax Window Files of CCH Canadian's Tax Library.

An explanation of these references is provided in Chapter 1. References to sections of the Act are provided for exercises and assignment problems. It should also be understood that in the course of their use within the paragraph of the text, all references preceded by such specific terms as "section", "subsection", "paragraph", "subparagraph", etc., without any indication of the pertinent statute, refer to the provisions of the *Income Tax Act*. Similarly, the provisions of the Income Tax Regulations are preceded by the term "Regulation" without specifying the relevant legislation. In the margin, these references are preceded by "ITA" and "ITR", respectively.

References to the *Excise Tax Act* are usually confined to the GST part of a chapter and are specifically indicated as being to that legislation. References in the margin are preceded by "ETA". An attempt has been made to integrate GST with relevant transactions discussed under the *Income Tax Act* in the chapters where these transactions are discussed.

Review Questions

A set of review questions is provided at the end of each chapter. These short-answer questions attempt to review key points made in the text or points that are not integrated into the example problems, multiple choice questions, exercises, or assignment problems in the chapter. Discussion notes on the review questions are provided in the Study Guide.

Multiple Choice Questions

Since multiple choice questions are common in professional examinations, this textbook provides six or seven such questions covering the material in each chapter, starting with Chapter 2, for a total of over 100 questions. Annotated solutions are provided in the Study Guide to enhance learning through self-study.

Exercises

Exercises have been provided at the end of each chapter. These usually consist of short problems to highlight particular areas of the chapter. They are designed to be fairly narrow in scope, to provide the student with an opportunity to apply the material in the chapter to a specific problem situation. Solutions to these exercises have been provided in the Study Guide.

Assignment Problems

Assignment problems are provided for each chapter of these materials. These problems are designed to have the student apply the material discussed in each chapter to an actual fact or problem situation. While these problems focus on the key elements of the chapter in much the same way that the solved example problems in the commentary do, the problems are not identical in their coverage or presentation. As a result, it will be necessary for the student to read the assignment problems very carefully in preparing a solution. Solutions to these problems are not available.

Suggested Approach

The authors suggest the following approach to the use of these materials. First, the students should identify the issue they need to research and then scan the headings of the particular chapter and look for the topics that relate to that issue. Once the relevant parts of the chapter are identified, students should read the commentary, including any referenced material such as sections of the Act or Regulations, Interpretation Bulletins, Information Circulars, and Advance Tax Rulings. Reviewing any example problems to see how the provisions work will also help develop understanding. The solutions provided for these problems will demonstrate the approach that can be taken for the type of example problem under consideration. The solutions can also be used as a check on the student's understanding as well as a means of providing further interpretation and explanation of the material covered. The exercises at the end of the chapter can be used in a similar manner. Once the parts of a chapter have been completed in this manner, the student should be sufficiently prepared to attempt the assignment problems relevant to a particular part or to the whole chapter. When reviewing material for examination or other purposes, the multiple choice questions at the end of each chapter can be attempted. The solutions in the Study Guide can then be checked. Review might also focus on the approaches used to address the various types of problems presented.

Learning Goals

To be a successful tax adviser it is not enough to just know the technical material found in the Act and supporting materials. You need to understand the purpose behind the rules so you can explain to others why your tax plan does not violate either the provision as it is written or purpose behind the provision. You also need to be able to blend a number of complex provisions into a comprehensive plan to accomplish the goals of your client or employer. As shown in the learning model below, you need to know the technical provisions and understand them well enough to be able to craft a comprehensive plan. The end goal is the successful application of knowledge and understanding.

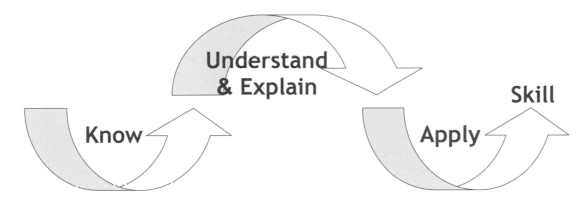

In each chapter of this book we will provide you with what you should Know, Understand & Explain, and Apply as a result of studying that chapter.

Materials at the introductory level on Canadian income tax legislation are not easy to study. A conscientious effort to do the work and, particularly, to do problems and apply what has been read is essential to a good understanding of this material. The authors have attempted to meet the challenge of presenting the material by setting out the work that must be done and by explaining, as best they can, the major provisions of the legislation. The challenge of learning the material is, of course, left to the student.

Toronto, Ontario   Robert E. Beam
Waterloo, Ontario   Stanley N. Laiken
Waterloo, Ontario   James J. Barnett

July 2009

Table of Contents

Chapter 1
Introduction

LEARNING GOALS

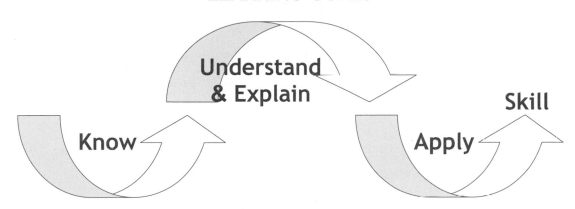

Know

By the end of this chapter you should know some of the history of income tax in Canada and how the *Income Tax Act* and the *Excise Tax Act* (pertaining to the goods and services tax) are structured, interpreted, and administered.

Understand and Explain

You should understand and be able to explain how to find what you need in the Act and how to put together the calculation of income for tax purposes and taxable income. In addition, you should be able to explain how to interpret tax legislation. Completing the Exercises (¶1,850) is a good way to deepen your understanding of the material.

Apply

You should be able to use your general knowledge and understanding of the calculation of income and the interpretation of tax laws to put together the calculation of income and taxable income and to find the meaning of certain words and phrases in the *Income Tax Act*. Completing the Assignment Problems (¶1,875) is an excellent way to develop your ability to apply the material in increasingly complex situations.

Chapter 1 — Learning Chart

Topic	Example Problem (✓)	Review Questions (N/A)	Multiple Choice (N/A)	Exercises (¶1,850)	Assignment Problems (¶1,875)
¶1,000 BACKGROUND AND INTRODUCTION					
¶1,001 History and Legislation—Canadian Tax System					
¶1,010 Brief history of the Income Tax Act					
¶1,015 Constitutional basis for income taxation					
¶1,020 Introduction to Income Tax Legislation					
¶1,021 The federal budgetary process					
¶1,022 Public submissions for change or amendment					
¶1,023 Adoption of specific proposals					
¶1,024 Federal Budget presentation to the House of Commons					
¶1,025 Passage of law					
¶1,030 Tax Principles and Concepts					
¶1,035 Classification of taxes					
¶1,040 Desirable characteristics of an income tax					
¶1,045 Tax reform guidelines					
¶1,100 STRUCTURE OF THE INCOME TAX ACT AND INTERPRETATION					
¶1,110 The Income Tax Act					
¶1,115 How do I reference the Act?					
¶1,120 Structure of the Income Tax Act				1	1
¶1,121 Parts I and I.2 — Income tax and tax on OAS benefits					
¶1,122 Special transaction taxes					
¶1,123 Non-residents					
¶1,124 Administration and interpretation					
¶1,130 Related References					
¶1,131 Historical footnotes					
¶1,132 Related matters					
¶1,133 Draft legislation: Pending amendments					
¶1,134 Income Tax Application Rules					
¶1,135 International tax conventions or treaties					
¶1,136 Income Tax Regulations					
¶1,140 Other Interpretive Sources					
¶1,141 Judicial decisions (common law)					
¶1,142 Forms					
¶1,143 CRA publications					
¶1,144 Technical notes and explanations					
¶1,145 Generally accepted accounting principles					
¶1,150 Interpretation of tax legislation					3
¶1,151 Precision					

Topic	Example Problem (✓)	Review Questions (N/A)	Multiple Choice (N/A)	Exercises (¶1,850)	Assignment Problems (¶1,875)
¶1,152 Plain and obvious meaning					
¶1,153 Intention of Parliament					
¶1,154 Remission orders					
¶1,155 Recent developments					
¶1,156 Form versus substance					
¶1,157 Exceptions override general					
¶1,158 Specific words followed by general					
¶1,159 Precedents					
¶1,160 Interpretation Act					
¶1,180 AREAS OF PRACTICE AND THE ROLE OF THE PROFESSIONAL ACCOUNTANT					
¶1,185 Why Study Taxation?					
¶1,190 The Practice of Taxation					
¶1,191 Compliance					
¶1,192 Legal interpretation					
¶1,193 Tax appeals and tax litigation					
¶1,194 Tax planning					
¶1,195 The Role of the Professional Accountant in Tax Matters					
¶1,200 INTRODUCTION TO INCOME TAX AND TAXABLE INCOME					
¶1,210 Approaches to Defining Income					
¶1,212 Income versus capital					
¶1,215 The economist's perspective					
¶1,220 The role of generally accepted accounting principles					
¶1,225 The doctrine of constructive receipt					
¶1,240 Computation of Income					
¶1,245 Aggregation formula					
¶1,250 Sourcing or tracing of income					
¶1,260 Determination of Income and Taxable Income	✓			2	2
¶1,300 GENERAL BACKGROUND ON ADMINISTRATION AND ENFORCEMENT OF THE ACT					
¶1,310 Onus of Proof					
¶1,320 Appeals					
¶1,325 Initial steps					
¶1,330 Tax Court of Canada					
¶1,335 Federal Court of Appeal					
¶1,340 Supreme Court of Canada					
¶1,350 Administration and Enforcement					
¶1,360 Tax Evasion, Avoidance, and Planning					
¶1,400 INTRODUCTION TO THE GOODS AND SERVICES TAX (GST)					
¶1,410 Overview and Basic Concepts					
¶1,420 Supplies					

Topic	Example Problem (✓)	Review Questions (N/A)	Multiple Choice (N/A)	Exercises (¶1,850)	Assignment Problems (¶1,875)
¶1,425 Zero-rated supplies					
¶1,430 Exempt supplies					
¶1,440 Input Tax Credits					
¶1,450 Note on Organization of Legislation and Availability of Interpretive Sources					
¶1,455 Excise Tax Act structure — Parts					
¶1,460 Structure of Part IX of the Excise Tax Act — GST legislation					
¶1,465 Schedules to the Excise Tax Act					
¶1,470 Reform of the GST and Provincial Harmonization					

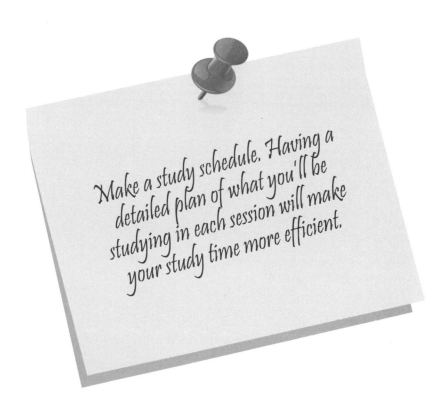

Make a study schedule. Having a detailed plan of what you'll be studying in each session will make your study time more efficient.

Study Notes

Chapter 1 — Solutions to Exercises

Exercise 1

The following summary is discussed in more detail below:

Case	Topic	Part	Division	Subdivision	Provision
(A)	Taxable capital gain	I	B	c	paragraph 38(*a*)
(B)	Membership dues	I	B	a	subparagraph 8(1)(*i*)(i)
(C)	Personal injury award	I	B	g	paragraph 81(1)(*g*.1)
(D)	Expense limit	I	B	f	section 67
(E)	Parent	XVII	—	—	subsection 252(2)
(F)	*Inter vivos* trust	I	B	k	subsection 108(1)
(G)	Filing deadline	I	I	—	paragraph 150(1)(*b*)
(H)	Shareholder benefit	I	B	b	subsection 15(1)
(I)	Non-arm's length	I	B	f	paragraph 69(1)(*b*)
(J)	Investment fees	I	B	b	paragraph 20(1)(*bb*)

(A) Part I, Division B, Subdivision c, paragraph 38(*a*): — Most definitions applicable to the Taxable Capital Gains and Allowable Capital Losses subdivision of Part I, Division B are found in section 54. However, this definition is set out at the beginning of Subdivision c. Definitions of terms used throughout the Act are found in subsection 248(1). If a term is not specifically defined in subsection 248(1) or in a section elsewhere in the Act, judicial precedents should be consulted for the meaning of the word.

(B) Part I, Division B, Subdivision a, subparagraph 8(1)(*i*)(i): — Employment income and deductions are set out in sections 5 to 8 of Part I, Division B, Subdivision a of the Act. All deductions from this source appear in section 8 with the major list of deductions occurring in subsection 8(1) and further explanation or restriction of these deductions appearing in subsections 8(2) to 8(11).

(C) Part I, Division B, Subdivision g, paragraph 81(1)(*g*.1): — Income from property acquired as personal injury award is one in a limited list of items found in section 81 which are not included in computing income.

(D) Part I, Division B, Subdivision f, section 67: — Inclusions and deductions in the computation of income are generally found in Part I, Division B, Subdivisions a, b, c, d or e. In this case, however, the rule is found in Subdivision f dealing with general rules relating to the computation of income from all sources.

(E) Part XVII, subsection 252(2): — The word "parent" appears throughout the Act, so the definition is most likely to be in Part XVII on "Interpretation."

(F) Part I, Division B, Subdivision k, subsection 108(1): — Trusts and their beneficiaries are dealt with in Subdivision k of Part I, Division B. The definitions section for this subdivision is section 108.

(G) Part I, Division I, paragraph 150(1)(*b*): This is a procedural matter generally handled in Division I of Part I of the Act dealing with Returns, Assessments, Payment and Appeals.

(H) Part I, Division B, Subdivision b, subsection 15(1): — A benefit received by a shareholder, if it is to be taxed, would likely be income from property which is handled in Subdivision b of Division B of Part I. Inclusions from that source are generally listed in sections 12 to 17.

(I) Part I, Division B, Subdivision f, paragraph 69(1)(*b*): — This provision can be found in the set of general rules pertaining to the computation of income in Subdivision f of Division B of Part I because it affects the computation of income from a variety of sources.

(J) Part I, Division B, Subdivision b, paragraph 20(1)(*bb*): — Investments provide income from property and deductions from such income are generally listed in subsection 20(1).

Exercise 2

DIVISION B

Par. 3(*a*)	*Subdivision a*			
	Sec. 5	Salary	$ 60,000	
	Par. 6(1)(*c*)	Director's fees	5,000	
	Ssec. 6(9)	Imputed interest	3,000	$ 68,000
	Less:			
	Par. 8(1)(*i*)	Professional engineering fees	$ 300	

Par. 8(1)(*m*)	Registered pension plan contributions . . .		4,000	4,300
				$ 63,700

Subdivision b

Sec. 9	Business income — share of partnership tax profits		$ 10,000	
Par. 12(1)(*c*)	Canadian bank interest		3,000	13,000

Subdivision d

Par. 56(1)(*a*)	Retiring allowance		20,000
	Total par. 3(*a*) income		$ 96,700

Par. 3(*b*) *Subdivision c*

Par. 38(*a*)	Taxable capital gain		$ 20,000	
Par. 38(*b*)	Allowable capital loss		(2,000)	18,000
				$114,700

Par. 3(*d*) *Subdivision b*

Ssec. 9(2):	Rental loss			
	Rental revenue		$ 25,000	
	Less: Expenses			
	Par. 20(1)(*c*)	Mortgage interest . . .	(23,000)	
	Par. 18(1)(*a*)	Taxes and insurance	(4,500)	
	Par. 18(1)(*a*)	Maintenance	(1,500)	(4,000)

Division B income			$110,700
Par. 110(1)(*j*)	Home relocation interest deduction	$ 1,000	
Par. 111(1)(*a*)	Non-capital loss	3,000	
Par. 111(1)(*b*)	Net capital loss	5,000	(9,000)
	Taxable income		$101,700

Federal tax after credits

Tax before credits		$ 20,333

Sec. 118	Personal credits		(3,096)
Sec. 118.7	CPP contributions credit		(318)
Sec. 118.7	EI premium credit		(110)
Sec. 118.5	Tuition credit		(68)
Sec. 118.6	Education and textbook credit transfer		(80)
Sec. 118.1	Charitable donation credit		(550)

Basic federal tax		$ 16,111

Chapter 2
Liability for Tax

LEARNING GOALS

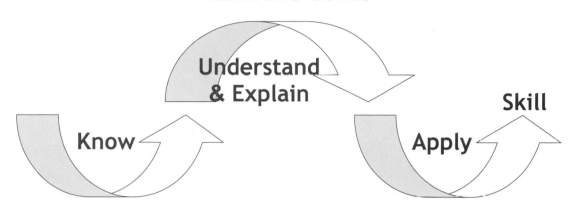

Know

By the end of this chapter you should know the basic provisions of the *Income Tax Act*, *Excise Tax Act*, and case law that relate to liability for tax and residency. Completing the Review Questions (¶2,800) and Multiple Choice Questions (¶2,825) is a good way to learn the technical provisions.

Understand and Explain

You should understand and be able to explain when an individual or a corporation is resident in Canada and whether they are liable for income tax or GST. Completing the Exercises (¶2,850) is a good way to deepen your understanding of the material.

Apply

You should be able to use your knowledge and understanding of residency and liability for income tax in a practical fact situation to determine whether a person is or is not liable for income tax. Completing the Assignment Problems (¶2,875) and the Advisory Case (¶2,880) is an excellent way to develop your ability to apply the material in increasingly complex situations.

Chapter 2 — Learning Chart

Topic	Example Problem (✓)	Review Questions (¶2,800)	Multiple Choice (¶2,825)	Exercises (¶2,850)	Assignment Problems (¶2,875)
¶2,000 LIABILITY OF INDIVIDUALS FOR INCOME TAX		1			
¶2,010 Liability of Individual Residents					
¶2,020 Full-Time Residence		3			
¶2,025 Deemed full-time residence					
¶2,030 Common law concept of full-time residence		2, 5	1, 2	1, 2, 3, 4	
¶2,035 Administrative practice					
¶2,040 Part-Year Residence		2, 5			
¶2,045 Applicable law					
¶2,050 Clean break or fresh start: The concept			4		
¶2,055 Liability of Non-Residents					
¶2,060 General determination of liability		9	3		
¶2,065 The meaning of carrying on business in Canada		4, 10, 11, 12			
¶2,070 International Tax Treaties and Individuals					
¶2,075 Services		15			
¶2,080 Resident and "tie-breaker" rules		13			
¶2,085 Permanent establishment					
¶2,090 Summary of the Residence Issue for an Individual					
¶2,100 Comprehensive Consideration of the Residence of an Individual					
¶2,105 Stages of involvement					
¶2,110 Consider both sides					
¶2,115 Form of advice					
¶2,120 Application	✓				
¶2,130 Non-Tax Factors Affecting Planning for the Residence of an Individual					
¶2,200 LIABILITY OF CORPORATIONS FOR INCOME TAX					
¶2,210 Charging Provision					
¶2,220 Residence of Corporations		6, 7, 8, 14	1	3	5
¶2,225 Deemed residence					
¶2,230 Common law concept of corporate residence					
¶2,240 Liability of Non-Resident Corporations				4	6, 7, 8
¶2,250 International Tax Treaties and Corporations					
¶2,260 Comprehensive Consideration of the Residence of a Corporation	✓				
¶2,300 REGISTRATION REQUIREMENTS AND LIABILITY FOR THE GOODS AND SERVICES TAX					
¶2,310 Liability for GST			6		
¶2,315 Supplies in Canada					

Topic	Example Problem (✓)	Review Questions (¶2,800)	Multiple Choice (¶2,825)	Exercises (¶2,850)	Assignment Problems (¶2,875)
¶2,320 Supplies by non-residents					
¶2,330 Registration Requirements for Residents					
¶2,335 Test for registration					
¶2,340 Definition of commercial activity					
¶2,345 Exclusions from commercial activity					
¶2,350 Exceptions from the registration requirements					
¶2,360 Registration and Collection Requirements for Non-Residents					
¶2,365 Meaning of non-resident					
¶2,370 Mandatory registration					
¶2,375 Voluntary registration					
¶2,380 Imports					

CHAPTER 2

Studying at the same time every day establishes a routine that becomes a regular part of your life. When the scheduled study time arrives, your mind and body will be prepared.

Study Notes

Chapter 2 —
Discussion Notes for Review Questions

(1) Canadian individuals are taxed based on residency and not their citizenship. Canadian residents are taxed on their world income.   ITA: 2(1)

(2) He or she will be deemed to be a resident only if he or she sojourned in Canada for 183 or more days during the year.   ITA: 250(1)

(3) You need to look at other factors to determine where they have a "continuing state of relationship", such as family and social ties and other personal property. The Interpretation Bulletin categorizes the type of facts that can be used to establish residential ties.   IT-221R3

(4) He or she would be considered to be a non-resident of Canada throughout the year. However, since he or she carried on business in Canada during the year while a non-resident, he or she would be taxable in Canada on his or her Canadian business profits for the year.   ITA: 2(3)

(5) If he or she is establishing a "fresh start" in Canada on March 31 then he or she becomes resident on that date and is taxed in Canada on his or her world income from that date. The sojourning rules would not apply since they only apply to non-residents who are in Canada on a temporary basis.

(6) The residency of a corporation is either determined by the common law test of "central management and control", or a corporation is deemed to be a Canadian resident if it is incorporated in Canada after April 26, 1965, or it meets the tests outlined in the Act if it was incorporated before that date.   ITA: 250(4)

(7) A corporation is deemed to be resident in Canada if it was incorporated in Canada after April 26, 1965. Reference to the tax treaty would be the next step but Canada does not have a tax treaty with Bermuda. Therefore, it would be resident in Canada and taxable in Canada on its world income.   ITA: 250(4)(*a*)

(8) Any company which was incorporated in Canada before April 27, 1965 and which carried on business in Canada in any year after that date is deemed to be resident in Canada. An extended meaning of carrying on business includes soliciting orders in Canada. The facts fit the meaning because of the continuity of the order solicitation over a period of years. Therefore, the company would be resident in Canada and taxable in Canada on its world income.   ITA: 250(4)(*a*)
ITA: 253(*b*)

(9) Subsection 2(3) refers to "employed in Canada in the year or a previous year". Therefore, section 115 of Division D requires the income from an office or employment to be taxed in Canada.   ITA: 115(2)(*c*)

(10) While the income would be business income, it would not be income from "carrying on" business under normal circumstances, since this term implies some ongoing activity which does not exist in this case. However, since the land was offered for sale in Canada it may fit into the extended definition of carrying on business in Canada, but this is unlikely since, in order to fit into this "extended" definition, he or she first has to be "carrying on business" which he or she is not. Therefore, the transaction cannot be included in the extended definition and would not be taxable in Canada.   ITA: 253

(11) The U.S. company is soliciting orders in Canada and, therefore, is carrying on business in Canada. The corporation is, thus, taxable in Canada on the profits related to these sales.   ITA: 2(3), 115, 253

(12) Under the extended meaning of carrying on business, the company would be resident in Canada. However, under the Canada–U.S. tax treaty, the U.S. company would not have a permanent establishment in Canada and, therefore, would not be taxable here.   ITA: 253

(13) Yes, a person can be a resident of more than one country since residency is determined under the laws of each country. Article IV of the Canada–U.S. tax treaty provides rules for resolving who collects the tax where a person is a resident of both the U.S. and Canada.

(14) Under Article VII of the Canada–U.S. tax treaty, it will only be subject to tax on the income attributable to that permanent establishment.

(15) Article XIV of the Canada–U.S. tax treaty will cause him to be taxed in the U.S. only if he has a "fixed base regularly available to him" in the U.S. Therefore, he will only pay tax in Canada on this income.

Chapter 2 —
Solutions to Multiple Choice Questions

Question 1

(B) is correct. Since X Ltd. is not incorporated in Canada, it is not deemed to be resident in Canada. Since the directors are not resident in Canada, X Ltd. is not resident in Canada under the common law "central management and control" rule.   ITA: 250(4)

(A) is incorrect because X Ltd. is deemed to be resident.   ITA: 250(4)(*a*)

(C) is incorrect because X Ltd. is resident under the common law "central management and control" rule.

(D) is incorrect because X Ltd. is deemed to be resident; the common law "central management and control" rule would also apply.   ITA: 250(4)(*c*)

Question 2

(C) is correct. Generally, the CRA will consider the individual not to have severed residential ties within Canada if he has a dwelling available for occupancy.   IT-221R3, par. 6

(A) is incorrect, because taking his wife and children with him to Germany is not feasible, since the couple is legally separated and the children are not dependent on him for support.   IT-221R3, par. 7

(B) is incorrect, because giving up Canadian citizenship has little relevance in determining residency.

(D) is incorrect. Although putting all his household furniture and personal effects into storage in Canada is a residential tie, the tie is a weaker one than that cited in (C).   IT-221R3, par. 8

Question 3

(B) is correct. Only the $50,000 of employment income earned in Canada would be reported on Mr. N's Canadian personal income tax return for the year.   ITA: 2(3), 115

(A) is incorrect. The $10,000 interest, earned by the non-resident, is not taxable under Part I. However, the interest would be subject to Part XIII tax withheld at source.

(C) is incorrect for the same reason as (A).

(D) is incorrect, because only residents of Canada are subject to Canadian income tax on their worldwide income.   ITA: 2(1)

Question 4

(C) is correct. Because Jay ceased to be a resident of Canada on April 30 of the year, only his worldwide income during the first four months of the year ($26,000 = $25,000 + $1,000) is subject to tax in Canada under Part I and would be reported on his Canadian personal income tax return for the year.   ITA: 2(1), 114

(A) includes income earned while not a resident of Canada: $58,000 = $25,000 + $1,000 + $30,000 + $2,000. The $30,000 of employment income earned in New Zealand and the $2,000 of Canadian interest earned from May 1 to December 31 of the year are not subject to Part I tax because Jay is not resident in Canada at that time. The $2,000 of Canadian interest is subject to tax under Part XIII, not Part I. Tax is withheld at source under Part XIII — no return is filed.   ITA: 2(1), 114

(B) includes the salary earned in New Zealand: $56,000 = $25,000 + $1,000 + $30,000. As in (A), above, the $30,000 of employment income earned in New Zealand is not subject to tax in Canada.

(D) excludes the worldwide income earned while Jay was a resident in Canada. As discussed in (A), above, this would be reported on his Canadian personal income tax return for the year.   ITA: 2(1), 114

Question 5

(B) is correct. Judy is a non-resident. She seems to have severed her residential ties to Canada (moving her belongings) and established new ties to London, England (buying a house).

(A) is incorrect. James is still a resident of Canada. There is no indication that James has severed his residential ties to Canada or established ties to London, England.

(C) is incorrect. Since ERT Limited was incorporated in Canada after April 26, 1965, it is deemed to   ITA: 250(4)(*a*)
be a resident of Canada.

(D) is incorrect. Doug is deemed to be a resident of Canada because he is a member of the Canadian   ITA: 250(1)(*b*)
armed forces.

Question 6

(C) is correct.

Sales (taxable at 5%)................................$250,000
Purchase of supplies from a registrant 30,000
$\underline{\underline{\$220,000}} \times 5\% = \$11,000.$

(A) incorrectly takes a deduction for salaries which is an exempt supply: $250,000 – $30,000 – $70,000 = $150,000. $150,000 × 5% = $7,500.

(B) incorrectly takes a deduction for interest expense: $250,000 – $30,000 – $20,000 = $200,000. $200,000 × 5% = $10,000.

(D) incorrectly includes exports (which are zero-rated) and takes a deduction for interest expense (an exempt supply): $250,000 + $100,000 – $30,000 – $20,000 = $300,000. $300,000 × 5% = $15,000.

Chapter 2 — Solutions to Exercises

Exercise 1

(A) Alpha is a part-year resident of Canada until August 27 of the year when he appears to have made a "clean break" with Canada. While in Canada he would not have been sojourning, so the deeming rule would not apply.

ITA: 250(1)(*a*)

(B) Beta has no residential ties with Canada. Citizenship is not a determining factor in establishing such ties.

(C) Gamma is a non-resident of Canada and is taxable only on employment income earned in Canada.

ITA: 2(3)(*a*), 115(1)(*a*)(i)

(D) Delta is either a part-year resident of Canada or a non-resident employed in Canada, depending on the facts of his stay in Canada. He is also taxable under paragraph 2(3)(*c*) because the shares are taxable Canadian property.

ITA: 115(1)(*b*)(iv)

(E) Epsilon is deemed a resident of Canada because of his relationship to his mother.

ITA: 250(1)(*c*)(i), 250(1)(*f*)

(F) Mu is not deemed to be a resident of Canada by any of the deeming rules. She has never been resident in Canada. Therefore, she is not a resident of Canada.

ITA: 250(1)

Exercise 2

[See: *MacDonald v. M.N.R.*, 68 DTC 433 (T.A.B.).]

(A) The full-time residence option→taxed in Canada on worldwide income for full year:

ITA: 2(1)

Criterion: residence is a question of fact dependent on the degree of permanency in the relationship between a person and a place;

Evidence:

(i) factors indicating this relationship between the appellant and Canada,

1. he sold his house in the United States and paid an American capital gains tax for not buying another residence,

2. his wife, upon arriving in Canada, rented premises pending the purchase of a house,

3. she and the children, whom the appellant was supporting to the extent of $600 per month, stayed in Canada all year-round,

4. he stayed in Canada when he was off-duty to the extent of 166 out of 180 days in 1964,

— full-time presence is not necessary,

5. other non-determining factors,

— joint account in Canada where pay cheques were deposited during his vacations,

— joint ownership of a car with New Brunswick registry,

— citizenship irrelevant;

(ii) factors detracting from a relationship with Canada,

1. a few rooms, without exclusive use, made available for him at his sister's house in the United States,

— not a permanent abode,

— an individual can have more than one residence,

2. U.S. citizen and previously and subsequently resided in the United States with a stated intention to return,

— but only 1964 in question on the facts,

— stated intention must be supported by behavioural facts,

— worked for a U.S. company and paid in U.S. currency,

— but not determining because a Canadian resident can be involved in such a situation, providing employment services abroad for a non-Canadian company,

   — memberships and investments including bank accounts, securities and pension plan in United States,

     — factors may indicate U.S. residence, but not determining and also possible for a person resident in Canada,

   — no Canadian memberships or investments and no application for family allowances,

     — not determining factors and also possible of a Canadian resident,

   — children living in United States,

     — married and apparently not dependent,

   — phone in wife's name in Canada,

     — a factor, but hardly determining,

   — neither employed in Canada nor carrying on business in Canada,

     — not necessary condition for full-time residence.

(This list of factors is longer but there is more substance for full-time residence.)

(B) The deemed residence option→taxed in Canada on worldwide income for full year: ITA: 2(1)

Criterion: the condition of sojourning an aggregate of 183 days or more;   ITA: 250(1)

Evidence: his total stay in Canada in the year was only for 166 days; therefore, the condition is not met.

(C) The part-year residence option→taxed in Canada on worldwide income for part of the year   ITA: 2(1), 114, 118.91
resident in Canada with deductions applicable to the period of part-year residence and non-refundable tax credits either prorated for or applicable to the period of part-year residence (as long as not resident in Canada during some other part of the year);

Criterion: clean break or fresh start during 1964;

Evidence: neither occurred.

(D) The non-residence option→taxed in Canada on income earned in Canada: ITA: 2(3)

Criteria: employed in Canada, carried on business in Canada or disposed of taxable Canadian property in the year;

Evidence: none of these conditions occurred in the year.   ITA: 2(3)

(E) Conclusion: if the taxpayer is to be found a resident it must be as a full-time resident:

   — the major factors indicate a relationship with Canada which would warrant a conclusion of such resident status.

Exercise 3

(A) Inch Incorporated is resident in Canada by virtue of the common law principle of central   ITA: 250(4)
management and control. The corporation cannot be deemed resident in Canada because it was not incorporated in Canada.

(B) Foot Limited is deemed resident in Canada because it was incorporated in Canada after   ITA: 250(4)(*a*)
April 26, 1965.

(C) Yard Incorporated is not resident this year by virtue of the common law principle of central management and control. Furthermore, the corporation cannot be deemed resident in Canada because it was not incorporated in Canada.

(D) Mile Limited is resident in Canada. The corporation was incorporated in Canada before   ITA: 250(4)(*c*)
April 27, 1965 and after that time it was resident by virtue of the central management and control rule.

Exercise 4

Canada levies tax on non-residents who carry on business in Canada. Carrying on business in   ITA: 2(3)
Canada is distinguishable from carrying on business with Canada. While Sam-son solicits sales from Canadians, it does not have a permanent establishment in Canada, nor does it employ a Canadian salesperson or agent. Given these facts, Sam-son is not liable for Canadian income taxes on the $76,000 profit originating from within Canada.

Chapter 3
Employment Income

LEARNING GOALS

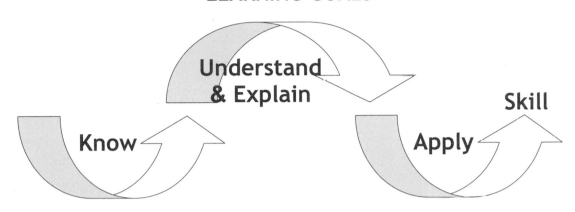

Understand & Explain

Skill

Know

Apply

Know

By the end of this chapter you should know the basic provisions of the *Income Tax Act* that relate to employment income and expenses. You should be able to calculate employment income and distinguish between a self-employed independent contractor and an employee. Completing the Review Questions (¶3,800) and Multiple Choice Questions (¶3,825) is a good way to learn the technical provisions.

Understand and Explain

You should understand and be able to explain how employment income and expenses are calculated and why the provisions are designed the way they are. Completing the Exercises (¶3,850) is a good way to deepen your understanding of the material.

Apply

You should be able to apply your knowledge and understanding of employment income and expenses to real life situations. Completing the Assignment Problems (¶3,875) is an excellent way to develop your ability to apply the material in increasingly complex situations.

Chapter 3 — Learning Chart

Topic	Example Problem (✓)	Review Questions (¶3,800)	Multiple Choice (¶3,825)	Exercises (¶3,850)	Assignment Problems (¶3,875)
¶3,000 BASIC RULES		1, 9			
¶3,010 Employed Versus Self-Employed or Independent Contractor	✓	2, 3		1, 2	1
¶3,015 Overview					
¶3,020 The economic reality or entrepreneur test		4			
¶3,025 Integration or organization test		5			
¶3,030 Specific result test		6			
¶3,035 Other considerations					
¶3,037 Defining the Taxation Year					
¶3,040 Salary, Wages, and Other Remuneration Including Gratuities					
¶3,050 Amounts Received		7, 8			3
¶3,060 Volunteer Services Exemption					
¶3,100 SPECIFIC INCLUSIONS		18			
¶3,110 Value of Board and Lodging					15
¶3,120 Other Fringe Benefits					
¶3,125 General rules				3, 7, 11	2, 3, 4, 10, 13, 15, 16
¶3,130 Housing loss and housing cost benefits				6	16
¶3,135 Employee loans	✓	11	4	8	2, 5, 8, 11, 15
¶3,140 Fringe benefits and administrative practice				3, 5	2, 3, 8, 10, 11, 13, 15, 16
¶3,150 Allowances					
¶3,155 Overview		12			2, 14, 15, 16
¶3,160 Exception of allowance for travelling expenses of sales/negotiating persons				14	
¶3,165 Exception of allowance for travelling expenses of other employees					16
¶3,170 Director's or Other Fees					8
¶3,180 Standby Charge and Operating Cost Benefit for Automobile Provided by Employer					
¶3,185 Calculation of the standby charge benefit from the use of the car itself		13	1	10	3, 6, 8, 13
¶3,190 Determining the operating cost benefit			1	10	3, 6, 8, 13
¶3,195 Summary of employer-provided automobile benefits					
¶3,200 Application of the rules	✓				6
¶3,210 Employee-Owned Automobile Operating Expense Benefit					
¶3,215 Vehicles Other Than Automobiles					
¶3,220 Benefit from Employer-Paid GST				15	

Topic	Example Problem (✓)	Review Questions (¶3,800)	Multiple Choice (¶3,825)	Exercises (¶3,850)	Assignment Problems (¶3,875)
¶3,230 Employment Insurance Benefits	✓	10			8, 10, 15
¶3,240 Payments by Employer to Employee	✓				9
¶3,250 Restrictive Covenants					
¶3,260 Stock Options					
¶3,265 General					
¶3,270 Rules applicable to stock options for all types of corporations					3, 4, 5, 10, 12, 14
¶3,275 Rules applicable to Canadian-controlled private corporations				9	16
¶3,280 Rules applicable to public corporations			5		3, 4, 5, 10, 12, 14
¶3,285 Valuation of shares					
¶3,287 Risk factors					
¶3,290 Summary	✓				
¶3,300 DEDUCTIONS FROM EMPLOYMENT INCOME					
¶3,310 Sales/Negotiating Person's Expenses		14	6	11, 13, 14	11, 12, 13, 14, 15
¶3,320 Any Employee's Travelling Expenses Other Than Motor Vehicle Expenses					
¶3,325 Overview					16
¶3,330 Conditions		15		14	16
¶3,335 Limitations				11, 13	12, 13, 14
¶3,340 Receipts by part-time employees for travelling expenses		16			
¶3,342 Dues and Other Expenses					10, 12, 14, 15
¶3,345 Work Space in Home		17	3	12	14
¶3,350 Other Expenses					
¶3,352 Legal expenses				4	
¶3,354 Clergy's residence					
¶3,356 Teacher's exchange fund					
¶3,358 Railway employees					
¶3,360 Transport employees					
¶3,362 CPP and EI premiums payable in respect of an assistant					
¶3,364 Retirement compensation arrangements					
¶3,366 Salary reimbursements					
¶3,368 Forfeitures					
¶3,370 Musical instrument costs					
¶3,372 Artist's expenses					
¶3,374 Tradesperson's tool expenses					
¶3,380 Registered Pension Plans					3, 10, 12, 13, 15, 16
¶3,385 Overview					

Topic	Example Problem (✓)	Review Questions (¶3,800)	Multiple Choice (¶3,825)	Exercises (¶3,850)	Assignment Problems (¶3,875)
¶3,400 SPECIFIC PROVISIONS FOR CAR ALLOWANCES AND EXPENSES					
¶3,410 Motor Vehicle Allowances Received from Employers					14
¶3,415 Overview					
¶3,420 Allowances for motor vehicles — Other persons					7, 8
¶3,425 Allowance deemed not to be reasonable			2		7, 8, 14
¶3,430 Expenses					
¶3,435 Overview				11	11, 14, 15, 16
¶3,440 Motor vehicle and aircraft — Interest and CCA				11, 14	11, 14, 15
¶3,445 Imputed interest deemed paid				8	11, 15
¶3,450 Interest on money borrowed for passenger vehicle					11, 14, 15
¶3,455 Capital cost for passenger vehicle				14	14, 15
¶3,460 Limitation re cost of leased passenger vehicle					14, 15, 16
¶3,465 Summary of interplay among deduction provisions					
¶3,470 Application of Rules	✓				
¶3,500 GST REBATE ON EMPLOYEE DEDUCTIONS	✓				16
¶3,600 APPLICATION OF RULES UNDER SUBDIVISION "A"	✓				

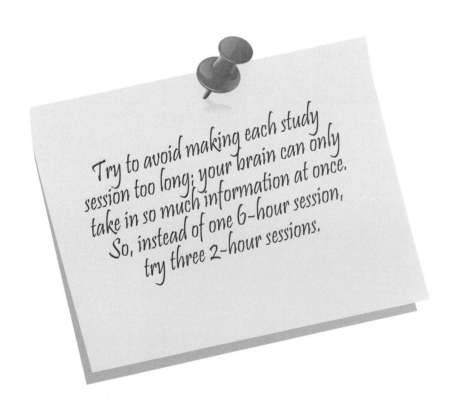

Try to avoid making each study session too long; your brain can only take in so much information at once. So, instead of one 6-hour session, try three 2-hour sessions.

Study Notes

Chapter 3 —
Discussion Notes for Review Questions

(1) The personal tax return (T1 General) does not include RPP contributions, union and professional dues and other paragraph 8(1)(*i*) deductions in the calculation of employment income. These are included under the heading "Net Income" in the personal tax return. It would be misleading to use the personal tax return format for this specific purpose, because certain deductions are limited to the amount of employment income in the year, such as the home office expense deduction.

(2) An employee can only deduct those expenses that are specifically allowed under section 8 whereas a self-employed individual may deduct all expenses incurred to earn business and property income as permitted by Subdivision b. Both the employee and the self-employed individual are subject to the reasonableness test.   ITA: 67

(3) No one test is conclusive in itself. All tests should be considered together before a conclusion is reached.

(4) The control subtest in the economic reality or entrepreneur test determines whether one person is in a position to order or require not only what is to be done but how it is to be done. Where such control, by the business over the individual, does exist, an employer–employee relationship is implied.

(5) The integration or organization test examines the degree of economic dependence of the individual on the organization. Where the individual is financially dependent on the organization, then an employer-employee relationship is implied.

(6) The specific result test looks at the expected results of the work performed. An employee–employer relationship usually contemplates the employee putting his or her personal services at the disposal of his or her employer during a given period of time without reference to a specified result and, generally, envisages the accomplishment of work on an ongoing basis. On the other hand, where a party agrees that certain specified work will be done for the other, it may be inferred that an independent contractor relationship exists.

(7) The Act uses the word "received" to determine the timing of the taxation of employment income. In this case, she will be considered to have received her bonus in the year she received the cheque. Just because she chose not to cash the cheque does not change the timing of when she received the payment.   ITA: 5

(8) The Act uses the word "received" to determine the timing of the taxation of employment income. The voluntary deferment of an unconditional right to receive the bonus is not an acceptable method of deferring income.   ITA: 5
Blenkarn v. M.N.R., 63 DTC 581 (T.A.B.)

(9) Employers cannot deduct all of the taxable benefits reported on the employee's T4. Items such as deemed interest benefits and standby charges for automobiles are not deductible to the employer since they are not expenses that are incurred for the purpose of earning income.   ITA: 80.4

(10) If the employer makes *any* of the premium payments then the benefit payments received will likely be taxable.   ITA: 6(1)(*f*); IT-428

(11) The CRA follows normal commercial practice such that the first day of the contract is counted and the last day is excluded for purposes of determining the number of days of interest. In this case the number of days from June 2 to June 29 inclusive will be used to determine the benefit, that is, 28 days.

(12) A reimbursement is a payment by an employer to an employee for expenses of the employer which have been paid by the employee and which are substantiated by receipts. This is normally accomplished by submitting an expense report. An allowance is a fixed amount which is paid to an employee in excess of his or her salary without the requirement that the employee be accountable for the amount expended.   IT-522R, pars. 40, 50

(13) The standby charge is calculated as follows:

$$\frac{20{,}004}{20{,}004} \times 2\% \times 12 \times (\$40{,}000 + \$3{,}200 + \$2{,}000) = \$10{,}848.$$

(14) The five conditions that a salesperson must meet in order to be able to deduct expenses are: ITA: 8(1)(*f*)

  (a) he or she must be employed in the year in connection with the selling of property or negotiating of contracts for his or her employer;

  (b) under the terms of his or her contract of employment he or she must be required to pay his or her own expenses;

(c) he or she must be ordinarily required to carry on his or her duties away from his or her employer's place of business;

(d) he or she is remunerated in whole or in part by commissions or other similar amounts fixed by reference to the volume of the sales made or the contracts negotiated; and

(e) he or she was not in receipt of a reasonable allowance for travelling expenses in respect of the taxation year that was not included in computing his or her income.

ITA: 6(1)(*b*)(v)

(15) The four conditions that must be met to allow an employee to deduct travelling expenses, other than car expenses, are:

ITA: 8(1)(*h*)

(a) he or she is ordinarily required to carry on his or her duties away from his or her employer's place of business or in different places;

(b) under his or her employment contract, he or she is required to pay the travelling expenses incurred by him or her in the performance of his or her duties;

(c) he or she was not in receipt of a reasonable allowance for travelling expenses that was not included in computing his or her income; and

ITA: 6(1)(*b*)(v), 6(1)(*b*)(vi), 6(1)(*b*)(vii)

(d) he or she did not claim any deduction for railway company employees, salespersons, or transport company employees.

ITA: 8(1)(*e*), 8(1)(*f*), 8(1)(*g*)

(16) There is nothing in paragraph 6(1)(*b*) that would exclude this allowance from income. However, another rule would apply to cause this receipt to be exempt from tax. In order to be exempt under this provision, the allowance must meet the following tests:

ITA: 81(3.1)

(a) he must deal at arm's length with his employer;

(b) he must have other employment or business income (not necessary in this case, since he is employed as a professor or teacher at a designated educational institution);

(c) the amount received must be reasonable and must relate only to travel to and from part-time employment; and

(d) the part-time location must be at least 80 km away from both the employee's ordinary place of residence and his principal place of employment or business.

(17) Neither word is defined in the Act. However, an Interpretation Bulletin interprets the word "principally" as more than 50%. Therefore, as long as the employment-use of the work space is its main or chief purpose, the test is met. "Exclusively" is not defined in the tax law, so reference is made to other sources. *Webster's English Dictionary* defines "exclusively" as "to the exclusion of all others" which is a much more onerous test.

IT-352R2, par. 2

(18) The Act deems that taxes withheld have been received at the time the bonus was paid. Therefore, even though the company still had the government's portion of the bonus, tax cannot be deferred on it. In addition, if the amount withheld in respect of the tax was not deemed to have been received by Ms. Smith, then she would not have received credit for the payment of this tax on her personal tax return.

ITA: 153(3)

Chapter 3 —
Solutions to Multiple Choice Questions

Question 1

(A) is correct: $12 \times 2\% \times \$34,500 = \$8,280$.

ITA: 6(2)

(B) and (C) are wrong because the operating cost benefit is computed as: 24 cents $\times$ 15,000 personal use km = $3,600. Part (B) incorrectly computes the operating cost benefit as: 15,000/20,000 $\times$ $3,300 = $2,475. Part (C) incorrectly computes the operating cost benefit as: 22 cents $\times$ 15,000 personal use km = $3,300.

ITA: 6(1)(*k*); ITR: 7305.1

(D) is wrong because he does not have more than 50% employment use.

ITA: 6(1)(*k*)(iv)

Question 2

(B) is correct: $50,000 salary + $3,500 allowance – $3,000 automobile expenses = $50,500. The car allowance is taxable because it is not based solely on kilometres driven. Since the car allowance is taxable, the automobile expenses can be deducted. The entertainment expenses are not deductible because she has no commission income.

ITA: 6(1)(*b*)(x), 8(1)(*f*), 8(1)(*h*.1)(iii)

(A) incorrectly excludes a deduction for automobile expenses: $53,500 = $50,000 salary + $3,500 allowance. The automobile expenses are deductible because the allowance is included in income.

ITA: 8(1)(*h*.1)
ITA: 6(1)(*b*)

(C) incorrectly includes a deduction for entertainment expenses: $49,500 = $50,000 salary + $3,500 allowance – $3,000 automobile expenses – $1,000 entertainment expenses. The entertainment expenses (50% $\times$ $2,000) are not deductible because she has no commission income or income from negotiating contracts.

ITA: 8(1)(*f*)

(D) incorrectly excludes the car allowance and the deduction for automobile expenses and incorrectly includes a deduction for entertainment expenses: $49,000 = $50,000 salary – $1,000 entertainment expenses.

Question 3

(A) is correct. Susanne Denholm can claim home office expenses because she is required by contract to maintain an office in her home and she works principally in her home (i.e., "most of the time"). The $500 correct amount of deductible home office expenses is calculated as follows:

ITA: 8(1)(*i*)(iii), 8(13)(*a*)(i)

Heat, hydro & maintenance: $5,000 $\times$ 10% = $500

Subsection 8(13) allows deductions under paragraphs 8(1)(*f*) or 8(1)(*i*). Since Susanne does not have any commission income, she can only deduct items under paragraph 8(1)(*i*). The distinction between (*f*) and (*i*) is that under (*f*) the expenses are fixed in nature and under (*i*) they are variable in nature (like supplies deductible under (*i*)). Since the only expenses that are variable with use are the heat, hydro, and maintenance, they are the only ones deductible. The mortgage interest is not deductible under either (*f*) or (*i*), since the only interest that is deductible as an employment expense is for automobiles and aircraft.

ITA: 8(1)(*j*), 8(2)

(B) incorrectly includes a deduction for property taxes and insurance: $1,100 = $500 + $200 insurance + $400 property taxes. The insurance (10% $\times$ $2,000) and property taxes (10% $\times$ $4,000) are not considered to be supplies. However, if Susanne had commission income, 10% of her insurance and property taxes would be deductible.

IT-352R2, par. 6
ITA: 8(1)(*i*)(iii)
ITA: 8(1)(*f*)

(C) incorrectly includes deductions for insurance, property taxes and the general telephone line: $1,400 = $500 + $200 insurance + $400 property taxes + $300 general telephone line. The insurance, property taxes and the cost of the general telephone line (50% $\times$ $600) are not deductible. If Susanne had commission income, the cost of the general telephone line would still not be deductible — only a special phone line and/or long distance calls would be deductible.

IT-352R2, pars. 6, 10(a)
ITA: 8(1)(*i*)(iii)

(D) incorrectly includes insurance, property taxes, the general telephone line and mortgage interest: $3,800 = $500 + $200 insurance + $400 property taxes + $300 general telephone + $2,400 mortgage interest. The insurance, property taxes, the cost of the general telephone line and mortgage interest (10% $\times$ $24,000) are not considered to be supplies. If Susanne had commission income, the mortgage interest would still not be deductible since the Act limits interest expense of an employee to interest on automobiles and planes.

IT-352R2
ITA: 8(1)(*i*)(iii)
ITA: 8(1)(*j*)

Question 4

(A) is correct. The loan qualifies as a home relocation loan. The benefit is computed using the lower of the prescribed interest rate at the time of the loan (4%) and the prescribed interest rate during the year (3%). Therefore the employment benefit is $1,000 (3% × $100,000 – 2% × $100,000 interest paid). ITA: 6(9), 80.4(1), 80.4(4)

(B) incorrectly computes the employment benefit using 4%: $2,000 = 4% × $100,000 – 2% × $100,000.

(C) incorrectly ignores the 2% interest paid in the computation of the interest benefit: $3,000 = 3% × $100,000.

(D) incorrectly computes the employment benefit using 4% rather than 3%. The 2% interest paid is not deducted: 4% × $100,000.

Question 5

(D) is correct. The stock option benefit is ($40 – $30) × 1,000 shares = $10,000. She meets the conditions for deferral because the option price was greater than the fair market value at the date of grant ($19 per share) in March 2008. She can therefore defer the employee benefit until she sells the shares. The benefit is, therefore, $10,000 in 2009.

(A) incorrectly reports the benefit in 2008 rather than 2009 and incorrectly subtracts a deduction (½ × $10,000) in computing the benefit ($10,000 – $5,000). This deduction is a Division C deduction. ITA: 110(1)(*d*)

(B) and (C) incorrectly compute the benefit based on the sales price of $38,000 ($38,000 – $30,000 = $8,000) rather than the price of the stock at the time of purchase. The benefit is $10,000. The $2,000 subsequent decline in value of the stock is a capital loss.

Question 6

(B) is correct.

Meals and entertainment (50% × $14,000)	$ 7,000
Driving costs (90% × $10,000)	9,000
Expenses eligible for deduction	$16,000

ITA: 8(1)(*f*)

Tim can either claim a deduction for these amounts to the extent of his commission income ($5,000) or he can claim a deduction for his automobile costs ($9,000) alone, without the commission limitation. The maximum deduction is therefore $9,000. ITA: 8(1)(*f*) 8(1)(*h*.1)

(A) is incorrect because it is the commission-limited amount. ITA: 8(1)(*f*)

(C) is incorrect because it is the full meals and entertainment amount ($14,000) and ignores the $5,000 commission limitation. ITA: 67.1

(D) is incorrect because it represents the expenses eligible as a salesperson ($16,000) but ignores the $5,000 commission limitation. ITA: 8(1)(*f*)

CHAPTER 3

Chapter 3 — Solutions to Exercises

Exercise 1

[See: *Isaac v. M.N.R.*, 70 DTC 1285 (T.A.B.)]

The following tests are applied to determine whether R.N. is an employee or an independent contractor.

Economic Reality or Entrepreneur Test

In applying the control subtest, the question is whether Canadian Forces Hospital, Halifax controlled not only what was done by R.N. but how it was done. In this case the Hospital exercised control over R.N. in connection with dividing up the patients to be cared for among the available nurses and imposing routine rules and regulations with regard to the administration of drugs and other medications. On the other hand, the Hospital did not exercise any control over the method in which R.N. did her work, which requires special knowledge, skill, and judgment. Accordingly, it does not appear that the Hospital exercised sufficient control to conclude that R.N. was an employee on the basis of this test alone.

However, the application of the other subtests is particularly revealing. R.N. does not run the risk of financing the equipment, supplying other assistants necessary to carry out her duties in the Hospital or seeking out clients. R.N. used the equipment and supplies furnished by the Hospital. She neither hired nor fired any of the nursing assistants who worked under her. She could only request that the Hospital hire additional staff to assist her. The clients were patients of the Hospital. R.N. was not in a position to substitute the services of another nurse if she was unable to perform her duties. All this evidence tends to establish that from an economic reality point of view R.N. was an employee, but this test may not be definitive in this case.

Integration or Organization Test

The Hospital deducted Canada Pension Plan contributions from her pay as they did with the nurses who were employed full-time by the Hospital. R.N. appeared to be economically dependent on the hospital, although she was not precluded from offering her services elsewhere. R.N. was subject to co-ordinational control of the hospital in terms of where to perform her services and when to do so. On the other hand, R.N. was not eligible for the regular benefits of a full-time nurse such as holidays, sick pay, retirement plan, etc. She was hired on a day-to-day basis at a *per diem* rate of pay. Her services could be terminated on 24 hours notice if full-time nurses became available. On the weight of the evidence it can be argued that R.N. is an employee of the Hospital based on the integration test.

Specific Result Test

On the one hand, it was R.N.'s personal services that were at the disposal of the Hospital. Her work was done on a continuous day-to-day basis without there being any limited or specified amount of work that she had, by contract, to accomplish. She could not substitute another person to perform her duties if she was unable to do so. On the other hand, R.N. was not a full-time nurse for any specified period of time. Her time was made up on a weekly basis in advance. She could be laid off on 24 hours notice. On balance, it appears that the evidence leads to the conclusion that, by applying the specific result test, R.N. was an employee. This conclusion is consistent with that for the integration or organization test.

Conclusion

The application of the control subtest of the economic reality or entrepreneur test leads to the conclusion that R.N was not an employee of the Hospital. The application of the other subtests of the economic reality test, the integration test and the specific result test leads to the inference that R.N. was an employee of the Hospital. (Your own conclusion after weighing all of these tests.)

Exercise 2

The courts generally rely on three tests to determine whether or not an individual is an independent contractor or an employee. Applying these tests should therefore help us determine the status of Ms. Capwell in relation to the architectural firm of Davies Ltd.

ITA: 248(1); *Wiebe Door Services Ltd. v. M.N.R.*, 87 DTC 5025 (F.C.A.)

(1) Economic Reality or Entrepreneur Test

(a) Control Test

The first test examines the day-to-day time commitment that is expected of an individual and the accountability of the individual to the corporation. In this instance, Ms. Capwell must work at least 14 days a month on the project (but the specific days appear flexible); however, she appears to be able to work under her own direction and on other projects on her days off. It does not seem to be conclusive as to whether or not Ms. Capwell is an employee given this test, but the evidence supports that she would be an independent contractor given the circumstances.

(b) Ownership of Tools

It is not clear, but Ms. Capwell appears to provide her own car, equipment, and technical expertise. We might also conclude that since she is working on the premises, many of her expenses, such as supplies and her place of work, will be covered by Davies Ltd. This test appears to support contractor status.

(c) Chance of Profit, Risk of Loss

This test assesses whether the individual incurs her own business risk, legal liability, and expenses. In this case, she is getting paid a flat fee of $4,000 per month, which we must assume is directly related to billable hours of work. She estimates that 30% of her contracting revenues will come from other sources, which is not entirely insignificant. This test is also not conclusive, and depending on the details, could go either way.

(2) Integration or Organization Test

This test determines whether or not the individual is economically dependent on the payer organization and is an integral part of the corporation. In this case, Ms. Capwell is not completely dependent on Davies for all of her income, but she retains an office on the premises and also receives some employee benefits in the form of underground parking. However, it's possible that the nature of the work demands she attend the company's offices. This test is inconclusive, but depending on the circumstances, slightly favours her being viewed as an employee.

(3) Specific Results Test

As the name suggests, the object of this test is to determine whether the individual's services were acquired to complete a specific task. In this case, there is no doubt that Ms. Capwell was taken on to complete a specific project, after which the contract will be fulfilled. Given this, she would appear to be an independent contractor.

Conclusion

The tests would seem to favour independent contract status, principally because of the flat fee for one specific project.

The results of the tests do not always provide us with a definitive answer as to whether or not an individual should be viewed as an employee. However, they can help guide us to make that determination. In this case, the facts lead toward the independent contractor conclusion. Given that the contract was drafted for a specific project, and that Ms. Capwell seems to be working independently, the courts would probably allow the designation of independent contractor status.

Exercise 3

(A) Specifically exempted.   ITA: 6(1)(*a*)

(B) Exempted; provincial employer health tax.   ITA: 6(1)(*a*)

(C) and (D) Exempted, since the premium was paid to a private medical plan.   ITA: 6(1)(*a*)

(E) Taxable. The Interpretation Bulletin only exempts tuition fees where the course is primarily for the benefit of the employer.   ITA: 6(1)(*a*), IT-470R, par. 18, 19

(F) Normally, taxable, but since the payment meets the conditions, namely that the Christmas gift is under $500 and is not cash or near cash, the CRA's position is that the gift is not a taxable benefit.   ITA: 6(1)(*a*)

(G) Partly taxable: The CRA takes the position that there will be no benefit if William had reimbursed the company the actual cost ($420). Since William did not completely reimburse the company for the actual costs, then the benefit would be calculated by taking the difference between the actual costs ($420) and the amount paid by William ($200) for a taxable benefit of $220.   ITA: 6(1)(*a*); IT-470R, par. 28

(H) Taxable, but the CRA takes the position that the amount would not be taxable if the membership was principally for the employer's advantage rather than the employee's.   ITA: 6(1)(*a*); IT-470R, par. 34

(I) Taxable unless the financial counselling was in respect of re-employment or retirement.   ITA: 6(1)(*a*), 6(1)(*a*)(iv)(B)

CHAPTER 3

Exercise 4

Paragraph 8(1)(*b*) allows for the deduction of legal expenses against employment income in the year, on account of legal expenses incurred by the taxpayer to collect or establish a right to salary or wages owed to the taxpayer that, if received by the taxpayer, would be required by this subdivision to be included in computing the taxpayer's employment income.

ITA: 6, 8

Paragraph 6(1)(*j*) requires any reimbursement to either be included in income or reduce the expense being claimed.

Legal expenses may also be deductible for other purposes such as to earn income from business or property or as another deduction [ITA 60(*o*), (*o*.1)], but only those expenses specifically listed in section 8 can be deducted from employment income [ITA 8(2)].

Other resources — IT-99R5, Legal and accounting fees; CRA Guide T4044, Employment Expenses

Exercise 5

The $6,000 merchandise discount is a taxable benefit. Administrative practice reflected in the Interpretation Bulletin does exempt discounts on merchandise, but they must be offered to all employees and not to just select groups. If there was an overall discount of 10% to all employees, it would seem reasonable in the circumstances to include only 25% in income; however, the Interpretation Bulletin is silent on this point.

IT-470R

IT-470R, par. 27

Exercise 6

The entire $5,500 is a taxable benefit. The exclusion for an eligible housing loss does not apply, because the loss was not incurred in an eligible relocation. The Interpretation Bulletin does provide some relief in this area, but only when an employee moves because he or she:

ITA: 6(1)(*a*), 6(19), 6(20), 248(1) "eligible relocation", IT-470R, par. 35

(a) has been transferred from one establishment of the employer to another; or

(b) has accepted another position at a location other than his or her former location.

If either of the above situations had existed, there would be no taxable benefit. Note that on the sale of the house, the loss cannot be greater than the actual loss to the employee, calculated as the amount by which the cost of the house exceeds the net selling price received.

IT-470R, par. 37

Exercise 7

Premiums paid:

(A) Group term life insurance premiums paid by an employer are a taxable benefit.

ITA: 6(1)(*a*), 6(4)

(B) and (C) The extended health care and dental care plans are private medical plans; hence, the premiums paid by the employer are not employment income.

ITA: 6(1)(*a*)

(D) Since the sickness or accident income protection plan is a group plan, premiums paid by the employer are exempt from employment income.

ITA: 6(1)(*a*)

Conclusion:

The following rearrangement would result in a lower tax cost:

(A) Company should pay for 100% of the extended health care and dental plan.

(B) Employees should pay the provincial medical plan premiums since company payments would be taxable benefits.

(C) Employees should consider paying the sickness or accident income protection premium themselves.

When an employer pays *any* portion of the premium for this type of plan, amounts that are paid out of the plan are taxable as employment income, less the employee's contribution to date. Conversely, if the employee pays all of the premiums, none of the amounts paid out of the plan are taxable. Since this particular plan has benefits of only 50% of the wages, the employee would be in a relatively poor cash position. The imposition of tax, even though at a lower rate, would certainly result in extreme hardship if the illness is prolonged.

ITA: 6(1)(*f*)

Exercise 8

Benefit would be the sum of:

ITA: 6(9), 80.4

(A) Car loan — prescribed rates

1st quarter	7% × $15,000 × 90/365	= $259	
2nd quarter	6% × $15,000 × 91/365	= 224	
3rd quarter	8% × $15,000 × 92/365	= 302	
4th quarter	7% × $15,000 × 92/365	= 265	$ 1,050

(B) Home purchase loan[1]
    The lesser of the prescribed rate at the time of the loan (i.e., 7%)
and the prescribed rate per quarter.

1st	7% × $100,000 × 90/365	= $ 1,726	
2nd	6% × $100,000 × 91/365	= 1,496	
3rd	7% × $100,000 × 92/365	= 1,764	
4th	7% × $100,000 × 92/365	= 1,764	6,750

(C) Other loan

1st	7% × $ 10,000 × 90/365	= $ 173	
2nd	6% × $ 10,000 × 91/365	= 150	
3rd	8% × $ 10,000 × 92/365	= 202	
4th	7% × $ 10,000 × 92/365	= 176	701
			$ 8,501

Less amounts paid[2]

(a) 6% × $ 15,000 × 365/365	$ 900	
(b) 4% × $100,000 × 365/365	4,000	
(c) 7% × $ 10,000 × 365/365	700	5,600
		$ 2,901

The Act would deem $150 of the car loan interest ($1,050 – $900) to be paid in the year and, therefore, eligible for an interest deduction, since the interest was deemed to be paid within 30 days of the year-end, as required.   ITA: 80.5   ITA: 8(1)(*j*), 80.4(1)(*c*)

An Interpretation Bulletin indicates that the deemed interest expense must be prorated for employment use.   IT-522R, par. 27

$$\frac{27,000 \text{ km}}{45,000 \text{ km}} \times \$150 = \$90$$

The interest deduction provision would deny a prorated deduction of the $900 paid on January 15 of the following year, since it was not paid in the taxation year in question. However, this amount would be eligible for a deduction in the following taxation year to the extent of the business use.   ITA: 8(1)(*j*)

The interest limitation restricts the interest to the lesser of (a) $90 and (b) $300 × $^{365}/_{30}$ × 27,000/45,000 = $2,190.   ITA: 67.2

— *NOTES TO SOLUTION*

   [1] If this loan had been as a consequence of an employment relocation, Division C of the Act would have provided a deduction for five years, equal to the imputed interest benefit on the first $25,000 of the "home relocation loan", as defined. As a result, in this particular case, the overall benefit on the housing loan would have been reduced by $1,688 (i.e., $25,000/$100,000 of $6,750). See Chapter 10 for a complete discussion of this provision. The "lesser of" comparison is made on a quarter-by-quarter basis.   ITA: 110(1)(*j*), 248(1)

   [2] The interest benefit is calculated on an aggregate basis. Any excess interest payment on one loan effectively reduces the deemed interest benefit on the other loans.   ITA: 80.4

Exercise 9

Year 1 — No tax effect.

Year 4 — No tax effect.

Year 5 — No tax effect, since the employer is a Canadian-controlled private corporation.

Year 6 — Must take into employment income under Division B the following: ITA: 7(1.1)

$$50,000 \text{ shares} \times (\$3 - \$1) = \underline{\$100,000}$$

— Will have a capital gain of

$$50,000 \text{ shares} \times (\$6 - \$3) = \underline{\$150,000}$$

— May be eligible for the capital gains deduction for qualifying small business corporation shares.

ITA: 110.6(1), 248(1)

— Since Katrina sold these shares within two years after the date of acquisition, she is not entitled to a deduction of one half of the subsection 7(1.1) inclusion. She is also not entitled to a general deduction since the exercise price of $1.00 was less than fair market value ($1.50) at the date the option was granted.

ITA: 110(1)(d), 110(1)(d.1)

Exercise 10

(a) Car benefit if business–use kilometres are 10,000

Standby charge

ITA: 6(1)(e), 6(2)

$$\frac{20,004 \text{ km}^{(1)}}{20,004 \text{ km}} \times [2\% \times (\$20,000 \times 12)] = \dots\dots\dots\dots\dots\dots \$4,800$$

Operating costs$^{(2)}$ (12,000 km × $0.24)	2,880	$7,680
Less: amount reimbursed		1,800
Total car benefit if business-use kilometres are 10,000		$5,880

ITA: 6(1)(k)(v)

(b) Car benefit if business-use kilometres are 20,000

Standby charge

ITA: 6(1)(e), 6(2)

$$\frac{12,000 \text{ km}^{(3)}}{20,004 \text{ km}} \times [2\% \times (\$20,000 \times 12)] = \dots\dots\dots\dots\dots\dots \$2,879$$

Operating costs$^{(4)}$ (50% × $2,879) =	1,440	$4,319
Less: amount reimbursed		1,800
Total car benefit if business-use kilometres are 20,000		$2,519

ITA: 6(1)(k)(v)

NOTES

(1) The employee does not qualify for the standby charge reduction since the car is not used more than 50% in the performance of employment duties when the business use is only 15,000 km. Therefore, in this outcome, the value of A in the formula (i.e., 12,000 km) is deemed equal to the value of B in the formula (i.e., 1,667 × 12 rounded).

(2) The election method is not available to the employee, since the car is not used more than 50% for business.

ITA: 6(1)(k)(iv)

(3) When the business-use kilometres is 20,000, the employee qualifies for the standby charge reduction and the numerator becomes the lesser of (a) 12,000 km, and (b) 1,667 km × 12 months.

(4) The operating benefit election at 50% of the standby charge is the same as $0.24 × 12,000 km = $2,880. The election method is available since employment kilometres comprise more than 50% of the total.

Exercise 11

Reille is limited in the amount he can claim to the $24,000 he made in commission income. Sales expenses (paragraph 8(1)(f)): Reille is permitted to claim 50% of the entertainment meals, and 50% of the out-of-town meals if he was out-of-town for more than a 12-hour period when he had these meals (subsection 8(4)). Reille may claim the $18,000 spent on hotels and airfare. Professional dues of $250 are deductible under paragraph 8(1)(i).

ITA: 8(1)(f), 8(1)(i), 8(4)

Hotel and airfare	$18,000
Out of town meals (4,000 × 50%)	2,000
Entertainment meals (2,500 × 50%)	1,250
Total sales expenses (paragraph 8(1)(f))	21,250
Professional dues (paragraph 8(1)(i))	250
Total employment expenses allowable	$21,500

The $21,250 is less than the $24,000 made in commissions so it, plus the $250 for professional dues, is deductible as employment expenses.

Exercise 12

The Act would appear to deny any deduction in respect of Calvin's work space in the home. In order for Calvin to avoid the restrictions, one of two conditions must be met, neither of which appear to be adhered to. The first alternative condition is that the work place in the home must be where the individual principally performs the employment duties. The second alternative condition is even more stringent, namely, that the work place must be used exclusively for employment income purposes and that the work place must be used on a regular and continuous basis as a meeting place for employment-connected persons.

ITA: 8(13)

If Calvin had met one of the conditions, then he would be able to deduct some of the expenses indicated as long as he met the conditions of paragraph 8(1)(*i*). First Calvin must have a contract with his employer indicating that he must pay for office rent and supplies and the employer completes and signs a T2200. However, of the expenses indicated, only the maintenance expense, including fuel, electricity, light bulbs, cleaning materials and minor repairs, on a prorated basis will be permitted. The imputed rent of $1,000 is not deductible; this position was confirmed in the *Thompson* case by the Federal Court–Trial Division.

ITA: 8(13)

IT-352R2, par. 2, 3
89 DTC 5439 (F.C.T.D.)

Exercise 13

Since the question refers to meal expenses for employees, you need to refer to subsection 8(4). A deduction for personal meals consumed while travelling is only allowed where the employee is away from the municipality/metropolitan area for a minimum of 12 hours. All meal costs, regardless of their nature and purpose, are also restricted by subsection 67.1(1) to 50% of the actual cost. However, long-haul truck drivers can deduct 65% in 2008 (increasing to 80% by 2011).

ITA: 8(4), 67.1(1)

Exercise 14

Allowances and related expenses: There are two conditions that must be met in order to permit the allowance to be excluded from income:

ITA: 6(1)(*b*)(vii)

(a) the allowance must relate to travel outside of the municipality in which the employer's office is situated;

(b) the allowance must be a reasonable amount.

The $10,000 accommodation allowance is a taxable allowance, since the amount is an unreasonable amount on the assumption that the incurred expenses of $12,000 were reasonable. Therefore, she is entitled to a deduction, since she meets the other conditions of this paragraph; namely, she ordinarily travels in respect of her employment duties and is required by her employment contract to pay for her own expenses.

ITA: 6(1)(*b*)(vii), 8(1)(*h*)

Total accommodation expenses	$12,000
Less: disallowed meal portion (50% × $4,500)	2,250
	$ 9,750

ITA: 67.1(1)

The car expenses are deductible since she meets the conditions of this paragraph which are quite similar to paragraph 8(1)(*h*), described above, to the extent of the following calculations:

ITA: 8(1)(*h.*1)

Gas	$1,500
Maintenance	500
Capital cost allowance (½ × 30% × $30,000 × 1.12)	5,040
Insurance	1,200
Licences	90

Interest — lesser of:

(a) $4,000

(b) $300 × $\dfrac{361 \text{ days}}{30}$ = $3,610

	3,610
	$11,940

Deductible car expenses:

$$\frac{15,000 \text{ km}}{21,000 \text{ km}} \times \$11,940 = \$8,529$$

Exercise 15

5/105 of the sum of:

(a) Deductible expenses including GST and PST but excluding exempt supplies:[1]

Accommodation and meals	$ 9,750
Gas and maintenance	1,429[2]
	$11,179
(b) Capital cost allowance	3,600[3]
	$14,779
(c) Less: any expenses for which a reasonable allowance was received	Nil
	$14,779
Rebate (5/105 of $14,779)	$ 704

Par. 6(8)(*c*) Employment income inclusion in year of receipt of rebate:

$$\frac{\$11,179}{\$14,779} \times \$704 = \underline{\underline{\$533}}$$

Par. 6(8)(*d*) Capital cost reduction under ssec. 13(7.1) in year of receipt:

$$\frac{\$ 3,600}{\$14,779} \times \$704 = \underline{\underline{\$171}}$$

— *NOTES TO SOLUTION*

[1] Exempt supplies: insurance, licences and interest in respect of car.

$$(2)\quad \frac{15,000 \text{ km}}{21,000 \text{ km}} \times (\$1,500 + \$500) = \underline{\underline{\$1,429}}$$

$$(3)\quad \frac{15,000 \text{ km}}{21,000 \text{ km}} \times \$5,040 \qquad = \underline{\underline{\$3,600}}$$

CHAPTER 3

Chapter 4

Income from Business:
General Concepts and Rules

LEARNING GOALS

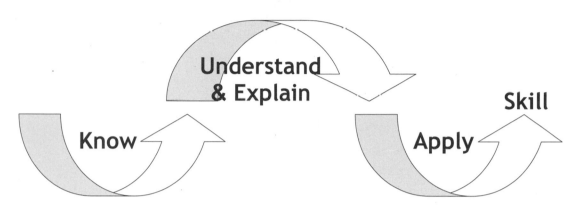

Know

By the end of this chapter you should know the basic provisions of the *Income Tax Act* that relate to the calculation of business income and expenses, and some of the GST implications for business activity. You should be able to start with accounting income and make the necessary adjustments to arrive at business income for tax purposes. Completing the Review Questions (¶4,800) and Multiple Choice Questions (¶4,825) is a good way to learn the technical provisions.

Understand and Explain

You should understand and be able to explain what business income and expenses are, when to recognize them, and why they are treated the way they are for tax purposes. Completing the Exercises (¶4,850) is a good way to deepen your understanding of the material.

Apply

You should be able to use your knowledge and understanding of business income and expenses to identify and resolve practical problems. Completing the Assignment Problems (¶4,875) and Advisory Case (¶4,880) is an excellent way to develop your ability to apply the material in increasingly complex situations.

Chapter 4 — Learning Chart

Topic	Example Problem (✓)	Review Questions (¶4,800)	Multiple Choice (¶4,825)	Exercises (¶4,850)	Assignment Problems (¶4,875)
¶4,000 BASIC RULES					
¶4,010 The Concept of Business Income					
¶4,015 Income from a business		2			
¶4,020 Business income versus capital receipt	✓	1	5	2, 5	1, 5, 6
¶4,021 Overview					
¶4,022 Objective of the analysis					
¶4,023 Observable behavioural factors or "badges of trade"					
¶4,024 Summary					
¶4,025 Damages as a receipt of income or capital		3, 4		4	2
¶4,026 Non-performance of business contracts					
¶4,027 Cancellation of agency agreements					
¶4,028 Loss of property					
¶4,030 Other receipts or benefits		5, 6			8
¶4,031 Profits from an illegal business					
¶4,032 Profits from betting, gambling, and windfalls					
¶4,033 Subsidies					
¶4,034 Forgiveness of debt rules					
¶4,035 Business income versus property income			6		
¶4,040 Inventory Valuation					
¶4,045 Basis of valuation	✓			6, 12	10, 11
¶4,050 Adjustment for depreciation allocation to inventory: absorption accounting	✓				
¶4,060 Sole Proprietorship					8
¶4,070 Conversion of Accounting Income to Net Business Income for Tax Purposes					
¶4,100 INCLUSIONS					4
¶4,105 Inclusions in Income for Tax Purposes					
¶4,110 Amounts Received and Receivable					8
¶4,120 Inducement Payments or Reimbursements					
¶4,130 Restrictive Covenants					
¶4,140 Partnership Income					
¶4,150 Barter Transactions and Inducement Payments					2
¶4,200 DEDUCTIONS					
¶4,205 Overview					
¶4,206 Disallowed or restricted deductions		7		1	
¶4,210 Deductibility of Expenditures				7	
¶4,215 General test — To gain or produce income			1, 2	10	7
¶4,220 Expenditure of a capital nature		10			5, 10, 14
¶4,222 Personal and living expenses			6		

Topic	Example Problem (✓)	Review Questions (¶4,800)	Multiple Choice (¶4,825)	Exercises (¶4,850)	Assignment Problems (¶4,875)
¶4,225 Other Prohibited Deductions		8	1, 2, 3	8, 9, 12	5, 6, 7, 8, 10, 14, 16
¶4,226 Reserves					
¶4,227 Payments on discounted bonds					
¶4,228 Use of recreational facilities and club dues					
¶4,229 Political contributions					
¶4,230 Automobile expenses					
¶4,231 Payments under the Act					
¶4,232 Prepaid expenses					
¶4,233 Expenses of investing in sheltered plans					
¶4,234 Work space in home					
¶4,235 Deductibility of provincial capital and payroll taxes					
¶4,236 Limitation on accrued expenses					
¶4,237 Reasonable Expectation of Profit (REOP)					3
¶4,238 Proposed amendments related to REOP					
¶4,239 Limitation on Amount of Deductions for Deductible Expenditures		9, 11	2, 3	1, 3	6, 8, 9, 10, 12, 13, 14, 16
¶4,240 Deductions Specifically Permitted	✓	12, 13	1, 4	10, 11, 12, 13	4, 7, 9, 11, 16
¶4,241 Write-offs of capital expenditures					
¶4,242 Interest					
¶4,243 Expenses of issuing shares or borrowing money					
¶4,244 Premiums on life insurance used as collateral					
¶4,245 Discount on debt obligations					
¶4,246 The system for reserves under the Act					
¶4,247 Employer's contribution to registered pension plan					
¶4,248 Employer's contribution under a deferred profit sharing plan					
¶4,249 Cancellation of lease					
¶4,250 Landscaping of grounds					
¶4,251 Expenses of representation					
¶4,252 Investigation of site					
¶4,253 Utilities service connection					
¶4,254 Disability-related modifications and equipment					
¶4,255 Convention expenses					
¶4,256 Application of the Rules for Deduction	✓				
¶4,257 Sales/Negotiating Person's Expenses Revisited					13
¶4,258 Automobiles					
¶4,260 Automobile allowances					
¶4,265 Office in the home					12, 13, 14

Topic	Example Problem (✓)	Review Questions (¶4,800)	Multiple Choice (¶4,825)	Exercises (¶4,850)	Assignment Problems (¶4,875)
¶4,270 Meals and entertainment	✓		2, 3		
¶4,275 Summary of Business Income Adjustments					
¶4,280 Ceasing to Carry on Business					
¶4,285 Sale of accounts receivable				14	
¶4,290 Sale of inventory					
¶4,300 Professional Business					
¶4,310 Scientific Research and Experimental Development					15, 16
¶4,315 Meaning of scientific research and experimental development (SR&ED)					
¶4,320 General deduction of expenditures					
¶4,325 Election method to determine deduction					
¶4,400 THE GST IMPACT ON BUSINESS ACTIVITY				15	17
¶4,410 Commercial Activity					
¶4,415 Carrying on business					
¶4,420 Adventure or concern in the nature of trade					
¶4,425 Exclusions from the definition of commercial activity					
¶4,430 Value for tax					
¶4,435 When GST is payable					
¶4,440 Automobile operating cost benefits paid by employer					
¶4,450 Input Tax Credits					
¶4,455 General rules					
¶4,460 Restrictions					
¶4,470 Adjustments to Net Tax					
¶4,475 Excess charges					
¶4,480 Price reductions					
¶4,485 Bad debts					
¶4,490 Lease of passenger vehicles					
¶4,495 Food, beverages, and entertainment expenses					
¶4,500 Application of the Rules	✓				

Study Notes

Chapter 4 —
Discussion Notes for Review Questions

(1) This type of transaction is commonly referred to as an "adventure in the nature of trade" and would result in business income, if the facts of the situation indicate that it has the "badges of trade". One of the indicators that a transaction is an adventure in the nature of trade is that the taxpayer has specialized knowledge in respect of the transaction. Mr. Flip is a real estate salesperson and, hence, on the surface appears to meet this test. Since "business" is defined to include "an adventure in the nature of trade", this transaction would be classified as business income.

ITA: 248(1)

(2) There is no requirement in the Act to use GAAP for tax purposes. The courts have, on occasion, rejected conformity between income for accounting and tax purposes, particularly in cases where GAAP is at variance with the court's concept of ordinary commercial trading and business principles and practices or common law principles. However, GAAP profits are usually used as the starting point for the calculation of net income for tax purposes.

(3) No. Since the performance of this contract would have been income to Opco if the customer had completed it, the damages received would also be treated as business income.

(4) The agreement was of such importance to Aco Ltd. that it would constitute a large part of the company's total business structure. As a result, the receipt may be treated as a capital transaction on the sale of eligible capital property with no cost base. Thus, 50% of the receipt is included in business income. (See Chapter 5.)

(5) No. Income from illegal activities is taxable. Subsection 9(1) does not impose conditions on how the profit is earned. See IT-256R for the CRA's position. See, also, the cases listed in the text on this issue.

(6) The subsidy is taxable as if it were an expense reduction to Opco. Refer to the CRA's position.

IT-273R2

(7) There are a number of limitations that restrict the deductibility of expenses even though they may have been incurred to earn income. Expenditures that are not deductible include:

ITA: 18

● capital outlay or loss;

ITA: 18(1)(*b*)

● use of recreational facilities and club dues;

ITA: 18(1)(*l*)

● political contributions; and

ITA: 18(1)(*n*)

● limitations on interest and property taxes.

ITA: 18(2), 18(3.1)

(8) A provision specifically prohibits the deduction of any amount paid or payable under the Act. As a result, the interest paid to the Receiver General will not be deductible.

ITA: 18(1)(*t*)

(9) Not necessarily. The Act also places a limitation on the amount of an outlay or expense. It can only be deducted to the extent that it is "reasonable in the circumstances."

ITA: 67

(10) If the replacement of the roof served to restore it to its original condition then the cost should be fully deductible in the year incurred. If the replacement roof was superior to the old roof, the cost could be considered capital in nature. This would result in an addition to the undepreciated capital cost pool. Then, the cost would be deductible over a number of years. An Interpretation Bulletin comments on the issue of income *versus* capital expenditures.

IT-128R

(11) No. Airplane, train, or bus fares are specifically excluded from the 50% limitation.

ITA: 67.1(4)(*a*)

(12) The reserve is only allowed if the company is the manufacturer of the product and pays an arm's length party to take over the obligations of the warranty for the company.

ITA: 20(1)(*m*.1)

(13) Yes. The deduction of certain expenditures of a capital nature made in Canada that are in respect of scientific research and experimental development is permitted. These expenditures do not include land.

ITA: 37(1)(*b*)

Chapter 4 –
Solutions to Multiple Choice Questions

Question 1

(D) is correct. A deduction for interest and penalties on late income tax payments is denied. ITA: 18(1)(*t*)

(A) is a deductible item. A deduction for amounts paid for landscaping business premises is allowed. ITA: 20(1)(*aa*)

(B) is a deductible item. A deduction for interest on money borrowed to finance the purchase of a factory for use in its business is allowed. ITA: 20(1)(*c*)

(C) is a deductible item. If the beneficiary of a $100,000 term life insurance policy on an employee is the employee's family, the cost of the insurance premium is part of the cost of the employee's remuneration package. As such, it is not denied as it is incurred for the purpose of earning income. ITA: 18(1)(*a*)

Question 2

(C) is correct. The entire $15,000 spent on three social events for all employees at a particular location is deductible as long as the number of events does not exceed six. ITA: 67.1(2)(*f*)

(A) The deduction for $11,000 of accrued legal fees for a pending law suit is not allowed, because it is a contingent liability. There is no legal liability to pay this amount. ITA: 18(1)(*e*)

(B) The deduction for $4,000 of donations to registered charities is denied because it is not incurred for the purpose of earning income. The donations would be deductible in the computation of taxable income. ITA: 18(1)(*a*), 110.1(1)(*a*)

(D) The deduction of $1,500 for golf club membership dues for employees is denied. ITA: 18(1)(*l*)

Question 3

(D) is correct, because the Act provides an exception to the 50% rule for the cost of meals and entertainment relating to a fund-raising event the primary purpose of which is to benefit a registered charity. ITA: 67.1(2)(*b*)

(A) is incorrect since donations to political parties are not deductible. The federal political donation would be eligible for a tax credit. ITA: 18(1)(*n*), 127(3)

(B) is incorrect, because accrued bonuses are not deductible if they are unpaid 180 days after year-end. ITA: 78(4)

(C) is incorrect, because the deduction for a financial accounting reserve for warranty expenses is denied. ITA: 18(1)(*e*)

Question 4

(A) is the correct answer. The $13,000 to be added back is computed as follows:

Legal expenses related to the purchase of an investment in shares	$ 5,000	ITA: 18(1)(*b*)
Legal expenses incurred to dispute a tax assessment	0	ITA: 60(*o*)
Legal expenses related to the issuance of debt	4,000	ITA: 20(1)(*e*)
Accounting fees in connection with the preparation of a prospectus	4,000	ITA: 20(1)(*e*)
	$13,000	

(B) incorrectly adds back $4,000 (instead of $5,000) for the legal expenses related to the purchase of an investment in shares: $12,000 = $4,000 + $4,000 + $4,000.

(C) incorrectly adds back nothing for either the legal expenses related to the issuance of debt or the accounting fees in connection with the preparation of a prospectus: $9,000 = $5,000 + $4,000.

(D) incorrectly adds back only the $5,000 legal expenses related to the purchase of an investment in shares.

Question 5

(D) is correct. Most of the facts support capital gains treatment: the nature of the asset (real estate), its use and intended use (rental), the 10-year holding period and the unsolicited offer for sale. As a result, the gain on the sale of the land will likely be treated as a capital gain for income tax purposes.

(A) is incorrect. Because Sam is a real estate agent, the CRA may argue that the gain on the sale of the land is business income (not a capital gain).

(B) is incorrect. The fact that the land has been held for 10 years supports capital gains treatment, not business income treatment.

(C) is incorrect. The unsolicited offer for sale supports capital gains treatment, not business income treatment.

Question 6

(A) is correct. Legal fees to defend a lawsuit brought by a customer would be deductible.   ITA: 18(1)(*a*)

(B) and (C) are incorrect because these items (accounting loss on the sale of capital property and the principal amount of a mortgage) are on account of capital and therefore not deductible.   ITA: 18(1)(*b*)

(D) is incorrect because personal and living expenses are not deductible.   ITA: 18(1)(*h*)

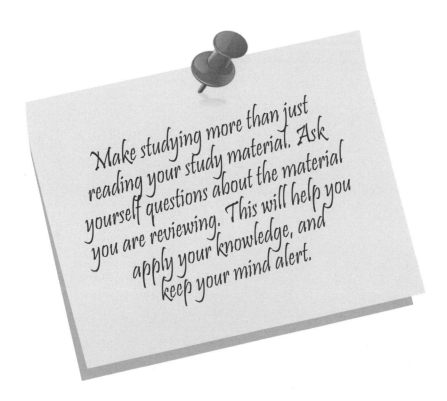

Make studying more than just reading your study material. Ask yourself questions about the material you are reviewing. This will help you apply your knowledge, and keep your mind alert.

Chapter 4 — Solutions to Exercises

Exercise 1

Employee Perk	Employee Taxable Benefit	Employer Impact	ITA: 9, 11, 18, 20
Tuition fees for the child of employee	$2,800 may be a taxable benefit, but jurisprudence possibly supports an exempt scholarship for the child.	Deductible as compensation expense	
Out-of-town meals	Not taxable to employee	50% deductible for employment duties	
Entertainment for clients	Not taxable to employee	50% deductible for employment duties	
Professional dues	Not taxable to employee	Deductible for employment duties	
Notebook computer for employment	Not taxable to employee	Deductible CCA for employment duties	
Membership for health club	Not taxable if employment-related	Not deductible for company	
Interest-free loan	$40,000 is subject to an imputed interest taxable benefit (deductible by the executive as was used to invest in company shares)	No impact on employer	
Life insurance premiums	$150 taxable benefit	Deductible as compensation expense	
Reimbursement for supplies	Not taxable to employee	Deductible CCA for employment duties	

Exercise 2

[See *Hiwako Investments Limited v. The Queen*, 78 DTC 6281 (F.C.A.)]

The intention of the taxpayer corporation in this case can only be inferred from the facts of the case. The nature of the asset involved in the transaction is of prime importance in this case. It was an income-producing asset that would have been regarded as a fixed capital asset had it been held longer. Normally, the increase in value on the sale of a capital asset is taxed as a capital gain. The gain represents an enhancement of value by realizing a security in the same sense that a growth stock may be sold for a gain that is regarded as a capital gain. Thus, the prospect of an increase in value does not, by itself, characterize the gain as income from business.

The nature of the activity surrounding the transaction could characterize it as an adventure in the nature of trade. However, it could be argued that an income-producing property was purchased as an investment and circumstances changed such that the investment had to be sold. This would not necessarily be regarded as a gain made in an operation of business in carrying out a scheme for profit-making.

The court indicated that the concept of "secondary intention" does no more than refer to a practical approach for determining certain questions that arise in connection with "trading cases". If property is acquired where there is no business or the purchaser has not considered how he or she will use it, then the sale may be regarded as an adventure in the nature of trade, supporting a secondary intention to sell at a profit. However, where the property in question is an active, profit-producing property, it may be more difficult to conceive of its having been held as a speculation in the sense of an adventure in the nature of trade.

The fact that the principal shareholder of the corporation had a long history of trading in real estate does not necessarily mean that his intention in the transaction at hand was to trade. That fact could be outweighed by the income-producing capital nature of the particular property in question.

The court held that the gain was not income from a business, based on the foregoing reasons. However, some believe that the arguments for business income are stronger in this case and that the decision in this case should be limited to its specific facts.

Exercise 3

(a) If the company leased the vehicle and provided it for Samuel, the company would be able to deduct the cost of the lease as a business expense. Samuel would have a taxable benefit that would consist of:

ITA: 9, 11, 18, 20

Standby charge	($400 × 12 × ⅔) =	$3,200
Operating cost benefit	(10,000 × $0.24) =	2,400
Taxable benefit		$5,600

(b) If the company purchased the vehicle, it would claim capital cost allowance using the CCA rate of 30%, thus receiving a tax reduction. This option requires the company to lay out cash and the company should do an analysis of which of the first two options is better for it for the period of time the automobile is needed. Samuel would have a taxable benefit that would consist of:

Standby charge	2% × $22,000 × 12 =	$5,280
Operating cost benefit	10,000 × $0.24 =	2,400
Taxable benefit		$7,680

(c) The allowance would cost the company $3,520, calculated as follows:

$0.52 × 5,000 km =	$2,600
$0.46 × 2,000 km =	920
Total	$3,520

This amount would be deductible as an expense for the employer as it is tied to the CRA's automobile expense deduction limits.

Samuel's operating costs incurred for business purposes = $1,029 ($2,500 × 7,000/17,000) plus depreciation. Samuel would be receiving $3,380 per year, which implies $2,491 ($3,520 - 1,029) for depreciation.

Exercise 4

The $225,000 would be considered a capital receipt based on the *Parsons-Steiner Limited v. M.N.R.* case.

62 DTC 1148 (Ex. Ct.)

The following paraphrased excerpt from that case will help explain the conclusion:

> On the whole therefore having regard to the importance of the franchise to Unloadum's business, the length of time the relationship had subsisted, the extent to which the appellant's business was affected by its loss both in decreased sales and by reason of its inability to replace it with anything equivalent, and the fact that from that time the appellant was in fact out of business, leads to a conclusion that this was a capital transaction. The payment in question was to replace "a capital asset of an enduring nature". It was one which Unloadum had built up over the years and which on the termination of the franchise they were obliged to relinquish. The payment received in respect of its loss was accordingly a capital receipt.

Exercise 5

Various factors must be examined in the determination of whether the dispositions should be considered income from a business or a capital gain.

ITA: 248(1)

Primary intention

The stated primary intention was to develop the properties into shopping plazas, thus, to earn income from these properties. However, this intention must be supported by objectively observable behavioural factors.

Behavioural factors

Relationship of the transaction to the taxpayer's business

AMC's main business appears to be the development and management of revenue properties. It also frequently engages in the sale of undeveloped properties. The fact that these transactions are closely related to AMC's main business and the fact that its major shareholder is a realtor and, therefore, heavily involved in buying and selling land, points to treatment of the sales as income from a business.

AMC often sells property when it is not feasible to develop and, as such, purchases land with good resale value. This focus on good resale value indicates an underlying intention of selling property for a gain. This indicates a treatment of the dispositions as business income.

Number and frequency of transactions

Transactions of buying and selling undeveloped land are frequently entered into as it is AMC's business to develop land. This frequency indicates treatment as income from a business.

Conclusion

It could be argued that AMC's primary intention was to hold the third parcel of land to develop it and earn income from it; therefore, its sale should be treated as a capital gain. But because of the likely secondary intention of earning a profit on its sale, the frequency of this type of transaction, and the closeness to AMC's primary business, it is likely the court would consider all the dispositions as income from a business. The court could say that AMC held onto the third parcel for six months only in order to get the best price and therefore to make a substantial profit.

Exercise 6

Since actual cost is known it must be used. Therefore, an assumption about cost is not appropriate. Market value is probably best reflected in net realization value for this inventory. The following calculation of inventory values could be used:

Item	Actual cost	Reg. 1801 Market	Ssec. 10(1) Each item at lower of cost or market
Mufflers	$1,120.00	$ 992.00	$ 992.00
Tailpipes	745.75	706.50	706.50
Exhaust system	633.75	604.50	604.50
Shock absorbers	4,979.20	5,056.00	4,979.20
Brackets	1,304.80	1,211.60	1,211.60
Clamps	1,134.90	1,396.80	1,134.90
Total		$9,967.40	$9,628.70

Either the $9,967.40 value can be used or the $9,628.70 value can be used. However, the ending valuation method used in a particular year must be the same as that used for the end of the preceding year.

ITR: 1801
ITA: 10(1), 10(2.1)

Exercise 7

(a) The *income-earning purpose test* is found in paragraph 18(1)(*a*) — the "general limitation" re: an outlay or expense made or incurred for the purpose of gaining or producing income from the business or property. Students can list any of the following related sections, ITs or ICs in their answer:

ITA: 18(1)(*a*), 18(1)(*b*), 18(1)(*c*), 18(1)(*e*), 18(1)(*h*), 67, 248(1)

Related sections: subsections 20(1), 20(16); subsection 21(1); subsection 26(2); section 30

ITs: IT-99R5; IT-185R; IT-211R; IT-261R; IT-357R2; IT-364; IT-467R2; IT-475; IT487; IT521

ICs: IC 77-11; IC 88-2

(b) The *capital test* is found in paragraph 18(1)(*b*) — no deduction is allowed for an outlay, loss, or replacement of capital, a payment on account of capital or an allowance in respect of depreciation, obsolescence or depletion except as expressly permitted by this Part.

Related sections: subsection 14(5); subsections 20(1), (10), (16); subsection 24(1); subsection 26(2); section 30

ITs: IT-187; IT-467R2; IT-475

ICs: none

(c) The *exempt income test* is found in paragraph 18(1)(*c*) — limits an outlay or expense to the extent it may reasonable be regarded as having been made or incurred for the purpose of gaining or producing exempt income.

Related sections: none

ITs: IT-467R2

ICs: none

(d) The *reserve test* is found in paragraph 18(1)(*e*) — no deduction for an amount as, or on account of, a reserve, a contingent liability or amount or a sinking fund except as expressly permitted by this Part.

Related sections: none

ITs: IT-215R; IT-321R; IT-467R2

ICs: none

(e) The *personal expenses test* is found in paragraph 18(1)(*h*) — no deduction for personal or living expenses of the taxpayer, other than travel expenses incurred by the taxpayer while away from home in the course of carrying on the taxpayer's business.

Related sections: subsections 20(1), (16); subsection 248(1) "personal or living expenses"

ITs: no primary ITs

ICs: none

(f) The *reasonableness test* is found in section 67, which states no deduction is allowed for an outlay or expense in respect of which any amount is otherwise deductible under this Act, except to the extent that it was reasonable in the circumstances.

Related sections: subsection 8(9); subsection 248(1) "amount"

ITs: no primary ITs

ICs: none

Exercise 8

(A) The deduction of these costs are prohibited, notwithstanding the argument that the lodge was used to produce income from client business.   ITA: 18(1)(*l*)

(B) The deduction of costs are allowed if they were incurred in the ordinary course of the company's business of providing the property for rent. The facts of this case *may* fit this exception.   ITA: 18(1)(*l*)

Exercise 9

First, it must be determined whether any expense incurred may be deducted in respect of the home office. To make this determination, the specific conditions outlined in subsection 18(12) are that: ITA: 18(12)

(i) the office is the principal place of business; or

(ii) it is used exclusively for the purpose of earning business income and is used on a regular and continuous basis for meeting clients, customers, or patients in respect to the business.

Since Karim performs only consulting work, the home office qualifies under condition (i). Although Amina teaches in addition to consulting, it is only part-time and her principal business is consulting. Therefore, she also qualifies under condition (i). Amina and Karim are carrying on separate self-employed businesses. Since they also live together, the home office expenses would be split on an agreed basis. Assuming that the split was agreed at 50%, both taxpayers would be permitted to deduct 50% of the eligible home office expenses. Eligible home office expense is equal to 500/2,000 square feet times the total home office costs. Supplies, materials, and software would be considered business expenses, not home office expenses. Therefore, Amina and Karim may **each** deduct the following as their 50% share of the expenses:

Home office expense (subsection 18(12))	$23,600 × 25% × 50% =	$2,950
Supplies and materials	$1,800 × 50% =	900
Computer and software lease	$2,300 × 50% =	1,150
Total		$5,000

Exercise 10

(A) — contribution may be made within 120 days of the end of 2009,

— an employer contribution to a defined-benefit RPP is deductible where it is made on the recommendation of an actuary in whose opinion the contribution is required so that the plan will have sufficient assets to provide benefits in accordance with its terms as registered,

— in this case, both the current service contribution and the lump-sum amount based on an actuarial valuation would be deductible in 2009, if they are in accordance with the plan.

(B) A full deduction of an amount paid in the year is permitted — or a taxpayer may elect to write it off in equal amounts over the 10-year period beginning in the current year.   ITA: 20(1)(*cc*) ITA: 20(9)

CHAPTER 4

(C) The deduction of the full amount of utilities connection costs is permitted. Since the taxpayer does not own the gas lines but the utilities company does, the amount is not eligible for capital cost allowance.

ITA: 20(1)(*ee*)

(D) Salary of an owner-employee's spouse is an allowable deduction to a corporation as long as it is reasonable in the circumstances. While $7,000 per month for full-time secretarial work is probably not reasonable, some lesser, reasonable amount would be deductible in this case. The amount in excess of a reasonable amount will not be deductible to the corporation, but will be included in the recipient's income from employment.

Exercise 11

Only ½ of the discount of $108.10 may be deducted because the bond was issued at less than 97% even though within the ⅓ × 9% or 12% yield range.

ITA: 20(1)(*f*)

Given that the discount is paid effectively on maturity when the principal amount is repaid, then the $54.05 is deductible in 2009.

Exercise 12

Net income per financial statements	$150,000	
Add: Items deducted in financial statements but not deductible for tax purposes:		
Provision for income taxes — current	25,000	ITA: 18(1)(*e*)
— future	130,000	
Depreciation expense	40,000	ITA: 18(1)(*b*)
Non-deductible interest — re interest on late taxes	2,500	ITA: 18(1)(*t*)
Bond discount	7,500	ITA: 18(1)(*b*), (*e*)
Inventory (closing) to FIFO basis	10,000	ITA: 10(1)
	$365,000	
Deduct: Items not deducted in financial statements but deductible for tax purposes:		
Landscaping costs $12,000		ITA: 20(1)(*aa*)
Inventory (opening) to FIFO basis 15,000	(27,000)	
		ITA: 10(1)
Net Income for tax purposes before CCA	$338,000	

Exercise 13

This transaction would likely involve a receipt of income because the intention is likely to make a profit on the purchase and sale of land. This would be substantiated by the frequency of transactions in land or, at least, the indication of an adventure in the nature of trade. During the year of sale the following income would be computed:

Revenue from the sale of land	$250,000	
Less: cost of land $107,500		
real estate commission 12,500	120,000	
Income from the sale of land	$130,000	ITA: 9
Less: reserve for amount not due until later year*		ITA: 20(1)(*n*)(ii)
$\frac{\$130,000}{\$250,000} \times (\$250,000 - \$110,000)$	72,800	
Income after reserve	$ 57,200	

* The reserve is not available, unless the sale occurred within 36 months of the end of the year in which a reserve is to be taken.

ITA: 20(8)(*b*)

Note that the minimum two-year repayment period does not apply on the sale of land which qualifies for the reserve. In the next year, the reserve of $72,800 would be taken into income.

ITA: 12(1)(*e*)(ii), 20(1)(*n*)(ii)

CHAPTER 4

Exercise 14

Since Mr. Flogger has sold substantially all of his business assets to a person who intends to carry on the business, a section 22 election is available. Note that Mr. Flogger and Mr. Sucker must elect jointly in prescribed form [T2022] to have section 22 apply. Mr. Flogger must include last year's doubtful debt reserve in income. Then, Mr. Flogger may deduct, as a business loss, the difference between the face value of the accounts ($45,000) and the consideration paid by Mr. Sucker which should be equal to their fair market value ($36,000). Hence, Mr. Flogger will have a deduction of $9,000. Mr. Sucker must include the same $9,000 difference in his business income for the taxation year of the purchase. However, Mr. Sucker will now be put in a position to deduct an appropriate reserve for doubtful debts at the end of the taxation year or to write off any of the accounts that can be established to have become bad debts, since an amount has been included in income in respect of these receivables.

ITA: 20(1)(*l*)
ITA: 12(1)(*d*)

ITA: 22(1)(*a*), 22(1)(*b*)

ITA: 20(1)(*l*), 20(1)(*p*)
ITA: 22(1)(*c*)

Mr. Flogger		Income Effect
Last year's reserve		$ 6,500
Loss on sale: Proceeds	$36,000	
Face amount	(45,000)	(9,000)
Net effect		$ (2,500)

Mr. Sucker	
Mr. Flogger's loss on sale included in income	$ 9,000
Face amount of receivables	$45,000

If the election is not used, the loss of $9,000 would be a capital loss, only ½ deductible as an allowable capital loss. Furthermore, an allowable capital loss can only be offset against a taxable capital gain.

ITA: 22

Exercise 15

Since the corporation is carrying on business, it is engaged in a commercial activity. Therefore, the corporation is required to register and collect GST on its supplies, i.e., sales of goods, which are "taxable supplies." As a registrant, the corporation is entitled to a full input tax credit (ITC) in respect of GST paid or payable on goods and services that it purchases exclusively for use in its commercial activity. If GST collected or collectible on its sales exceeds its ITCs, the corporation must remit the difference. On the other hand, if ITCs exceed GST collected or collectible, a refund of the excess is available.

ETA: 123(1)

ETA: 169(1)

The following is the appropriate GST treatment of the items listed:

(a) Net income per financial statements would have been increased by GST charged which is included in revenue and reduced by GST paid or payable which is included in costs. GST charged net of ITCs from GST paid or payable must be remitted.

(b) There are no GST implications for the provision for income taxes.

(c) GST paid on the purchase of depreciable property provides an ITC, as discussed in Chapter 5. When the cost of the asset is subsequently written off through depreciation or capital cost allowance, there are no further GST implications.

The following costs would involve payment of GST on taxable supplies and, hence, would give rise to an ITC:

(a) inventory of goods purchased, and

(b) landscaping goods and services.

The following costs would not involve the payment of GST, since they are for exempt supplies:

(a) interest paid on income tax due results from a financial service, and

(b) bond interest also results from a financial service.

Chapter 5
Depreciable Property and Eligible Capital Property

LEARNING GOALS

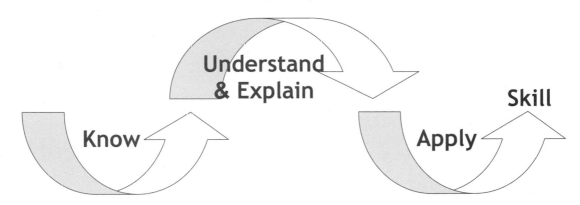

Know

By the end of this chapter you should know the basic provisions of the *Income Tax Act*, and the *Excise Tax Act*, pertaining to the GST, that relate to depreciable and eligible capital property. Completing the Review Questions (¶5,800) and Multiple Choice Questions (¶5,825) is a good way to learn the technical provisions.

Understand and Explain

You should understand and be able to explain how to calculate capital cost allowance and cumulative eligible capital amount, which is the tax equivalent of amortization for capital and intangible property. Completing the Exercises (¶5,850) is a good way to deepen your understanding of the material.

Apply

You should be able to use your knowledge and understanding of depreciable and eligible capital property to advise taxpayers on the tax implications of the purchase of these assets. Completing the Assignment Problems (¶5,875) is an excellent way to develop your ability to apply the material in increasingly complex situations.

Chapter 5 — Learning Chart

Topic	Example Problem (✓)	Review Questions (¶5,800)	Multiple Choice (¶5,825)	Exercises (¶5,850)	Assignment Problems (¶5,875)
¶5,000 THE CAPITAL COST ALLOWANCE SYSTEM					
¶5,010 Basic Rules	✓				
¶5,012 Eligibility for capital cost allowance					
¶5,015 Classes of assets for tangible capital property	✓	1, 4, 5, 6, 7, 8		4, 8	2, 7, 8, 9
¶5,020 Taxation year less than 12 months		9		6	
¶5,025 Ownership of property				1	
¶5,030 Disposition of property		2, 3		5	2, 6, 7, 8
¶5,035 Automobiles used in employment or business		10	1	2, 3, 8, 9	1, 2, 6
¶5,040 Comparison of capital cost allowance and accounting amortization					
¶5,045 Separate class rule for electronic office equipment					
¶5,050 Computer equipment acquired after March 22, 2004 and before March 19, 2007				8	
¶5,051 Computer equipment acquired on or after March 19, 2007					
¶5,052 Computer equipment acquired on or after January 28, 2009					
¶5,054 Example	✓		5	4	2, 7, 8
¶5,056 Transfers to another class — Avoiding recapture					
¶5,057 Interest expense					
¶5,058 Capital cost reduction for cost assistance		11			
¶5,059 Inducement payments					
¶5,060 Exceptions to the Declining Balance Method					
¶5,065 Leasehold improvements			2, 4	4, 6, 8	2, 7, 8
¶5,070 Class 14 limited-life intangibles		12	6	4, 6, 8	2, 7
¶5,075 Manufacturing and processing machinery and equipment					
¶5,080 Insurance Proceeds Expended on Damaged Depreciable Property					
¶5,090 Involuntary and Voluntary Dispositions					
¶5,095 Involuntary dispositions				7	10
¶5,100 Voluntary dispositions	✓				
¶5,110 Change in Use and Part Disposition Rules					
¶5,115 Change from income-producing to other purpose					
¶5,120 Change from non-income-producing to income-producing purpose					3
¶5,125 Property acquired for multiple purposes					
¶5,130 Change in proportion of use for producing income and other purposes	✓				

Topic	Example Problem (✓)	Review Questions (¶5,800)	Multiple Choice (¶5,825)	Exercises (¶5,850)	Assignment Problems (¶5,875)
¶5,135 Non-arm's length transfer of depreciable property					
¶5,150 Franchises and Similar Property					
¶5,200 ELIGIBLE CAPITAL PROPERTY					
¶5,210 Basic Rules		13	3	1	
¶5,220 Similarities with Capital Cost Allowance System					
¶5,230 Illustration of the Rules	✓			10, 11	2, 4, 5
¶5,235 Common aspects		14			
¶5,240 Non-arm's length transactions					
¶5,250 Election re: Capital Gain	✓				
¶5,300 CAPITAL PERSONAL PROPERTY AND THE INPUT TAX CREDIT SYSTEM UNDER GST					
¶5,310 Basic Rules					
¶5,320 Passenger Vehicles and Aircraft					
¶5,325 Passenger vehicles owned by registrants other than individuals and partnerships					
¶5,330 Passenger vehicles and aircraft owned by registrants who are individuals or partnerships					

CHAPTER 5

Study Notes

Chapter 5 —
Discussion Notes for Review Questions

(1) The full amount of the capital cost is added to the CCA class. The half-year rule makes a separate adjustment for purposes of calculating CCA in the year of acquisition, but this adjustment does not affect the capital cost.

ITR: 1100(2)

(2) A terminal loss is allowed only when the asset sold is the last asset in the class. Otherwise, the proceeds are credited to the UCC of the class under the definition of "undepreciated capital cost" and CCA is claimed on the remaining balance.

ITA: 13(21), 20(16)

(3) "Cost amount" reflects the tax value of an asset at a particular moment in time. With respect to depreciable property, cost amount is that proportion of the UCC that the capital cost of the asset is of the capital cost of all the assets in the class. Capital cost is not defined, but as used here, it means the laid-down cost which includes the actual cost plus all costs of preparing the asset for use.

ITA: 248(1) "cost amount"

ITA: 13(21)

(4) The "capital cost" is the amount that is added to the CCA class when the asset is first acquired [item A in the definition of "undepreciated capital cost"]. See (3) above for a broadly worded definition.

ITA: 13(21)

(5) Certain exceptions to the half-year rule are found in the Regulations. However, regulations for leaseholds and for classes like Classes 24 and 27 provide their own version of the half-year rule.

ITR: 1100(2)
ITR: 1100(1)(*b*), 1100(1)(*t*), 1100(1)(*ta*)

(6) The half-year rule is a simple, arbitrary adjustment that is made to reflect a period of ownership during the year. It is a simpler alternative to prorating CCA for the number of days the asset is owned during the year.

(7) Normally, the statement is true. However, the "available-for-use" rules do not allow CCA to be claimed until the asset is available for use by the taxpayer.

ITA: 13(26)–(32)

(8) An Information Circular provides the CRA's position on when the CCA claim for prior years can be changed. If the change results in a lower taxable income for the year, it must be requested within the normal time limits for appeals (see Chapter 14). If the change does not result in a lower taxable income, as, for example, the case of a loss year, the change will be allowed.

IC 84-1, par. 9, 10

(9) A regulation provides for this daily proration in the case of the short taxation year of a business, as might occur, for example, in the start-up year.

ITR: 1100(3)

(10) Normally, this statement is true. However, a regulation allows a CCA claim equal to one-half the normal CCA in the year of disposition, as compensation for the inability to claim a terminal loss on the disposal of a Class 10.1 automobile. To qualify, the taxpayer must have sold an auto that was in Class 10.1 and that was owned by him or her at the end of the preceding year.

ITR: 1100(2.5)

(11) Your client is correct. The Act reduces the capital cost of depreciable property for grants, subsidies, forgivable loans, deductions from tax, investment allowances or other assistance received on the acquisition of the property.

ITA: 13(7.1)

(12) There are four choices available for the legal costs of obtaining the patent:

(a) deduct them as expenses of representation;

ITA: 20(1)(*cc*)

(b) deduct the costs equally over 10 years;

ITA: 20(9)

(c) capitalize them in Class 14 by an election not to include them in Class 44 and depreciate them over the life of the patent; or

ITR: 1103(2h)

(d) capitalize the costs in Class 44 and depreciate them at a 25% declining-balance rate.

Any deduction under paragraph 20(1)(*cc*) or subsection 20(9) is subject to recapture.

ITA: 13(12); IT-99R5

(13) There is only *one* CEC pool for all eligible capital expenditures for each business. Since Mrs. Smith is only carrying on one business within her corporation, the additions to the company's CEC account in the year will be 75% of $10,800.

(14) He is able to deduct the full CEC balance as a business loss in the year that he ceased to carry on business.

ITA: 24

Chapter 5 —
Solutions to Multiple Choice Questions

Question 1

(C) is correct. The maximum CCA is: ½ × 30% × $30,000 = $4,500.   ITA: 13(7)(*g*); ITR: 7307(1)

(A) incorrectly uses the $50,000 cost of the vehicle to compute CCA: ½ × 30% × $50,000 = $7,500.

(B) incorrectly ignores the half-year rule: 30% × $30,000 = $9,000.

(D) incorrectly uses the pre-2001 maximum Class 10.1 cost of $27,000: ½ × 30% × $27,000 = $4,050.

Question 2

(A) is correct. $10,000 is the lesser of ⅕ × $80,000 = $16,000 and $80,000/8 = $10,000. For 2009,   ITR: 1100(1)(*b*), Sch. III
the year the cost was incurred, the maximum CCA = 50% of $10,000 = $5,000.

(B) is incorrect. It is 50% of the $16,000 amount calculated in (A).

(C) is incorrect because the $10,000 figure does not take into account the 50% rule.   ITR: 1100(1)(*b*)

(D) is incorrect for the reasons outlined for (B) and (C) combined.

Question 3

(D) is correct. The maximum CECA claim is: 75% × $100,000 × 7% = $5,250.

(A) is incorrect: $100,000/40 = $2,500. Forty years is the maximum period for amortization of goodwill for accounting purposes only.

(B) is incorrect: ½ × $100,000 × 7% = $3,500. The ½ rate does not apply for purposes of additions to the CEC pool.

(C) is incorrect: 7% × $100,000 = $7,000. Only 75% of the cost is used before multiplying by 7%.

Question 4

(B) is correct because the remaining lease term in 2009 is three years and the first renewal period is three years. The maximum CCA claim is $5,000, calculated as follows:

Lesser of: (i)   1/5 × $60,000   = $12,000
           (ii) $60,000/(3 + 3)   = $10,000

For 2009, the year the cost was incurred, the maximum CCA is: 50% of $10,000 = $5,000.   ITR: 1100(1)(*b*)

(A) is incorrect, because it uses the initial 5-year term of the lease in the calculation in place of the remaining lease term of three years: $60,000/(5 + 3) = $7,500 × 50% = $3,750.

(C) is incorrect, because the greater ($12,000), as opposed to the lesser ($10,000), of the two amounts calculated has been used: $6,000 = 50% × $12,000.

(D) is incorrect, because it uses the initial 5-year term of the lease in the calculation in place of the remaining lease term of three years and ignores the 50% rule in Regulation 1100(1)(*b*): $60,000/(5 + 3) = $7,500.

Question 5

(B) is correct. Under the Regulations, dies and moulds and software are not excepted from the half   ITR: 1100(2)
net-amount rule, but the other Class 12 items are: linens are listed in paragraph (*g*), cutlery and dishes are listed in paragraph (*b*) and kitchen utensils costing less than $500 are listed in paragraph (*c*)). ½ ($1,200 + $600) + $15,000 + $400 = $16,300.

(A) is incorrect because it uses the half net-amount rule on all Class 12 assets: ½ ($1,200 + $600 + $15,000 + $400) = $8,600.

(C) is incorrect because it ignores the half net-amount rule on the dies and moulds: $1,200 + ½ × $600 + $15,000 + $400 = $16,900.

(D) is incorrect because it ignores the half net-amount rule on the dies and moulds and software: $1,200 + $600 + $15,000 + $400 = $17,200.

Question 6

(D) is not available, since the property is not eligible capital property.

(A), (B), and (C) are all options for the treatment of patent costs.

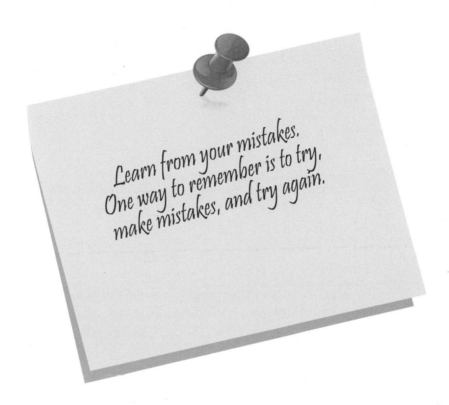

Chapter 5 — Solutions to Exercises

Exercise 1

The overpass is not eligible for capital cost allowance, since the owners have no title to the land on which the footings are placed and capital cost allowance cannot be claimed on assets that are not owned (see *Saskatoon Community Broadcasting Co. Ltd. v. M.N.R.*). The cost of the overpass qualifies as an eligible capital expenditure.   58 DTC 491 (T.A.B.)

Exercise 2

Harrison's automobile is defined as a passenger vehicle for CCA purposes. Passenger vehicles with a cost in excess of $30,000 (2009 amount) must be placed into a separate CCA class, Class 10.1. The depreciation rate for class 10.1 assets is 30%. However, CCA may only be taken on the deemed capital cost of the vehicle up to a maximum of $30,000 (paragraph 13(7)(*a*) and ITR 7307(1)). Harrison's maximum CCA claim for the first and second year of owning the car would be calculated as follows: ITA: 13(7); ITR: 7307(1)

Year 1

Capital cost of additions	$30,000
Less CCA (30,000 × 30% × 50%*)	4,500
UCC, end of year 1	$25,500

* Half-year rule applied.

Business use CCA (CCA × usage %) = $4,500 × 40% = $1,800

Year 2

UCC, Beginning of Year 2	$25,500
Less CCA @ 30%	7,650
UCC, end of Year 2	$17,850

Business use CCA (CCA × usage %) = $7,650 × 40% = $3,060

Exercise 3

No terminal loss can be deducted for an automobile in Class 10.1. The special "half-year rule" to compute capital cost allowance in the year of disposition applies to Class 10.1.   ITA: 20(16.1); ITR: 1100(2.5)

(A)	Jan.	1/09	UCC (Class 10.1)	$ 18,475
		2009	CCA (½ × .30 × $18,475)	(2,771)[1]
			Proceeds of disposition	(12,000)
			Terminal loss of $3,704 denied	Nil
(B)		2009	Purchase ($36,000) (new Class 10.1) max.	$ 33,900[2]
	Dec.	31/09	UCC before adjustment	$ 33,900
			One-half of net amount (½ × $33,900)	(16,950)
			UCC before CCA	$ 16,950
			CCA @ 30% of $16,950	(5,085)[3]
			Add: ½ net amount	16,950
	Jan.	1/10	UCC	$ 28,815

— *NOTES TO SOLUTION*

[1] Note that 75% of $2,771 or $2,078 is the deduction based on business use.

[2] Limited to $30,000 plus PST (8%) and GST (5%) or $33,900, since it was acquired after 2000.

[3] Note that 75% of $5,085 or $3,814 is deductible, since CCA claimed is not subject to the limitation on sales/negotiating person's expenses.   ITA: 8(1)(*f*), 8(1)(*j*)

Exercise 4

	Cl. 1: 4%	Cl. 8: 20%	Cl. 10: 30%	Cl. 13: S.L.	Cl. 14: S.L.	Cl. 29: 50%
Jan. 1/09						
UCC	$120,000	$75,000	$40,000	$42,000	$54,400	Nil
2009 Purchases:						
— mfg. equip.						$50,000
— off. equip.		10,000				
Disposals:						
— building	(100,000)[1]					
— equip.						
Dec. 31/09						
UCC before adjustment	$ 20,000	$85,000	$40,000	$42,000	$54,400	$50,000
½ net-amount...........	Nil	(5,000)	Nil	Nil	N/A	(25,000)
UCC before CCA	$ 20,000	$80,000	$40,000	$42,000	$54,400	$25,000
CCA..................	(800)	(16,000)	(12,000)	(1,250)[2]	(3,400)[3]	(12,500)
½ net-amount...........	Nil	5,000	Nil	Nil	N/A	25,000
Jan. 1/10						
UCC	$ 19,200	$69,000	$28,000	$40,750	$51,000	$37,500

NOTES TO SOLUTION

[1] Capital gain on disposition of building of $50,000.

[2] Lesser of: (a) ⅕ of $50,000 .... $10,000
(b) $50,000/40 (max.) .... $ 1,250 } $1,250
— not reduced by ½ because not first year of ownership.

[3] $\dfrac{\$68,000}{(20 \times 365)} \times 365 = \$3,400$

Exercise 5

The proceeds from the sale of Liam's building are greater than the UCC of the building. This would indicate that, although Liam claimed CCA in previous years, the market value of the building did not decline. Accordingly, CCA claimed in previous years must be recaptured and added to income for tax purposes in the current year. Liam must report recaptured depreciation of $15,500, calculated as follows:

ITA: 13

Class 1-4%		
UCC, beginning of year		$144,500
Less disposition at lesser of:		
Capital cost	$160,000	
Net proceeds	$180,000	160,000
Recaptured depreciation..............................		$(15,500)

Note that no CCA may be claimed in the year as a result of the disposition and recapture.

Exercise 6

(a)(i) $100,000 × 20% × ½ = $10,000

ITA: 20(1)

(ii) $100,000 × 20% × ½ × (90/365) = $2,466

In (ii), CCA is prorated because the taxation year is less than 365 days.

(b) Leasehold improvements — CCA is lesser of

(1) $25,000 × ⅕ × ½ = $2,500

(2) $25,000 \times \frac{1}{12} \times \frac{1}{2} = \$1,042$

(Twelve years is the denominator; this includes the initial lease term and the first renewal period.)

(c) The franchise is for a limited term, hence it is a Class 14 asset. The CCA on Class 14 assets is computed on a straight-line basis over the remaining life of the asset. The half-year rule does not apply to Class 14. CCA allowed to July 31 (153 days) is:

$25,000 \times \frac{1}{15} \times (153/365) = \$699$

Exercise 7

			Cl. 3: 5%	
Jan. 1, 2008	UCC		$ 221,000	
	Disposal[(1)]			
	lesser of:			
	(a) capital cost $300,000			
	(b) proceeds $295,000		(295,000)	
Dec. 31, 2008	UCC		$ (74,000)	
	Recapture		74,000	
Jan. 1, 2009	UCC		Nil	
Aug. 2009	File an amended return for 2008 as follows:			ITA: 13(4)
Jan. 1, 2008	UCC		$ 221,000	
	Deemed proceeds			ITA: 13(4)(*c*)
	lesser of:			
	(a) capital cost	$300,000		
	(b) proceeds	$295,000 → $295,000		
	reduced by lesser of:			
	(a) recapture			
	($295K – $221K)	$ 74,000 → $ 74,000		
	(b) replacement cost	$400,000	$(221,000)	
Dec. 31, 2008	UCC		Nil	
	Recapture		Nil	
Jan. 1, 2009	UCC		Nil	
			Cl. 1-NRB: 6%[(2)]	
2009	Purchase of new building	$400,000		
	Less: reduction above	74,000	$ 326,000	ITA: 13(4)(*c*)
Dec. 31, 2009	UCC		$ 326,000	
	CCA @ 6% of [$326,000 – ($\frac{1}{2} \times$ $326,000)]		(9,780)	
Jan. 1, 2010	UCC		$ 316,220	

— *NOTES TO SOLUTION*

(1) The CRA appears to require that even if a replacement property is purchased before the tax return for the year of disposition must be filed (i.e., within six months of the taxation year-end), the recapture must be reported in the year of disposition. The taxpayer can request a reassessment if and when the replacement is purchased within the specified time limits. In lieu of paying tax initially on the recapture, the CRA will take acceptable security until the final determination of tax is made.

IT-259R3, par. 3

(2) Note how the rules allow for a replacement with an asset of another class.

ITA: 13(4)

Exercise 8

ITA: 20(1)

a.   **Class 1** ($208,895 + $\frac{1}{2}$ ($20,000)) $\times$ 4% = $ 8,756

b.　**Class 13 — Leasehold Improvements**
Lesser of:

(i) $\frac{1}{10} \times \frac{1}{2} \times 70,000$　　　　　$\underline{\$3,500}$

(ii) $\frac{1}{5} \times \frac{1}{2} \times 70,000$　　　　　$\underline{\$7,000}$

CCA for the year　　　　　　　　　　$\underline{\$\ 3,500}$

c.　**Class 45 (Computer equipment)**

UCC, beginning of year	$40,000
Additions	0
	$40,000
CCA 40,000 × 45%	18,000
UCC, end of year	$22,000

d.　Class 10 (trucks)

UCC, beginning of year	$25,000
Less dispositions ($10,000 – $1,000)	(9,000)
	$16,000
CCA 30%	4,800
UCC, end of year	$11,200

e.　**Class 14 — License**

$30,000 \times \frac{1}{15} \times (122*/365)$　　　　　$\underline{\$\ \ \ \ 668}$

* Number of days from June 1 to September 30.

Exercise 9

The change in use rules could be applied as follows:　　　　　　　　ITA: 13(7)(*d*)

			Cl. 10:[1] *30%*
2007	Purchase (85% of $14,600)		$12,410
Dec. 31, 2007	UCC		$12,410
	CCA @ 30% of [($12,410 – (½ × $12,410)]		(1,862)
Jan.　1, 2008	UCC		$10,548
2008	Disposal (5% of $12,200)[2]		(610)
Dec. 31, 2008	UCC		$ 9,938
	CCA @ 30% of $9,938		(2,981)
Jan.　1, 2009	UCC		$ 6,957
2009	Purchase (10% of $9,800)[3]		980
Dec. 31, 2009	UCC		$ 7,937
	CCA @ 30% of [$7,937 – (½ × $980)]		(2,234)
Jan.　1, 2010	UCC		$ 5,703

In practice, however, the following calculation of capital cost allowance might be made:

		Cl. 10: 30%	*Business deduction of CCA*
2007	Purchase	$14,600	
Dec. 31, 2007	UCC	$14,600	
	CCA @ 30% of ½ × $14,600	(2,190)	85% of $2,190 = $1,862
Dec. 31, 2008	UCC	$12,410	
	CCA @ 30%	(3,723)	80% of $3,723 = $2,978
Dec. 31, 2009	UCC	$ 8,687	
	CCA @ 30%	(2,606)	[80% + ½ (90% – 80%)][4] of $2,606 = $2,215
Jan.　1, 2010	UCC	$ 6,081	

—NOTES TO SOLUTION

(1) Since the automobile cost less than the prescribed limit, it is placed in Class 10.   ITA: 13(7)(g)

(2) Lesser of proceeds at fair market value and capital cost.

(3) Since fair market value is less than cost, the increase in capital cost is based on fair market value.

(4) An increase in use for business represents an addition to the class which is subject to the half-year rule. In practice, the CCA may be computed simply as 90% of $2,606 or $2,345.

Exercise 10

The cumulative eligible capital account would be affected as follows:

Year	Opening balance	Par. 20(1)(b) deduction[1]	Ssec. 14(1) business income inclusion	Closing balance
1996	$ 8,100	$ 567		$7,533
1997[2]	7,533	527		7,006
2008	7,006	490		6,516
2009	6,516	—	$18,684[3]	
Total		$1,584		

2009 Opening balance	$ 6,516
Sale (¾ × $45,000)	(33,750)
Negative balance	(27,234)
Minus: previous CECA claims	1,584
Balance	$(25,650)
Income inclusion:	
Previous CECA claims	$ 1,584
⅔ × $25,650	17,100
Total	$ 18,684

—NOTES TO SOLUTION

(1) 7% of the declining balance.

(2) No amortization deductions taken in the 1998–2007 period because of business losses.   ITA: 20(1)(b)

(3) The sale in 2009 would result in $18,684 of business income which is equal to the sum (rounded) of par. 20(1)(b) deductions ($1,584) plus ½ of the gain of $34,200 ($45,000 – $10,800).

Exercise 11

Jan. 1, 2001	Purchase of goodwill (¾ × $40,000)	$ 30,000
Dec. 31, 2001	Cumulative eligible capital amount @ 7%	(2,100)
Jan. 1, 2002	Cumulative eligible capital	$ 27,900
Dec. 31, 2002	Cumulative eligible capital amount @ 7%	(1,953)
Jan. 1, 2003	Cumulative eligible capital	$ 25,947
June 1, 2003	Purchase of license (¾ × $50,000)	37,500
	Cumulative eligible capital	$ 63,447
Dec. 31, 2003	Cumulative eligible capital amount @ 7%	(4,441)
Jan. 1, 2004	Cumulative eligible capital	$ 59,006
Dec. 31, 2004	Cumulative eligible capital amount @ 7%	(4,130)
Jan. 1, 2005	Cumulative eligible capital	$ 54,876
Mar. 1, 2005	Purchase of trademark (¾ × $20,000)	15,000
	Cumulative eligible capital	$ 69,876

Dec. 31, 2005	Cumulative eligible capital amount @ 7%	(4,891)	
Jan. 1, 2006	Cumulative eligible capital	$ 64,985	
Nov. 1, 2006	Purchase of goodwill (¾ × $50,000)	37,500	
	Cumulative eligible capital	$ 102,485	
Dec. 31, 2006	Cumulative eligible capital amount @ 7%	(7,174)	
Jan. 1, 2007	Cumulative eligible capital	$ 95,311	
Sept. 7, 2007	Sale of goodwill (¾ × $100,000)	(75,000)	
	Cumulative eligible capital	$ 20,311	
Dec. 31, 2007	Cumulative eligible capital amount @ 7%	(1,422)	
Jan. 1, 2008	Cumulative eligible capital	$ 18,889	
Dec. 31, 2008	Cumulative eligible capital amount @ 7%	(1,322)	
Jan. 1, 2009	Cumulative eligible capital	$ 17,567	
Aug. 3, 2009	Sale of license (¾ × $150,000)	(112,500)	
	Sale of trademark (¾ × $200,000)	(150,000)	
Dec. 31, 2009	Cumulative eligible capital	$(244,933)	ITA: 14(1)
	Business income	172,433	
	Non-taxed ⅓ of "gain" [⅓ × ($244,933 − 27,433)]	72,500	
Jan. 1, 2010	Cumulative eligible capital	$ Nil	

The business income in 2009 is calculated as:

The total of:
(a) the lesser of:
    (i) the negative amount .... $ 244,933

    and

    (ii) the total of: ....

all cumulative eligible capital deductions......	$ 27,433	
less: all recaptured deductions in prior years...	Nil	
	$ 27,433	
The lesser is		$ 27,433

and
(b) ⅔ of (negative amount less recaptured in deductions in
(a)(ii), above [⅔ × ($244,933 − 27,433)] 145,000*

Business income $172,433

* This is the same as:

Proceeds ($100,000 + $150,000 + $200,000)	$ 450,000
Cost ($40,000 + $50,000 + $20,000 + $50,000)	(160,000)
Gain	$ 290,000
½ = ...	$ 145,000

Chapter 6
Income from Property

LEARNING GOALS

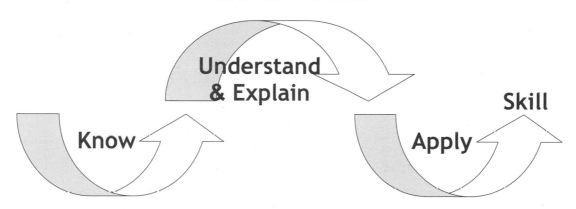

Know

By the end of this chapter you should know the basic provisions of the *Income Tax Act* that relate to property income and the income attribution rules that are uniquely applicable to property income. It is important to know the distinction between property income and business income, since they are two separate sources of income on which different income tax rules may apply. You should also know a little about how the GST affects some property income issues. Completing the Review Questions (¶6,800) and Multiple Choice Questions (¶6,825) is a good way to learn the technical provisions.

Understand and Explain

You should understand and be able to explain the tax treatment of specific types of property income and expenses, including the basic questions of who will pay the tax, and when and how much tax will be paid. You should also understand some basic tax planning strategies that can be utilized in real life to maximize the after-tax return on investment. Completing the Exercises (¶6,850) is a good way to deepen your understanding of the material.

Apply

You should be able to apply your knowledge and understanding of property income to real life situations. Completing the Assignment Problems (¶6,875) and Advisory Cases (¶6,880) is an excellent way to develop your ability to identify tax issues and to apply the material in increasingly complex situations.

Chapter 6 — Learning Chart

CHAPTER 6

Topic	Example Problem (✓)	Review Questions (¶6,800)	Multiple Choice (¶6,825)	Exercises (¶6,850)	Assignment Problems (¶6,875)
¶6,000 INCLUSIONS					
¶6,005 Specific Inclusions of Property Income					
¶6,010 Interest Income		1, 2		1	2, 7, 10
¶6,015 The meaning of interest					
¶6,020 Method of reporting income					
¶6,025 Accrual rules for individuals	✓				
¶6,030 Other interest income provisions					
¶6,032 Purchasing a corporate bond at a discount	✓				
¶6,033 Treasury bills	✓				
¶6,034 Zero-coupon bonds	✓				
¶6,035 Timing and recognition of interest income	✓				
¶6,036 Purchasing an accrued interest bond	✓				11
¶6,040 Payments Based on Production or Use					1
¶6,045 Concept of the provision	✓				
¶6,050 Dividends from Corporations Resident in Canada			1, 5		2, 7, 8, 10
¶6,052 Overview					
¶6,055 The issue					
¶6,060 Overview of the Canadian dividend taxation system	✓				
¶6,065 Dividends Received from Non-Resident Corporations			5		7, 8
¶6,070 Income Attribution		3, 4	3, 6	2	2, 9, 10, 11
¶6,075 The reason for attribution rules					
¶6,080 Definition of related persons					
¶6,085 Transactions subject to income attribution	✓				
¶6,090 Avoiding income attributions					
¶6,095 Anti-avoidance rules relating to attribution					
¶6,100 More types of income subject to attribution					
¶6,102 "Second-generation" income from property					
¶6,105 Loans or transfers to non-arm's length individuals who are 18 years of age or older					
¶6,110 Summary of income attribution rules					
¶6,115 Tax on split income earned by persons under 18 years of age (the "Kiddie Tax")	✓				
¶6,120 What else can be income split?					
¶6,200 DEDUCTIONS					
¶6,210 Carrying Charges on Land					
¶6,215 Limitation on deduction — Vacant land	✓	5		3	3, 11
¶6,220 "Soft Costs" Relating To Construction of Buildings or Ownership of Land					5

Topic	Example Problem (✓)	Review Questions (¶6,800)	Multiple Choice (¶6,825)	Exercises (¶6,850)	Assignment Problems (¶6,875)
¶6,230 Rental Properties		6	2	4, 5, 7	4, 7, 10
¶6,235 Separate classes — Rental property costing over $50,000					
¶6,240 Losses from rental property	✓				
¶6,250 Depreciation-Based or Similar Tax Shelters					
¶6,260 Interest Deduction		7			
¶6,265 Proposed legislation					
¶6,270 Loss of the source of income	✓	10			
¶6,275 Capitalization of interest					
¶6,290 Personal Loan Planning and Interest Deductibility		8, 9	4	6	10, 11, 12
¶6,295 Deductibility of interest expenses					
¶6,300 Commentary on two Supreme Court decisions on interest deductibility — Singleton and Ludco					
¶6,305 Tax planning	✓				
¶6,310 Carrying charges					
¶6,315 Investment counsel fees					
¶6,320 Legal and accounting fees					
¶6,325 Foreign non-business income tax					
¶6,400 DIFFERENCES BETWEEN BUSINESS AND PROPERTY INCOME					
¶6,410 Applicable to Business Income Only					
¶6,420 Applicable to Property Income Only					
¶6,500 GST AND PROPERTY INCOME					
¶6,510 Interest and Dividends					
¶6,520 "Soft Costs"					6

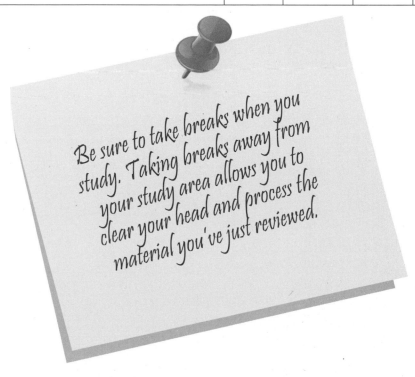

Be sure to take breaks when you study. Taking breaks away from your study area allows you to clear your head and process the material you've just reviewed.

Study Notes

Chapter 6 —
Discussion Notes for Review Questions

(1) The principal would be separated from the accrued interest and cause the interest to be included in Billy's income as interest income. The purchaser can deduct the same amount that the vendor included in income.

ITA: 20(14)(*a*)
ITA: 20(14)(*b*)

(2) Interest accrued annually to the anniversary date of the bond is taxable, requiring tax to be paid from some other source of funds, since no interest will be received on the compound interest bond. Your client may wish to invest in the type of Canada Savings Bonds that pay interest annually. Note that the annual accrual rules may not present a cash flow problem if the holder of the bond is not taxable on the accrued interest due to a low level of total income.

ITA: 12(4)

(3) Attribution would not appear to apply to cause any income allocated to Mrs. Soleprop to be reallocated to her husband since there is no attribution of business income. (It should be noted that, if she is not actively involved in the business, then she will not be a specified member of the partnership and the income from the partnership will be deemed to be income from property.)

ITA: 74.1(1)

ITA: 248(1), 96(1.8)

(4) Although the corporation is carrying on a business, Mrs. Smith is not. She will be earning property income (i.e., dividends on the shares), so the exception to the attribution rules for business income does not apply. Attribution as a result of guarantees would only cause the attribution rules to apply if the loan was not at commercial rates. If the bank is charging commercial interest rates, then the attribution rules will not apply.

ITA: 74.5(7)
ITA: 74.5(1)

(5) The interest on the 10 acres would be capitalized since it is not used in business and there is no revenue from the land.

ITA: 18(2)

(6) CCA cannot be claimed to create or increase a loss on rental property. However, those loss limitation rules do not apply to a corporation whose principal business was the leasing, rental, development or sale, or any combination thereof, of real property owned by it. In this case, Rent Co. will be able to claim CCA to create or increase a loss.

ITR: 1100(11)–(14)

(7) No interest is deductible if Ms. Cautious is considered to realize a capital gain on the sale of the gold. Since capital gains are not income from business or property, she does not meet the requirements and cannot deduct the interest. Also, there is no provision that would allow her to capitalize the interest to the cost of the gold. On the other hand, if the gain on the sale of the gold is considered to be income from business or property, the interest would be deductible. Note that the CRA would allow her to choose income treatment for these transactions.

ITA: 9(3)
ITA: 20(1)(*c*)
ITA: 53
IT-346R, par. 8

(8) In the *Attaie* case, the Federal Court–Trial Division agreed that the interest expense was deductible. However, the Federal Court of Appeal reversed this decision and decided that the interest was not deductible, since there was not a direct link between the borrowed funds and the income from property.

87 DTC 5411 (F.C.T.D.)
90 DTC 6413 (F.C.A.)

(9) Under the proposed plan, the interest would not be deductible since the money is not being used to earn income. However, if your client were to borrow from the bank the $100,000 needed to loan to the purchaser in order to complete the sale of his existing house, then at least the interest would be deductible up to 8%. The purchaser would then be in a position to pay the full purchase price for the new residence.

(10) Since the corporation that your client invested in has gone out of business, there is no longer a possibility of earning income from business or property. However, the amount of the lost capital would be deemed to continue to be borrowed for the purpose of earning income and, hence, would allow the interest in this case to continue to be deductible. Refer to IT-533, paragraph 19.

ITA: 20.1(1)

CHAPTER 6

Chapter 6 —
Solutions to Multiple Choice Questions

Question 1

(B) is correct. The calculation is as follows:

Grossed up dividend ($12,000 × 1.25)	$15,000
Combined tax rate	× 46%
	$ 6,900
Dividend tax credit	(3,000)
Net tax	$ 3,900

(A) incorrectly ignores provincial tax: $15,000 × 29% − $3,000 = $1,350.

(C) incorrectly ignores the dividend tax credit:

$$\$15,000 \times 46\% = \$6,900$$

(D) incorrectly ignores the gross-up and the dividend tax credit: $12,000 × 46% = $5,520.

Question 2

(B) is the correct answer. The calculation is as follows:

	Property			
	1	*2*	*3*	*Total*
UCC at Jan. 1st	$100,000	$75,000	$150,000	
Rental revenue for the year	$ 58,000	$22,000	$ 20,000	
Expenses for the year	50,000	20,000	20,000	
Income before CCA	$ 8,000	$ 2,000	(Nil)	$10,000
CCA: 4% × UCC	$ 4,000	$ 3,000	$ 6,000	$13,000
Maximum CCA [Reg. 1100(11)]				$10,000

(A) is incorrect. $13,000 is the CCA calculation ignoring the rental property restriction.   ITR: 1100(11)

(C) is incorrect. $7,000 is the maximum CCA calculation on the first two buildings only. This calculation ignores the fact that the CCA on the third property can be claimed against the net rental income on the first two properties.

(D) is incorrect. It is one-half of the $13,000 calculated in (A) above.

Question 3

(B) is the correct answer. The $12,000 of dividend income will be attributed to Mr. P. Mabel and   ITA: 56(4.1)
Mr. P are related and it can reasonably be considered that one of the main reasons for making the loan was to reduce tax.

(A) is incorrect. The $3,000 of interest income will not be attributed. Peter is not under 18 years of age and, therefore, attribution does not apply. If it had been a loan, instead of a gift, subsection 56(4.1)   ITA: 74.1(2)
would apply and may attribute the income.

(C) is incorrect. Even though an interest-free loan was made to which attribution would apply,   ITA: 56(4.1)
there is no property income from the cottage to attribute.

(D) is incorrect. Even though a gift was made to a spouse to which attribution would apply, there is   ITA: 74.1(1)
no property income from the chequing account to attribute.

Question 4

(B) is correct. The premium paid on a $100,000 term life insurance policy on the taxpayer's life   ITA: 20(1)(e.2)
which is required as collateral for a $100,000 bank loan used to purchase a $100,000 investment in common shares is deductible.

(A) is incorrect because commissions paid on the purchase of an investment in common shares are capitalized as part of the cost of the shares.   ITA: 18(1)(*b*)

(C) is incorrect because the Act does not allow a deduction for interest expense on a loan to invest in a registered retirement savings plan.   ITA: 18(11)(*b*)

(D) is incorrect because commissions paid on the sale of an investment in common shares are a selling cost deducted in computing the capital gain on the sale of the shares. One-half of a capital gain is a taxable capital gain which is computed under Subdivision c of Division B of Part I of the Act, whereas income from business or property is computed under Subdivision b.

Question 5

(D) is correct: $20,000 × 1.25 + $8,500 + $1,500 tax withheld = $35,000.   ITA: 82(1)

(A) is incorrect because it ignores the gross-up on the dividend and the foreign income: $20,000.

(B) is incorrect because it ignores the gross-up on the dividend and the foreign tax withheld: $20,000 + $8,500 = $28,500.

(C) is incorrect because it ignores the gross-up on the dividend: $20,000 + $8,500 + $1,500 = $30,000.

Question 6

(D) is correct.

(A) is incorrect because the tax on split income only applies to taxpayers under age 18 throughout the year. Since Ron is 18, the tax on split income will not apply.   ITA: 120.4 "specified individual"

(B) is incorrect because the only exemption regarding inherited shares is for shares inherited from a parent. If Ron had been under 18 at any time in the year, the tax on split income would have applied to dividends received on the shares.   ITA: 120.4 "excluded amount"

(C) is incorrect because the tax on split income does not apply to capital gains.   ITA: 120.4 "split income"

Chapter 6 — Solutions to Exercises

Exercise 1

(A) In its June 30, 2009 taxation year, the corporation would be required to include in income the interest received March 31, 2009 for the period October 1, 2008 to March 31, 2009 plus interest accrued from April 1 to June 30, 2009. Accrued interest from October 1, 2008 to January 1, 2009 (the period prior to acquisition), which was purchased with the bond, would give rise to a deduction. ITA: 12(3), 20(14)

(B) The Act would require accrued interest from November 1, 2009 to October 31, 2010 to be included in income in 2010. ITA: 12(4)

(C) The anniversary day would be December 31, 2009. Accrued interest from the date of purchase to December 31, 2009 would be included in 2009 income.

(D) The first anniversary day would occur October 31, 2010 and accrued interest would be included at that time. The CRA has, in the past, administratively allowed Canada Savings Bond interest to be accrued on a "bond year" basis. The Act gives legislative effect to this practice. IT-396R, par. 25; ITA: 12(4)

(E) The $80 received each year would be included in income. On November 30, 2009, there will be an anniversary day, but all of the interest accrued to that day will have been included in income as interest received in the year. ITA: 12(1)(c)

Exercise 2

(A) (i) The Act would attribute the income on the bond to him even though she is legally entitled to receive it, since a gift is considered to be a transfer and is not a fair market value exchange which would be exempt. ITA: 74.1(1), 74.5(1)

    (ii) Since a sale is also considered to be a transfer, attribution would apply except that, in this case, the transfer would be exempt because it was for fair market value consideration, as long as they elect jointly not to have the rollover apply. ITA: 74.1(1), 74.5(1)(a), 73(1)

    (iii) This situation still involves a sale directly between husband and wife and is, therefore, a transfer subject to the attribution of income. A non-interest bearing demand note would not qualify for the exception because a commercial rate of interest was not charged. ITA: 74.1(1), 74.5(1)(b)

    (iv) The loan of funds would result in attribution, because the exception would not apply since a commercial rate of interest was not charged on the loan. ITA: 74.1(1), 74.5(2)

(B) If the loan was to a non-arm's length minor or a niece or nephew who is also a minor, then attribution would apply to transfers or loans by means of a trust to or for the benefit of a minor in the same way as spousal attribution applied in part (A), above. However, there are special rules pertaining to transfers or loans to a trust which will be discussed in Chapter 18. ITA: 74.1(2)
ITA: 74.1(1)

(C) Attribution of income does not apply to a transfer involving an individual who is 18 or older. However, another provision might apply to transactions (iii) and (iv) involving loans. The key condition for this rule to apply is that one of the main reasons for the loan was to reduce or avoid tax on income from property or substituted property. A loan bearing a commercial rate of interest would be exempt from attribution. ITA: 74.1(2)
ITA: 56(4.1)

Exercise 3

(i) The deductibility of carrying charges is not limited because the land is being used in the course of the hotel business. ITA: 18(2)

(ii) The Act will limit the deductibility of carrying charges to 75% of their total (i.e., to the amount of the net revenues) so as not to create a loss by their deduction, unless the land is owned by a corporation whose principal purpose is the rental of real property (i.e., land and building) owned by it. This is not the principal purpose of a hotel corporation. ITA: 18(2)(e)

ITA: 18(2)(f)

(iii) The deductibility of carrying charges may be limited in the same manner as in (ii), above, until the property is used in the business. ITA: 18(2)

Exercise 4

	Class 1: 4% Building 1	Class 1: 4% Building 2[(1)]	Class 8: 20%	Total
UCC, January 1	$148,000	—	$25,000	
Purchases	—	$137,500	—	
UCC, December 31	$148,000	$137,500	$25,000	
CCA	5,920	2,750[(2)]	4,350[(3)]	$13,020
UCC, January 1	$142,080	$134,750	$20,650	

— *NOTES TO SOLUTION*

(1) Separate class for rental building costing $50,000 or more.   ITR: 1101(1ac)

(2) 4% of [$137,500 − (½ × $137,500)].

(3)

Net rental income before CCA ($9,270 + 3,750)		$13,020
CCA on rental building and leasing properties (i.e., furniture and fixtures) limited to $13,020 [$13,020 − ($5,920 + $2,750) = $4,350]		(13,020)
Net income from rental properties		Nil

Note that where less than maximum capital cost allowance is taken, the less than maximum amount should be taken in classes with relatively higher CCA rates, so that the UCC carried forward to the following year is eligible for CCA at the higher rate in that subsequent year.

Exercise 5

(A)

	Property A	Property B	Total
UCC, January 1	$330,000	$480,000	
Disposal	(336,000)	—	
UCC, December 31	$ (6,000)	$480,000	
Recapture	6,000	—	
CCA @ 4% (Class 1) — see below	—	(12,000)	
UCC forward	Nil	$468,000	
Revenue	$ 13,500	$ 22,500	$36,000
Recapture	6,000	—	6,000
Expenses before CCA	(11,250)	(18,750)	(30,000)
Net	$ 8,250	$ 3,750	$12,000
CCA (4% of $480,000 = $19,200; limited to net above)			(12,000)
Net income from property			Nil

(B)   The rule to defer recapture applies on a voluntary disposition of a "former business property". A   ITA: 13(4), 248(1)
rental property is excluded from the definition and, hence, the deferral rule does not apply.

Exercise 6

Interest expenses are deductible if there is a reasonable expectation of earning income from   ITA: 20(1)(c)
property.

Investment	Not deductible	Deductible
Common shares		$20,000[(1)]
Gold bullion	$25,000[(2)]	
Corporate bond		20,000[(3)]
Preferred shares (RRSP)	10,000[(4)]	

Common shares		30,000[5]
Paintings	15,000[6]	
GICs		20,000[5]
Total	$50,000	$90,000

Deductible interest = $90,000 × 8.5% = $7,650

— NOTES TO SOLUTION

[1] As there is often an expectation of dividend income on common shares, the interest is deductible.

[2] As capital treatment has been chosen for gains/losses on the gold bullion, the interest is not deductible.

[3] The corporate bond is income-producing and the associated interest would be deductible.

[4] The preferred shares were purchased in an RRSP; deduction of interest is disallowed.

[5] The associated interest on the common shares and GICs would be deductible, as there is the expectation of earning property income.

[6] The paintings from well-known galleries would be considered an investment for earning future capital gains and, therefore, the associated interest would not be deductible.

Exercise 7

Since the rule relates to capital cost allowance, Regulations Part XI, Capital Cost Allowances, would be a starting point. More specifically, ITR 1101(1ac) deals with the separate classes rule related to rental properties having a cost of at least $50,000.   ITR: 1100(11), 1101(1ac)

The other special rule is ITR 1100(11), which states that capital cost allowance on rental properties can only be deducted to the extent that it does not create or increase a net loss from all rental properties combined. Note that Interpretation Bulletin IT-195R4, *Rental Property — Capital Cost Allowance Restrictions*, provides further details.

Chapter 7
Capital Gains: An Introduction

LEARNING GOALS

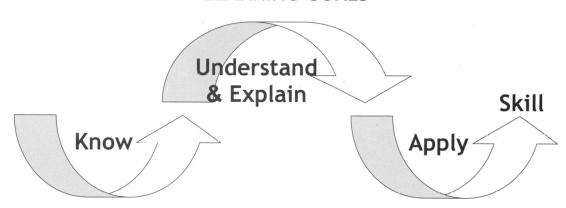

Know

By the end of this chapter you should know the basic provisions of the *Income Tax Act* that relate to capital gains and losses. Completing the Review Questions (¶7,800) and Multiple Choice Questions (¶7,825) is a good way to learn the technical provisions.

Understand and Explain

You should understand and be able to explain

- how to calculate proceeds of disposition and the adjusted cost base to determine the capital gain or loss;
- how capital gains and losses are taxed;
- the special rules for principal residences, personal-use property, and listed personal property;
- the special case of an allowable business investment loss; and
- how capital gains and losses fit in to the calculation of income for tax purposes.

Apply

You should be able to apply your knowledge and understanding of the rules pertaining to capital gains and losses in a way that accomplishes a client's goals. Completing the Assignment Problems (¶7,875) is an excellent way to develop your ability to apply the material in increasingly complex situations.

Chapter 7 — Learning Chart

Topic	Example Problem (✓)	Review Questions (¶7,800)	Multiple Choice (¶7,825)	Exercises (¶7,850)	Assignment Problems (¶7,875)
¶7,000 OVERVIEW OF THE TAXATION OF CAPITAL GAINS					
¶7,010 History					
¶7,012 Capital Property					
¶7,013 General considerations					
¶7,014 Personal-use property					
¶7,015 Listed personal property					
¶7,016 Other capital property					
¶7,017 Schematic classification					
¶7,018 Restrictions					
¶7,020 Capital Receipt Versus Income Receipt Revisited		1, 2, 3, 4, 5			1
¶7,025 Primary intention					
¶7,030 Secondary intention					
¶7,035 Badges of trade or behavioural factors					
¶7,040 Terminology					
¶7,050 Capital Gains Deduction					
¶7,060 Election re: Disposition of Canadian Securities					
¶7,070 Avoidance					
¶7,100 GENERAL RULES					
¶7,110 Computation of Capital Gains and Capital Losses					
¶7,115 Proceeds of disposition		6			
¶7,120 Adjusted cost base and capital cost					
¶7,122 Mutual funds and DRIPs	✓			9	7
¶7,125 Reserves	✓		1		2, 7
¶7,130 Adjustments to the Cost Base		7			
¶7,200 SPECIFIC PROVISIONS FOR THE TAXATION OF CAPITAL GAINS					
¶7,210 Principal Residence Exemption	✓	8	4	1, 2	3, 6
¶7,220 Personal-Use Property	✓	9, 10	2, 6	3, 4, 7, 10	5, 6
¶7,230 Listed Personal Property	✓	10	6	3, 4, 7, 10	5, 6
¶7,235 Disposition of Depreciable Property	✓				
¶7,236 Capital Losses — General					
¶7,240 Pooling of Identical Assets Purchased After 1971	✓		3, 6	5, 6, 8	4, 8
¶7,250 Disposition of Shares Acquired Under a Stock Option					
¶7,255 Disposition of newly acquired securities	✓				
¶7,260 Adjusted cost base of shares acquired under a stock option					7
¶7,265 Identical properties exempt from cost-averaging rule	✓				

Topic	Example Problem (✓)	Review Questions (¶7,800)	Multiple Choice (¶7,825)	Exercises (¶7,850)	Assignment Problems (¶7,875)
¶7,270 Cost of Certain Properties	✓	11, 13, 14	5	8	4, 8
¶7,271 General consideration					
¶7,272 Dividends in kind					
¶7,273 Stock dividends					
¶7,280 Adjustments to the Cost Base					
¶7,290 Superficial Losses	✓				4, 8
¶7,295 Transfer of Property to an RRSP					
¶7,300 COMPUTATIONAL RULES					
¶7,310 Section 3 Revisited		12		10	7
¶7,320 Allowable Business Investment Losses	✓				7
¶7,900 SUPPLEMENTAL NOTES					
¶7,910 Cost of Assets Owned on December 31, 1971					
¶7,920 Additional Rules for a Residence Owned On and After December 31, 1981	✓				
¶7,930 Principal Residence on Farm Land					
¶7,940 GST Rules for Dispositions of Residential Property and Used Goods					
¶7,945 Sales of used residential or personal-use real property					
¶7,950 Sales of used goods and acceptance of trade-ins					

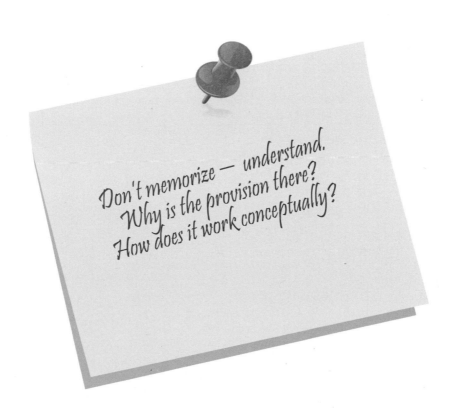

Don't memorize — understand.
Why is the provision there?
How does it work conceptually?

Study Notes

Chapter 7 —
Discussion Notes for Review Questions

(1) The transaction will probably be an income receipt. The partnership appears to have been set up specifically to buy and hold the land. The partnership agreement seems to confirm that their primary intention was to make a profit, since the agreement specifically states how the income is to be split. If, after five years, they still have done nothing to develop the land to earn rental or other income, then it would appear to be a speculation gain and, therefore, income.

(2) The transaction will probably be an income receipt. Rachel has used her specialized knowledge, derived from her normal occupation, to make the large profit. This factor, combined with her trading history, would weigh heavily in favour of income treatment.

(3) Normally, stock market transactions are treated as capital gains or losses. However, his intention seems to be to make a profit in trading shares, thereby indicating an income receipt. He may elect to have these transactions treated as capital gains. However, Winston should be careful that the CRA does not subsequently deem him to be a "trader" and thereby revoke his election.

ITA: 39(4), 39(5)

(4) The transaction would probably be an income receipt. Her primary intention is to develop the shopping centre for sale which would be an income transaction. Therefore, the sale of the land prior to development would also be an income transaction.

(5) Capital receipt (not taxable). Doug's $15,000 net winnings should not be treated as income because his actions are more in the nature of a hobby, not making a profit. If this was his business, the profits would be taxable.

IT-334R2, par. 10

(6) "Proceeds of disposition" is defined to include the principal amount of the mortgage that is owed to the mortgage company. This transaction may trigger recaptured CCA or a terminal loss.

ITA: 13(1), 13(21.1), 20(16), 54 "proceeds of disposition" (*h*)

(7) Whenever the adjusted cost base becomes negative there will be an immediate capital gain. The only exception to this rule is for a partnership interest in a general partnership (but not a limited partnership).

ITA: 40(3)

(8) Until the end of 1981 each individual could own and claim a principal residence. After that time the principal residence exemption is restricted to one residence per family. The rules provide the framework for deciding which residence should be claimed for which years in order to maximize the exemption. Mr. Confused and his wife must choose one residence or the other for the exemption.

ITA: 54 "principal residence" (*c*)
ITA: 40(2)(*b*)

(9) The cottage is considered to be "personal-use property" (PUP). Any loss on the disposal of PUP cannot be deducted. The losses are considered to arise as a result of normal personal use over time.

ITA: 40(2)(*g*)(iii), 54

(10) For the purpose of calculating the capital gain or loss on any disposal of PUP the taxpayer's cost is deemed to be the greater of the adjusted cost base of the property and $1,000. Similarly, the taxpayer's proceeds of disposition are deemed to be the greater of actual proceeds and $1,000. Listed personal property (LPP) is defined to be a subset of PUP; therefore, the $1,000 rule also applies to LPP.

ITA: 46(1)

ITA: 54

(11) The dividend should be included with the gross-up in income. The amount of the dividend before the gross-up will increase the cost base of the shares and effectively reduces the capital gain or increase the capital loss when the shares are sold.

ITA: 53(2)

(12) The result of the taxable capital gains minus the allowable capital losses cannot be negative. Any negative amount is a "net capital loss" that can be carried back three years or forward indefinitely.

ITA: 3(*b*) of Div. B; 111(1)(*b*), 111(8) of Div. C

(13) You would be deemed to have acquired the prize at a cost equal to its fair market value at the time you received it.

ITA: 52(4)

(14) The car has a cost base equal to the $35,000 benefit included in her income as a shareholder benefit.

ITA: 15(1), 52(1)

Chapter 7 —
Solutions to Multiple Choice Questions

Question 1

(B) is correct. The gain is: $600,000 – $100,000 = $500,000. The maximum 2009 reserve is computed using the lesser of the percentage of proceeds payable after the end of the year ($510K/$600K or 85%, in this case) and four fifths ($\frac{4}{5}$). Since the lesser amount is four fifths, the reserve is $400,000 ($\frac{4}{5}$ × $500,000) and the capital gain is therefore $100,000 ($500,000 – $400,000). The minimum taxable capital gain is therefore $50,000 ($\frac{1}{2}$).

ITA: 40(1)(*a*)

(A) is incorrect, because the capital gain must be multiplied by $\frac{1}{2}$ to compute the taxable capital gain.

(C) is incorrect, because it uses the 85% figure to compute the reserve and does not multiply the result by $\frac{1}{2}$: $500,000 – 85% × $500,000 = $75,000.

(D) is incorrect, because it uses the 85% figure to compute the reserve: $75,000 × $\frac{1}{2}$.

Question 2

(C) is correct. The loss on the automobile is not allowed since it is personal-use property (PUP). The $1,000 rule means that the gain on the boat (which is PUP) is $500, the gain on the painting (which is listed personal property (LPP)) is $300, and the loss on the jewellery (which is LPP) is $400. Since the deductible portion of the $400 LPP loss is limited to the LPP gain in the year ($300), the capital gain is: $500 + $300 – $300 = $500. The $100 LPP loss can be carried over against LPP gains.

ITA: 2, 41(1), 46(1), 54

(A) is incorrect, because it ignores the $1,000 rule and computes the gain on the boat (PUP) as $900, the gain on the painting (LPP) as $700, and the loss on the jewellery (LPP) as $1,200. The LPP gain is then offset by a portion of the LPP loss, leaving the $900 gain.

(B) is incorrect, because it does not subtract the deductible portion of the LPP loss from the LPP gain: $500 + $300 = $800.

(D) is incorrect, because it deducts the full LPP loss ($400) against all the gains: $500 + $300 – $400 = $400.

Question 3

(A) is correct since only the gift to the son will result in a taxable capital gain.

The ACB of Mike's stock is:

100 × $3.11 plus $39 commission (incl. sec. 7 benefit)	$350
100 × $4 plus $50 commission	450
200	$800 = $4 ACB per share.

ITA: 47, 53(1)(*i*)

His taxable capital gain on the gift to his son is: $\frac{1}{2}$ ($6 – $4) × 100 = $100.

There is no taxable capital gain on the gift to his wife, because the transfer occurs at his $4 ACB since no special election was filed.

ITA: 73(1)

(B) incorrectly excluded brokerage commissions from the ACB of his shares as: $\frac{1}{2}$ ($6 – $711/200) × 100 = $122.

(C) incorrectly computes a capital gain on the gift to Mike's wife: $\frac{1}{2}$ ($6 – $4) × 200 shares = $200.

(D) is incorrect, because it incorrectly computes a capital gain on the gift to his wife and does not apply the $\frac{1}{2}$ fraction to compute the taxable portion of the gain: ($6 – $4) × 200 = $400.

Question 4

(B) is the correct answer. Since Amanda had no capital gain on her house, she must have designated it as her principal residence for all but one of the years 2000 to 2008. She therefore has two years to designate in respect of the cottage: one of the years not used on the house (say, 2008) plus 2009. Since she owned the cottage eight years (2002 to 2009), the principal residence exemption for the cottage is: $\frac{3}{8}$ × $80,000 = $30,000 (3 = 2 years designated + "one-plus rule"). Therefore, Amanda's taxable capital gain is $25,000 ($\frac{1}{2}$ × ($80K – $30K principal residence exemption)).

(A) is incorrect, because $80,000 is the capital gain before the exemption.

(C) is incorrect, because it uses $\frac{2}{8} \times \$80,000 = \$20,000$ as the principal residence exemption: $\frac{1}{2} \times$ ($80K – $20K) = $30,000.

(D) is incorrect, because $50,000 is the capital gain, not the taxable capital gain.

Question 5

(B) is correct. The amount of the dividend is $4, the increase in the paid-up capital, and this is also the cost of the shares (ssec. 53(3)). However, the individual's net income would increase by $5.80, since it is a taxable dividend: $4 × 1.45 gross-up = $5.80.   ITA: 82(1)

(A) is incorrect because although $4 is the amount of the dividend, the amount included in net income is the grossed-up dividend (1.45 × $4 = $5.80).

(C) is incorrect because the amount of the dividend is not based on the $10 fair market value of the share.

(D) is also incorrect because the amount of the dividend is not based on the $10 fair market value of the share and the amount included in income is the increase in paid-up capital grossed up by 1.45, not the fair market value grossed up by 1.45.

Question 6

(C) is correct.

Shares		$1,600
Personal-use property		700
Listed personal property	$500	
Listed personal property	(140)	
Listed personal property losses of prior year	(100)	260
Shares		(820)
Personal-use property		Nil
Capital gain		$1,740
Taxable capital gain (½)		$ 870

(A) is incorrect because it deducts the $1,000 personal use property loss: ½ ($1,740 – 1,000) = $370.

(B) is incorrect because it deducts the $1,000 personal use property loss and does not multiply by the ½ fraction: ($1,740 – $1,000) = $740.

(D) is incorrect because it does not deduct the listed personal property loss of other years: ½ × ($1,740 + $100) = $920.

CHAPTER 7

Chapter 7 — Solutions to Exercises

Exercise 1

Step 1: Determine gain per year of ownership

	City home		Cottage	
Par. 40(2)(*b*) gain				
P of D		$ 517,500		$ 375,000
ACB		(400,000)		(250,000)
Gain		$ 117,500		$ 125,000
Gain per year	$\frac{\$117,500}{12 \text{ years}}$ = $ 9,792		$\frac{\$125,000}{7 \text{ years}}$ = $ 17,857	

Step 2: Assignment of no-option years

In the five taxation years 1998 to 2002, Ms. Twoholmes owned only the Regina home. Therefore, there is no option in those years but to designate the city home as her principal residence.

Step 3: Gain determined under paragraph 40(2)(*b*)

The gain per year of ownership for the cottage ($17,857) exceeds that for the city home ($9,792). If all seven years are assigned to the cottage, however, one year will be wasted. Hence, the city home should be designated for one of the years 2003 to 2009.

	City home	Cottage
Gain	$ 117,500	$ 125,000
Exemption	(68,542)[1]	(125,000)[2]
Capital gain	$ 48,958	Nil
Taxable capital gain	$ 24,479	Nil

— *NOTES TO SOLUTION*

[1] $\frac{1 + 5 + 1}{12}$ × $117,500 = $68,542; years designated — 1998–2002 and one of 2003–2009

[2] $\frac{1 + 6}{7}$ × $125,000 = $125,000; years designated — all but one of 2003–2009

Exercise 2

Step 1: Determine gain per year of ownership

	City home		Cottage		
P of D		$ 247,000		$ 164,000	ITA: 40(2)(*b*)
ACB	$ 180,000		$ 90,000		
SC	12,000	(192,000)	6,000	(96,000)	
Gain		$ 55,000		$ 68,000	
Gain per year	$\frac{\$55,000}{16 \text{ years}}$ = $ 3,438		$\frac{\$68,000}{11 \text{ years}}$ = $ 6,182		

Step 2: Assignment of no-option years

In the five taxation years 1994 to 1998, Peter owned only the city home. Therefore, there is no option in those years but to designate the city home as his principal residence.

Step 3: Gain determined   ITA: 40(2)(*b*)

The gain per year of ownership for the cottage ($6,182) exceeds that for the city home ($3,438). If all 11 years are assigned to the cottage, however, one year will be wasted. Hence, the city home should be designated for one of the years 1999 to 2009.

	City home	Cottage
Gain	$ 55,000	$ 68,000
Exemption	(24,063)[1]	(68,000)[2]
Capital gain	$ 30,937	Nil

— *NOTES TO SOLUTION*

[1] $\frac{1 + 5 + 1}{16}$ × $55,000 = $24,063; years designated — 1994–98 and one of 1999–2009

[2] $\frac{1 + 10}{11}$ × $68,000 = $68,000; years designated — all but one of 1999–2009

Exercise 3

	Painting		Antique clock		Outboard motor		Gold coin	
P of D		$2,000		$1,200		$1,000		$1,000
ACB	$1,000		$1,000		$1,000		$1,000	
SC	100	(1,100)	20	(1,020)	15	(1,015)	10	(1,010)
CG (CL)		$ 900		$ 180		$ (15)		$ (10)

Net taxable capital gain:

LPP — Painting	$ 900
— Gold coin	(10)[1]
	$ 890
— ½	$ 445
PUP — Antique clock (½ × $180)	90
	$ 535

— *NOTE TO SOLUTION*

[1] Listed personal property losses, whether current or carried-over, are applied at the full capital gain (capital loss) amount.

Exercise 4

	Cost	Proceeds	CG (CL)	Taxable amount
Listed personal property:				
Oil painting	$ 2,500	$ 1,000	$(1,500)	
Rare coin	1,300	1,000	(300)	
Bible	1,000	5,000	4,000	
			$ 2,200	
2006 LPP — CL			(1,200)[3]	
			$ 1,000	$500
Personal-use property:				
Canoe	$ 1,000	$ 1,000	Nil	
Antique car[1]	15,000	10,000	Nil [2]	
Antique chair[1]	1,000	1,200	200	
Antique table[1]	1,500	2,000	500	
			$700	350
				$850

— *NOTES TO SOLUTION*

[1] Antiques are not listed personal property under the definition in section 54.

[2] Losses on personal-use property assets are not allowed.

[3] Listed personal property loss carryovers are netted against capital gains, not taxable capital gains.

Exercise 5

(A)　P of D 200 shares @ $25 .... $5,000

　　　ACB 200 shares @ $33[1] $6,600

　　　SC .... 75　(6,675)

　　　CL[2] (Superficial loss of $1,675) .... ___Nil___

(B)　Adjusted cost base of shares

$$
\begin{array}{lll}
50 \text{ shares @ } \$33 & = & \$1,650 \\
200 \text{ shares @ } \$26 & = & 5,200 \\
\text{superficial loss} & & \underline{1,675} \\
& & \underline{\$8,525} \div 250 \text{ shares} = \underline{\$34.10}
\end{array}
$$

— *NOTES TO SOLUTION*

[1]　$$
\begin{array}{lll}
100 \text{ shares @ } \$30 & = & \$3,000 \\
150 \text{ shares @ } \$35 & = & \underline{5,250} \\
& & \underline{\$8,250} \div 250 \text{ shares} = \underline{\$33}
\end{array}
$$

[2]　Since Ivan acquired additional shares of Solid Investments within the 30-day period.

Exercise 6

(a) For identical properties acquired after 1971, the weighted "moving average" basis is to be used　　ITA: 47(1)
to calculate the ACB of each individual property (subsection 47(1)).

High Growth Co.

Date	Shares Purchased	Share Price	Adjusted Cost Base	ACB/Share
Jan. 1/03	1,000	$3.00	$ 3,070	$3.07
Jun. 5/04	3,000	2.80	8,490	
	4,000		11,560	2.89
Aug. 5/04	1,500	3.80	5,770	
	5,500		17,330	3.15
Dec. 3/05	1,000	5.10	5,220	
	6,500		22,550	3.47
May 1/06	(3,000)	3.47	(10,410)	
Nov. 8/07	1,000	5.75	5,880	
	4,500		18,020	4.00
Jan. 9/08	(1,500)	4.00	(6,000)	
	3,000		$12,020	4.00

Note: The disposition of shares has no effect on the moving average cost.

(b)

HIGH GROWTH CO. ACB:

Jan. 10/03	(20,000 × $0.25) + $200 =	$5,200
Jan. 14/03	(4,000 × $0.80) + $75 =	$3,275
Totals	24,000 shares	$8,475

May 20/09		
	Proceeds	$7,200
	ACB	(8,475)
	Broker fees	(150)
	Capital loss	$(1,425)
	Allowable capital loss	$(712.50)

Exercise 7

		With Sale		ITA: 3, 5, 6, 7, 8, 9
Paragraph 3(*a*)	Sources of income			
Sections 5-8	Employment income	$23,000		
Section 9	Business income	10,000		
Paragraph 3(*b*)	Taxable capital gains			
	Sale of antique painting			
	(.50 × (29,000 − 9,000))	10,000		
Section 3	Net income for tax purposes	$43,000		

Exercise 8

Adjusted cost base:

1,000 shares @ $35	$35,000
brokerage	500
1984 — stock dividend (50 shares × Nil)	Nil
1992 — stock dividend — 105 shares (10% × 1,050) × $10..........	1,050
2006 — stock dividend — 231 shares (20% × 1,155) × $10..........	2,310
	$38,860

Shares (1000 + 50 + 105 + 231) = 1,386
ACB per share: $38,860 ÷ 1,386 = $28.04

Exercise 9

2008:	Capital gain allocated.................................	$ 96.37
	Taxable capital gain (½ × $96.37)	$ 48.19

The taxable capital gain of $48.19 must be included in her income for 2008.

2009:	P of D (25 units)	$ 718.00
	ACB (25 units @ $27.38[1])	(684.50)
	CG.......................................	$ 33.50
	TCG (½ × $33.50).................................	$ 16.75

— *NOTE TO SOLUTION*

[1] Adjusted cost base of units:

72.788	units..	$2,000.00
3.774	units @ $25.535	96.37
76.562	units..	$2,096.37

Weighted average: $2,096.37 ÷ 76.562 = $27.38

Exercise 10

		2008	*2009*
Par. 3(*a*)	Income from non-capital sources (non-negative):		
	Employment income	$25,000	$30,000
	Property income	10,000	—
	Business income — other	8,000	—
		$43,000	$30,000

CHAPTER 7

		2008	*2009*
Par. 3(b)	Net taxable capital gains (non-negative):		

Taxable capital gain —
personal-use property
  ($\frac{1}{2} \times \$8,000$) . . . . $ 4,000   —

Plus

Listed personal property gain	$4,000		—
Less: LPP loss carryforward — 2005	(1,000)		
LPP loss carryback — 2009	(1,500)		
	$1,500		

Taxable net gain — $\frac{1}{2}$ thereof   1,750

               $ 4,750

Public corporation — allowable capital loss . . . .   (4,750)   Nil[1]

   — taxable capital gain . . . . $ 4,500[2]

                     $43,000 $34,500

Par. 3(d)	Losses from non-capital sources:		
	Property loss	—	(4,000)
	Business loss	—	(9,000)
	Allowable business investment loss	(3,000)[3]	(1,000)[4]
	Division B income	$40,000	$20,500

— *NOTES TO SOLUTION*

[1] Of the $6,000 allowable capital loss ($\frac{1}{2} \times \$12,000$), $1,250 cannot be claimed in 2008 and will be carried back or forward under Division C as a "net capital loss" to be discussed in Chapter 10.

[2] $\frac{1}{2} \times \$9,000$

[3] $\frac{1}{2} \times \$6,000$

[4] $\frac{1}{2} \times \$2,000$

Chapter 8
Capital Gains: The Finer Points

LEARNING GOALS

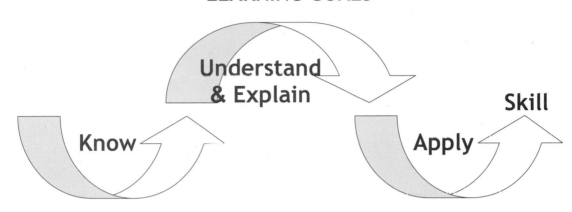

Know

By the end of this chapter you should know some more advanced provisions of the *Income Tax Act* that relate to capital gains and losses. Completing the Review Questions (¶8,800) and Multiple Choice Questions (¶8,825) is a good way to learn the technical provisions.

Understand and Explain

You should understand and be able to explain

- Some of the finer points related to capital gains;
- Bad debts on capital property;
- Non-arm's length transfers and the attribution rules; and
- Death of a taxpayer issues for capital property.

Apply

You should be able to apply your knowledge and understanding of the rules pertaining to capital gains and losses in a way that accomplishes a client's goals. Completing the Assignment Problems (¶8,875) is an excellent way to develop your ability to apply the material in increasingly complex situations.

Chapter 8 — Learning Chart

Topic	Example Problem (✓)	Review Questions (¶8,800)	Multiple Choice (¶8,825)	Exercises (¶8,850)	Assignment Problems (¶8,875)
¶8,000 VARIOUS CAPITAL GAINS PROVISIONS					
¶8,010 Foreign Exchange Gains and Losses	✓	1		1	
¶8,020 Part Disposition		2			
¶8,030 Exchanges of Property		3, 4, 5	1	2	1, 2
¶8,035 The basic deferral	✓				
¶8,040 Election for additional deferral	✓				
¶8,050 Proceeds on Disposition of Building	✓			11	3, 4
¶8,060 Election on Change in Use	✓	6	6		
¶8,070 Change in Use of a Principal Residence		7		3	5
¶8,075 Application of the change-in-use elections	✓				
¶8,080 Interpretation Bulletin IT-120R6 — Principal residence					
¶8,085 Section 54.1 — Extended designation		8	6	3	
¶8,090 Subsection 40(4) — Transfer between spouses	✓				
¶8,100 Leaving and Entering Canada		9, 10	4	4	
¶8,110 Options	✓	11, 12		5	
¶8,120 Debts Established to be Bad Debts		13		10	
¶8,130 Convertible Properties		14			
¶8,140 Capital Gains Deferral	✓				
¶8,150 Certain Shares Deemed to be Capital Property					
¶8,200 NON-ARM'S LENGTH TRANSFERS AND THE ATTRIBUTION RULES REVISITED					
¶8,210 Non-Arm's Length Transfers					
¶8,215 Who does not deal at arm's length?				6	
¶8,220 Transactions with non-arm's length individuals		15, 16	2	7, 9	6, 8
¶8,230 Attribution Rules					6
¶8,235 Capital gains on spousal transfers or loans			3		
¶8,240 Recapture					
¶8,245 Summary of provisions					
¶8,300 DEATH OF A TAXPAYER					
¶8,310 Deemed Disposition on Death			5	8	9
¶8,400 INCOME RECONCILIATION REVISITED	✓				7

Study Notes

Chapter 8 —
Discussion Notes for Review Questions

(1) The loss on foreign currency is a capital loss. However, as an individual, she must deduct $200 from the loss in arriving at her capital loss. In this case her capital loss is $2,300.

ITA: 39(2)(*b*)

(2) One way to approach this question is to assume that the cost was allocated equally to each acre. Therefore, the cost of the three acres sold would be ½ of the original cost of the six acres or $12,000. However, the CRA, in applying the law, may consider that $12,000 is too high an amount to be "reasonably regarded as attributable to that part," since the lake-front portion would usually be more valuable than the non-lake-front property assuming that access is still available to both parcels. This, then, becomes a valuation issue.

ITA: 43

(3) He has to replace the land before the end of the second taxation year after the initial year. If they finally agreed to the price in 2009 then he has until December 31, 2011 to replace the property. The initial year is the year that the "amount has become receivable as proceeds of disposition", i.e., 2009 in this case.

ITA: 44(1)(*c*)

ITA: 44(1), 44(2)

(4) Yes. In order for these rules to apply the destroyed equipment must be either property that was stolen, destroyed or expropriated or a "former business property". The definition of former business property only refers to real property which has a common law definition of "land and building." Equipment is not included in that definition. However, if the property is stolen, destroyed or expropriated, it only has to meet the definition of "property." In this case the equipment meets this definition and the replacement property rules can apply. Of course, any potential recapture would be offset, by the normal rules, because the purchase of the new machine was made in the year of loss.

ITA: 248(1) "former business property"

(5) Under the definition of "former business property" the advice she received was incorrect. This building qualifies as a former business property, since it is rented to a related corporation and is used in the related corporation's business.

ITA: 248(1) "former business property", 251

(6) A change in use does not include a transfer of property from one income-producing use to another. In this case the property is being transferred from earning property income to earning business income. As a result there is no income to report on July 1 of last year when zoning was applied for. However, when the property is eventually sold an assessment will need to be done at July 1 of last year since the increase in value up to that point will be a capital gain and any profit after that date will be business income from the sale of the condominiums.

ITA: 13(7), 45(1); IT-218R

(7) If Mrs. Smith did not make any structural changes to the house, then there will not be any change in use. The house will still remain her principal residence. She will have to declare the rental income and can deduct the expenses that relate to it.

IT-120R6, par. 30

(8) Since she was moved by her employer nine years ago and was still employed by that employer when she moved back this year, the Act modifies paragraph (*d*) of the definition of "principal residence" to allow her to continue to claim her house as her principal residence for more than the 4 years generally allowed on a normal change in use under the definition. All years qualify since she was still resident in Canada, as required. She still has to make the election not to have a change in use in the year they moved. As a result, on the sale of the house, she will be able to claim the full principal residence exemption.

ITA: 45(2), 54, 54.1

ITA: 40(2)(*b*)

(9) The Act causes a deemed disposition on all her property other than certain property and certain items that are subject to withholding tax. In this case the term deposits will be deemed to be disposed of, but since there is no capital gain, there would not be any tax.

ITA: 128.1(4)

(10) Mr. State will be excepted from the deemed disposition rules on the shares of his U.S. employer since he was in Canada less than 60 months in the past 10 years.

ITA: 128.1(4)

(11) The Act generally treats the sale of this option as a disposition with the cost base being nil. Therefore, the capital gain will be equal to the proceeds and will be taxed in the year the option is sold.

ITA: 49(1)

(12) On the granting of an option there is a disposition and the ACB is deemed to be nil. He does not have the alternative of reducing the cost base.

ITA: 49(1)

(13) Ms. Sorry can elect to have disposed of her note when it is established to have become uncollectible. This will result in a capital loss equal to $100,000 and the note will then have a cost equal to nil. All or some of this loss can then be carried back under Division C to be applied against the previous capital gain. If the original property disposed of was personal-use property then the debt would have been "personal-use property". Then the Act allows a capital loss only to the extent of the capital gain on the original disposition.

ITA: 50(1), 54 "personal-use property"

ITA: 50(2)

(14) A rollover on the exchange of the common shares for the debentures is provided as long as the debenture had the conversion feature built into its terms and no cash was received. The shares will have

ITA: 51

a cost base of $10 each, so the accrued gain of $10 per share will be deferred until the common shares are sold.

(15) If a person sells something to someone with whom he or she does not deal at arm's length then the proceeds will be deemed to be the fair market value. Related parties do not deal at arm's length, but in this case the two are not related. However, it is a question of fact whether persons not related to each other are dealing at arm's length. In this case there is no evidence of hard bargaining and the transaction is obviously not at fair market value. Therefore, it would be unlikely that they would be considered to be dealing at arm's length and the proceeds would likely be deemed to be $100,000. Her friend will have a cost base equal to what she paid for the land of $50,000. As a result there will be double taxation.

ITA: 69, 251, 251(1)(*c*)

(16) At the time of the gift, Bill will be deemed to have sold the shares at their fair market value. Scott will be deemed to have received the shares at a cost to him equal to the fair market value at the time of the gift. Since the shares were a gift, the attribution rules applicable to an income-splitting loan will not apply.

ITA: 69(1)(*b*), 69(1)(*c*)

ITA: 56(4.1)

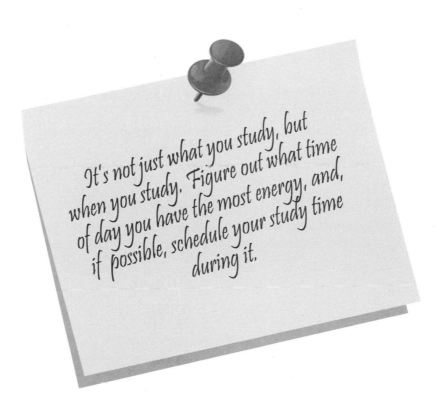

It's not just what you study, but when you study. Figure out what time of day you have the most energy, and, if possible, schedule your study time during it.

Chapter 8 –
Solutions to Multiple Choice Questions

Question 1

(D) is the correct answer. Since the expropriation is an involuntary disposition, the property must be replaced by the later of two years and 24 months from the end of the taxation year in which the disposition took place. Since the relevant taxation year was May 31, 2010, the two-year deadline is May 31, 2012.   ITA: 44(1)(*c*)

(A) incorrectly uses the one-year deadline which is applicable for voluntary dispositions.

(B) incorrectly uses two years from the disposition date as the deadline.

(C) incorrectly uses two years from the end of the calendar year of the disposition as the deadline.

Question 2

(A) is correct.   ITA: 74.1(2)

(B) is incorrect, because capital gains or losses do not attribute on loans or gifts to minors.

(C) is incorrect, because there will be a capital gain on the gift.   ITA: 69

(D) is incorrect. $100,000 is the capital gain. The taxable capital gain is:

$$\frac{1}{2} \times \$100{,}000 = \$50{,}000.$$

Question 3

(C) is correct. There is a superficial loss because Ms. Y has incurred a loss and an affiliated person (Mr. Y) acquired the shares within 30 days of the disposition.   ITA: 40(2)(*g*), 54

(A) is incorrect, because it ignores the superficial loss rule and computes the loss as $\frac{1}{2} \times$ ($800K – $900K).

(B) is not correct, because Ms. Y elected out of the interspousal rollover.   ITA: 73(1)

(D) is not correct. There is no attribution because she elected out of the subsection 73(1) rollover and received fair market value consideration (i.e., $800,000 cash).   ITA: 74.5

Question 4

(B) is correct, because the taxable capital gain is computed as follows: listed shares of a public corporation resident in Canada (= $\frac{1}{2} \times$ ($40,000 – $10,000) = $15,000) + painting (= $\frac{1}{2}$ ($10,000 – $6,000) = $2,000) = $17,000.

The rental real estate in Canada and the registered retirement savings plan are specifically exempted from the deemed disposition rules.   ITA: 128.1(4)

(A) incorrectly excludes the taxable capital gain on the painting.

(C) incorrectly includes $\frac{1}{2}$ of the gain on the RRSP ($10,000).

(D) incorrectly includes a $25,000 taxable capital gain on the rental real estate in Canada.

Question 5

(C) is correct. The calculation is as follows:

	Division B income
Toronto home (no capital gain; principal residence)	—
Rental property in London, Ontario	
— Land: $\frac{1}{2}$ ($100,000 – 50,000)	$25,000
— Building: recapture = $25,000 – $2,000	23,000
Taxable capital gain = $\frac{1}{2}$ ($35K – $25K)	5,000
Mutual fund units: $\frac{1}{2}$ ($60K – $12K)	24,000
Shares of a public company: $\frac{1}{2}$ ($100K – $90K)	5,000
	$82,000

(A) incorrectly ignores recapture: $82,000 – $23,000 = $59,000.

(B) incorrectly multiplies the recapture by the ½ taxable capital gains fraction: $25,000 + ½ × $23,000 + $5,000 + $24,000 + $5,000 = $70,500

(D) incorrectly includes a capital gain on the principal residence: $82,000 + ½ × ($240K – $100K) = $152,000

Question 6

(B) is correct. Because Gary made the election to be deemed not to have changed the use in respect of the property, there is deemed to be no change in use in 2003. The only disposition occurs in 2009 on the date of sale. The Act allows Gary to designate the property as his principal residence for up to four years where the election was made. The gain on the property is $500,000 ($850K – $350K) and the total years of ownership were 18 (1992 to 2009) and the maximum number of years that can be designated is 16 (1991 to 2002 plus 4). Therefore, the principal residence exemption is [(16 + 1)/18] × $500,000 or $472,222. The capital gain is therefore $27,778 ($500K – $472,222) and the taxable capital gain is $13,889 (½ × $27,778). *ITA: 45(2)* *ITA: 54* *ITA: 45(2)*

(A) is incorrect because there is a taxable capital gain to report in 2009 because not all years of ownership qualify as years eligible for a principal residence. The extension of the four-year rule does not apply, because Gary did not move back into the residence before it was sold. *ITA: 54.1*

(C) incorrectly calculates taxable capital gains of $50,000 in 2003 [½ ($550K – $350K)] and 2009 [½ ($850K – $550K)]. The timing is wrong because there is no deemed disposition in 2002 because of the election. The amount is also wrong because 12 years (1992–2003) can be designated in respect of the residence. *ITA: 45(2)*

(D) correctly calculates the gain in 2009 as $500,000 without claiming any principal residence exemption, resulting in a taxable capital gain of $250,000 (½ × $500K).

Chapter 8 — Solutions to Exercises

Exercise 1

Sale of car

P of D — Canadian dollars ($10,000 × 1.25)	$12,500
ACB — Canadian dollars	(4,000)
CG	$ 8,500
TCG (50%)	$ 4,250

Currency

P of D — Canadian dollars received	$13,000
ACB — Canadian dollars at time of sale	(12,500)
Gain	$ 500
Exempt portion	(200)
CG	$ 300
TCG (50%)	$ 150

Exercise 2

(A) During the years prior to the settling of the claim, Tax Processing Ltd. is deemed to own the destroyed asset. Hence the company can continue to take capital cost allowance.   ITA: 44(2)

		Class 10: 30%
UCC before the fire		$17,150
CCA — 2007	$ 5,145	
CCA — 2008	3,601	(8,746)
UCC before proceeds received		$ 8,404

(B) In the second year after the fire (2009) when the company received the proceeds, the company would be deemed to have sold the computer for $60,000 with the following tax consequences:

Taxable capital gain:

P of D		$60,000
ACB		(50,000)
CG		$10,000
TCG (½ × $10,000)		$ 5,000

Recapture:

UCC before proceeds received		$ 8,404
Less the lesser of:		
(i) Capital cost	$50,000	
		(50,000)
(ii) P of D	$60,000	
Recapture		$41,596

(C) In the year of purchase of the new computer (2011), which is within the 24-month time limit for an involuntary disposition, Tax Processing Ltd. would file an amended return for the 2009 year in which the taxable capital gain and recapture were recognized.

Taxable capital gain:
  ½ of the lesser of:

(1) capital gain (see above)		$10,000⎤		
(ii) P of D	$60,000	⎬	= Nil	
less replacement cost	70,000	Nil⎦		

    ACB of new computer in 2011: ($70,000 – $10,000) = $60,000   ITA: 44(1)(*f*)

Recapture: ITA: 13(4)

Class 10: 30%

UCC before proceeds received (see above calculation)		$ 8,404	
Less deemed disposal:			ITA: 13(4)(*c*)
lesser of (i) cost ($50,000)			
(ii) P of D ($60,000)	$50,000		
Less the lesser of:			
(i) the recapture			
($8,404 – $50,000) $41,596			
(ii) replacement cost 70,000 41,596	8,404		
UCC after proceeds received, Dec. 31, 2009		Nil	

Class 50: 55%

2011 addition:		
Capital cost of replacement property	$70,000	
Less reduction for deferred gain	10,000	ITA: 44(1)(*f*)
Deemed capital cost	$60,000	
Less reduction for deferred recapture	41,596	ITA: 13(4)(*d*)
UCC before CCA	$18,404	
CCA (55% of ½ × $18,404)	(5,061)	
UCC after CCA	$13,343	

Exercise 3

When Howard rents his home, he is deemed to have changed the use of the home and a capital gain may be triggered. However, Howard can designate the home with the appropriate number of years and should not be taxed on the gain. Under this course of action, Howard would now have a rental property from which he must declare the income less all his expenses. However, a rental loss could not be generated with capital cost allowance on the home and equipment therein.   ITA: 45(1)   ITR: 1100(15))

Alternatively, Howard could elect to defer the gain until he either sells the home or rescinds his election. Note that the CRA normally permits a retroactive election at the time of sale. In this situation, Howard would not be allowed to claim any capital cost allowance on the home or the election to be deemed not to have changed the use would be invalid.   ITA: 45(2)   IT-120R6   ITA: 45(2)

The election would permit Howard to designate his Vancouver home as his principal residence for at least four extra years depending upon whether he is self-employed or employed.   ITA: 45(2)

(A) Self-employed

Paragraph (*d*) in the definition of a "principal residence" permits Howard to designate his Vancouver home as his principal residence for four years, while it is being rented, if he elects to be deemed not to have changed the use according to paragraphs (*b*) and (*d*) of the definition.   ITA: 54   ITA: 45(2)

Howard might consider rescinding his election after the fourth year. This course of action would enable Howard to claim capital cost allowance after the fourth year subject to the loss restrictions discussed above.

(B) Employed

The Act waives the four-year restriction discussed above if Howard (or his wife) has moved at least 40 km closer to his new work location. Howard then can designate his Vancouver home as his principal residence during all the rental years if: ITA: 54.1

(i) Howard subsequently resumes ordinary habitation of his home while employed with the same employer; or

(ii) Howard subsequently resumes ordinary habitation of his home within one year from the end of the year in which he terminates employment with that employer; or

(iii) Howard dies.

Note that "ordinarily inhabited" means any time during the year according to the CRA, but Howard cannot temporarily move back in order to qualify for this exemption.

IT-120R6

Exercise 4

Capital property A

(A) If Mr. Emigrant departs prior to June 1, 2009, there will be no capital gain on the capital asset which he brought from the U.S. by virtue of the 60-month short-term exemption.

ITA: 128.1(4)

(B) If he departs subsequent to June 1, 2009, there will be a taxable capital gain on $\frac{1}{2}$ of the excess of the proceeds of disposition ($12,000) over the fair market value at the time of entry ($5,000), namely, $3,500.

Capital property B

(A) First, it is necessary to determine whether the capital property acquired in Canada is exempt from immediate departure tax but will be taxed on its ultimate disposition.

ITA: 2(3)

(B) If the property is not exempted then the taxpayer will be taxed at the time of exit from Canada.

Exercise 5

Doctor Quick

July 1, 2008 — acquired an option (capital property) with an adjusted cost base of $5,000.

Feb. 1, 2009 — transaction resulted in a capital loss of $3,000 (i.e., $2,000 – $5,000) of which only $1,500 would be recognized since 50% of the option was for a principal residence.

Doctor Slow

Feb. 1, 2009 — acquired an option with an adjusted cost base of $2,000.

May 1, 2009 — acquired a property with an adjusted cost base and a capital cost of $102,000 ($100,000 + $2,000).

Devalued Properties Ltd.

July 1, 2008 — received business income of $5,000; not a capital gain.

May 1, 2009 — received business income of $100,000; not a capital gain. May subtract the cost of property inventory to arrive at income for tax purposes.

— note that section 49 is not applicable if the gain is not a capital gain.

Exercise 6

(A) Since they are related by marriage, they are not at arm's length.

ITA: 251(2)(*a*), 251(6)(*b*)

(B) Since they are not considered to be related by blood, they are at arm's length.

ITA: 251(6)(*a*)

(C) Since they are still legally married, they are not at arm's length.

(D) The facts of a situation can determine that two unrelated persons are not at arm's length.

ITA: 251(1)(*b*)

Exercise 7

	James *(seller or transferor)*	*Hayden* *(purchaser or transferee)*
(A) sale at $2,000	has proceeds of $2,000 and, hence, a capital gain of $800 (i.e., $2,000 – $1,200)	deemed [par. 69(1)(*a*)] to have acquired at $1,500 resulting in potential double-counting of $500 gain
(B) sale at $1,200	deemed [par. 69(1)(*b*)] to have proceeds of $1,500 and, hence, a capital gain of $300	acquired at $1,200 resulting in potential double-counting of $300 gain

	James *(seller or transferor)*	*Hayden* *(purchaser or transferee)*
(C) gift	deemed [par. 69(1)(b)] to have proceeds of $1,500	deemed [par. 69(1)(c)] to have acquired at $1,500

Exercise 8

Property received as an inheritance has an ACB equal to the FMV when acquired. In this case, the ACB is $60,000.

ITA: 40(1)(a), 69(1)(c)

Mary Jane has correctly calculated her capital gain. However, she only received $50,000 of the proceeds in 2009 and the balance is not due until 2011. Therefore, she can consider claiming a reserve under subparagraph 40(1)(a)(iii), calculated as follows:

$$\frac{\text{Amount not due}}{\text{Proceeds}} \times \text{capital gain}$$

$$\frac{\$150,000}{\$200,000} \times \$140,000 = \$105,000$$

OR

$\frac{4}{5}$ of gain

$\frac{4}{5} \times \$140,000 = \$112,000$

Capital gain = $140,000 – $105,000 = $35,000

Mary Jane can claim a reserve of $105,000. This reserve will then be included in income in 2010 and a reserve calculated based on proceeds not yet due. Mary Jane must file Form T2017 with her 2009 income tax return.

Exercise 9

(A) (i) Since a gift is a transfer, the interspousal rollover would automatically deem that Alice's proceeds of disposition are equal to her adjusted cost base ($12,000), resulting in no capital gain.

ITA: 73

(ii) Alice would be subject to the income attribution rules on any dividends from the shares, because a gift would not meet the exception, since the fair market value of the property transferred exceeded the fair market value of the consideration received and an election out of the interspousal rollover was not made.

ITA: 74.1, 74.5(1)(a)

ITA: 73(1)

(iii) Alice would also be subject to capital gains attribution for the same reason as discussed in part (A)(ii), above. There would be full capital gains attribution on all substituted property.

ITA: 74.2; IT-511R, par. 27

(B) (i) Since Alice does elect out of the interspousal rollover, the non-arm's length transfer rule, with which the transaction conforms, will apply, since the cash consideration ($15,000) was equal to the fair market value of the property transferred. A capital gain of $3,000 would be triggered.

ITA: 73(1)
ITA: 69(1)(b)(ii)

(ii) There would be no income or capital gains attribution, because Alice has conformed with the attribution rule exception. The fair market value of the property transferred did not exceed the fair market value of the consideration received and an election out of the interspousal rollover was made.

ITA: 74.5(1)(a)

ITA: 73(1)

(C) (i) Unless Alice elects not to have the provisions of the interspousal rollover apply, there will be no capital gain triggered on the transfer to her husband.

ITA: 73

(ii) Although Alice has received consideration (debt) with a face value ($15,000) equal to the fair market value of the property transferred, the interest rate must be at least equal to the prescribed rate at the time or a commercial rate. In addition, the Act requires that Alice elect out of the interspousal rollover. Therefore, Alice will be subject to both income and capital gains attribution.

ITA: 74.5(1)(b)(i)

74.5(1)(c)

(D) The result would be the same as in (A), above, since the shares would be considered substituted property for a transfer of cash for no consideration.

(E) The result would be the same as in (C), above, since the shares would be considered substituted property.

Exercise 10

If section 22 is not used, Mr. Flogger must still include in income last year's reserve of $6,500. However, the loss of $9,000 will be regarded as a capital loss which is only fractionally deductible and can be offset only against taxable capital gains. Since Mr. Sucker has not included any amount as income in respect of these accounts receivable, he will not be allowed a deduction for a reserve or for bad debts because the conditions of the reserve for doubtful debts or the bad debt expense rules will not be met. If Mr. Sucker collects more than the $36,000 fair market value, the excess will be a capital gain and, if he collects less than $36,000, the difference will be a capital loss.

ITA: 20(1)(*l*), 20(1)(*p*)

Exercise 11

Sienna Research Inc. has what, at first, appears to be a terminal loss on the building and a capital gain on the land. When this occurs, subsection 13(21.1) reallocates the proceeds so that the terminal loss is reduced by the capital gain on the land.

ITA: 13(21.1)

Without adjustment	Land	Building	Total
Proceeds per contract	$ 895,000	$ 385,000	$ 1,280,000
ACB, UCC	345,000	438,700	
Capital gain, terminal loss	550,000	(53,700)	

With subsection 13(21.1) adjustment	Land	Building	Total
Adjusted proceeds	$ 841,300	$ 438,700	$ 1,280,000
ACB, UCC	345,000	438,700	
Capital gain, terminal loss or recapture	$ 496,300	Nil	

There are no tax implications on the disposition of the building. Even though the deemed proceeds are less than the capital cost of the building, a capital loss can never arise on the disposition of depreciable property.

CHAPTER 8

Chapter 9
Other Sources of Income and Deductions in Computing Income

LEARNING GOALS

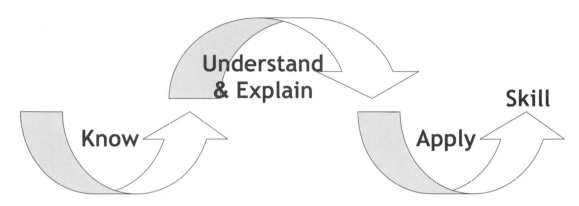

Know

By the end of this chapter you should know the basic provisions of the *Income Tax Act* that relate to other income and other deductions. Completing the Review Questions (¶9,800) and Multiple Choice Questions (¶9,825) is a good way to learn the technical provisions.

Understand and Explain

You should understand and be able to explain:

- The nature of income such as pensions, retiring allowances, support payments, and scholarships and bursaries; and
- The nature of other deductions such as RRSPs, moving expenses, child care expenses, and the disability support deduction.

Apply

You should be able to apply your knowledge and understanding of these forms of income and deductions in a way that accomplishes a client's goals. Completing the Assignment Problems (¶9,875) is an excellent way to develop your ability to apply the material in increasingly complex situations.

Chapter 9 — Learning Chart

Topic	Example Problem (✓)	Review Questions (¶9,800)	Multiple Choice (¶9,825)	Exercises (¶9,850)	Assignment Problems (¶9,875)
¶9,000 OTHER SOURCES OF INCOME					
¶9,010 Benefits in the Nature of Pensions					
¶9,015 Income splitting — Canada Pension Plan					
¶9,020 Income splitting — Pension income					
¶9,030 Retiring Allowances and Other Payments on Termination of Employment		1, 2, 17	1		5, 6, 10
¶9,040 Support Receipts and Payments		3, 4		1	
¶9,045 Overview					
¶9,050 Spousal support					
¶9,055 Child support					
¶9,060 Legal fees in connection with support payments					
¶9,070 Annuity Payments					
¶9,080 Amounts Received from Deferred Income Plans					
¶9,085 Inclusion provisions					
¶9,090 Registered education savings plan (RESP)					
¶9,095 Registered disability savings plan (RDSP)					
¶9,100 Education Assistance Payments		5			9
¶9,110 Other Inclusions		6			
¶9,120 Indirect Payments		7			
¶9,125 Overview					
¶9,130 Conditions					
¶9,140 Restrictive Covenants [Proposed]					
¶9,145 Inclusion					
¶9,150 Exclusion					
¶9,155 Schematic of the system for restrictive covenants					
¶9,200 AMOUNTS NOT INCLUDED IN COMPUTING INCOME					
¶9,210 Specific Examples					
¶9,220 Tax-Free Savings Account (TFSA)					1
¶9,300 DEDUCTIONS IN COMPUTING INCOME					
¶9,310 Capital Element of Annuity					6
¶9,320 Registered Retirement Savings Plans				4	1, 3, 5
¶9,325 Objectives of pension reform					
¶9,330 Types of tax-assisted retirement plans		8, 9, 10			
¶9,355 Types of RRSPs					
¶9,340 Integration of limits		11, 12, 13			
¶9,345 Contribution limits for RRSPs			2	3, 6	2, 6, 10, 11
¶9,350 Definition of earned income for RRSPs			5	2	5, 6
¶9,355 Calculation of the pension adjustment (PA)					
¶9,360 RRSP contribution room carried forward					6
¶9,365 Excess contribution		14			5
¶9,370 Contributions of property					

Topic	Example Problem (✓)	Review Questions (¶9,800)	Multiple Choice (¶9,825)	Exercises (¶9,850)	Assignment Problems (¶9,875)
¶9,375 Application	✓				
¶9,380 Contributions to spousal (or common-law partner) RRSP				3	
¶9,385 Attribution on spousal (or common-law partner) RRSPs				5	5
¶9,390 Withdrawals before retirement		15			
¶9,395 Home Buyers' Plan (HBP)	✓				4
¶9,400 Tax-free RRSP withdrawals for lifelong learning plan (LLP)					
¶9,405 Retirement options					
¶9,410 RRIFs					
¶9,415 Treatment of RRSPs and RRIFs on death		16			
¶9,420 Transfers of Retirement Income and Sheltered Amounts					
¶9,425 Direct transfer				6	
¶9,430 Retiring allowances	✓			6	
¶9,440 Overpayments and Other Deductions					
¶9,445 Overpayments included in income					
¶9,450 Objections and appeals					
¶9,455 Legal fees to establish a right					
¶9,460 OAS clawback					
¶9,470 Moving Expenses			4, 6	7, 9	4, 7, 9, 10
¶9,475 Deductible expenditures					11
¶9,480 Flat-rate deductions by administrative practice	✓				
¶9,485 Eligible relocation					
¶9,490 Child Care Expenses			3, 5	8	4, 8, 9, 10
¶9,495 Eligibility					
¶9,500 Limitations					
¶9,505 Deduction calculation					11
¶9,510 Encouragement for parent to attend school	✓				
¶9,515 Application					
¶9,520 Disability Support Deduction	✓				
¶9,530 Expenses of Residents Absent from Canada					

CHAPTER 9

Study Notes

Chapter 9 —
Discussion Notes for Review Questions

(1) The payment was made to Ms. Tired "upon or after retirement of a taxpayer from an office or employment in recognition of her long service" and as such should qualify as a retiring allowance and be included in income. An Interpretation Bulletin states that "the cessation of employment for any reason is considered as being retirement or loss of employment." Therefore, even though she quit, this amount should still qualify as a retiring allowance.

ITA: 56(1)(*a*)(ii), 248(1) "retiring allowance"

IT-337R4, par. 2

(2) The accumulated sick days will qualify as a "retiring allowance" and be taxed as such. However, the unused vacation days will not qualify under this definition, according to the Interpretation Bulletin, and will be taxed as employment income.

ITA: 6(3), 56(1)(*a*)(ii), 248(1) "retiring allowance"; IT-337R4 par. 5

(3) Since the $3,000 per month is contained in the written agreement and the $1,200 mortgage payment is part of the "allowance," the full amount should be deductible. However, the deductibility for the mortgage payment is limited to ⅕ of the original principal. In this case, ⅕ × $120,000 = $24,000. After 20 months ($24,000/$1,200), Charles will no longer be able to deduct the payments related to the mortgage and Dee will no longer have to take them into income.

ITA: 60.1(2)

(4) Under this agreement, the $500 in monthly fees paid to the financial institution will qualify as an allowance since Mark does have the discretion as to where the $500 is paid. In addition, this amount is part of the monthly spousal maintenance payment specified in the agreement.

(5) The loan would have to be included in employment income when received. Such amounts are not awards and are not subject to the rules for scholarships and research grants. As a result, neither the full exemption for scholarships nor research expenses are available as deductions. Any repayment of this repayable award is deductible provided the conditions of that paragraph are met.

ITA: 5(1), 6(3), 8(1)(*n*); IT-340R

ITA: 56(1)(*n*), 56(1)(*o*)

(6) The OAS Supplement would fall into the category of "social assistance payments" since it is based on an income test. As a result, the payments are included in net income, but there is a corresponding deduction to exclude it from taxable income. The effect of these two provisions is to raise Mrs. Smith's income to a point that no one can claim her as a dependant, but at the same time not to make Mrs. Smith taxable on this amount.

ITA: 56(1)(*u*), 110(1)(*f*)

(7) The $15,000 will be taxed in Mr. Slippery's hands on an indirect payment and not in Mrs. Slippery's hands.

ITA: 56(2)

(8) Defined benefit pension plans are approved by and registered with the CRA. Once the CRA has agreed to the terms of the plan, the amount that the company can deduct is determined by an actuary who certifies the amount that is necessary to fund the accruing benefits of the plan.

(9) The maximum benefit that may be provided to an individual under a defined benefit plan is 2% of the individual's average best 3 years of remuneration times the number of years (normally a maximum of 35 years) of pensionable service, with a dollar limit of $85,555 in 2009.

(10) Under a defined benefit plan, the benefit that is to be paid is defined, usually in regard to a certain percentage of an employee's earnings in the last few years of employment, regardless of the cost to the employer or the earnings experience of the plan. The benefit that is tax-assisted is limited to an annual maximum pension of $85,555 in 2009. Under a money purchase plan, the contribution that is required by the employer and the employee is defined rather than the benefit. The retirement benefit of the employee is based on the amount accumulated in the plan at retirement and the annuity that this amount can buy at that time.

(11) The "18%" part of the limit for RRSP contributions was arrived at as follows:

(a) it is assumed that $9 of contributions buys $1 of annual pension income,

(b) pension income is limited to 2% of income per year up to an effective maximum of 35 years,

therefore, to get $1 of pension income in the future you will need a contribution of 18% (9 × 2%) of current income.

(12) The "$20,000" part of the RRSP limit was arrived at as follows:

(a) it is assumed that $9 of contributions buys $1 of annual pension income,

(b) pension income is limited to 2% of income per year up to an effective maximum of 35 years,

(c) the maximum pension available out of a defined benefit plan is $81,667 for 2008 (prior year),

(d) the maximum number of years that are eligible for the defined benefit calculation is normally 35 years at the 2% rate, this amounts to $81,667/35 years = $2,333 per year. Thus, to fund the maximum pension of $81,667, a contribution of $2,333 × 9 = $21,000 is needed.

(13) The explanation is based on the fact that the two pension systems are integrated and the integration is based on how rich your pension plan is. The richness of your pension plan is determined by the Pension Adjustment calculation. For this system to work, the pension calculation has to come first. So, your maximum pension contribution is based on your current income. Then, early in the following year your pension adjustment (PA) is calculated. Finally, your RRSP limit is determined, based on your earned income and PA, both of which relate to the prior year.

(14) Using the assumptions given in the question, the calculation would be as follows:

    (a) $2,000 compounded at 10% for 15 years within the RRSP minus 46% tax on withdrawal equals $4,511.

    (b) $2,000 compounded at 5.4% after tax for 15 years outside the RRSP equals $4,402.

If the rate of return was only 8% the funds would have to be left in the plan for about 18.5 years:

    (a) $2,000 compounded at 8% for 18.5 years within the RRSP minus 46% tax on withdrawal equals $4,485.

    (b) $2,000 compounded at 4.32% after tax for 18.5 years outside the RRSP equals $4,374.

(15) The Regulations set the withholding rates based on the amount of the withdrawal — 10% of the amount if it is $5,000 or less; 20% if the amount is between $5,000 and $15,000; and 30% if the amount exceeds $15,000. The rates are one-half of these amounts in Quebec. Based on this formula, the withholdings would be 30% of $20,000 or $6,000. Instead, if she were to withdraw four payments of $5,000, then the tax withheld would amount to only 10% of $20,000 or $2,000. In both cases the $20,000 withdrawn will have to be included in her income for the year and the same amount of ultimate tax will have to be paid. The tax will have to be funded from other sources to allow for the $20,000 to be spent for the car. Alternatively, the withdrawal will have to be increased for the amount of the tax to be paid. The necessary withdrawal would be $20,000/(1 – t), where t is her marginal tax rate. ITR: 103(4), 103(6)

(16) Since he left his RRSP to an adult child, the estate will have to pay tax on the basis that the full amount of the RRSP was included in income in the year of death. At a 50% tax rate, this will amount to $75,000 of tax which will come out of the residue or Jim's share of the estate. As a result, Kim will receive $150,000 of cash and Jim will receive the residue of the estate minus the $75,000 of tax and any other tax that may be payable. Mr. Mort should have calculated the division of property based on the after-tax values to the estate.

(17) The following items would show up on her personal tax return:

    (a) the $40,000 would be included in income as a retiring allowance;

    (b) $35,000 could be deducted as a transfer of a retiring allowance in respect of pre-'96 years of service to an RRSP; and ITA: 60(j.1)

    (c) $5,000 of the $8,000 of legal fees could be deducted. ITA: 60(o.1)

The full amount of the legal fees was deductible; however, the deduction is limited to the net of the retiring allowance less the amount transferred to the RRSP and deducted. She should have only contributed $32,000 to her RRSP from the retiring allowance. ITA: 60(j.1)

Chapter 9 —
Solutions to Multiple Choice Questions

Question 1

(B) is the correct answer and is calculated as follows: ITA: 60(*j*.1)

21 years employed before 1996 (1975 – 1995) × $2,000	$42,000
14 years employed before 1989 when no RPP or DPSP benefits vested (1975 – 1988) × $1,500	21,000
	$63,000

(A) incorrectly ignores the $1,500 rule for pre-89 years where RPP or DPSP benefits have not vested.

(C) incorrectly includes 1996 and 1989: 22 × $2,000 + 15 × $1,500 = $66,500.

(D) incorrectly counts 1996 to 2009 in the calculation: 35 × $2,000 + 14 × $1,500 = $91,000.

Question 2

(C) is correct. The $6,000 is calculated as follows:

The lesser of:		
the 2009 RRSP dollar limit		$21,000
18% of earned income for 2008:		
Income from employment	$44,000	
RPP contributions	1,000	
Support received	3,600	
Real estate rental income	1,400	
	$50,000 × 18%	$ 9,000
The lesser amount	$ 9,000	
minus 2008 PA.........................	(4,000)	
add unused deduction room	1,000	
	$ 6,000	

(A) incorrectly uses $44,000 as earned income: 18% × $44,000 – $4,000 PA + $1,000 = $4,920.

(B) incorrectly excludes the unused deduction room: $9,000 – $4,000 = $5,000.

(D) incorrectly ignores the earned income calculation: $20,000 – $4,000 + $1,000 = $17,000.

Question 3

(A) is correct. The calculations are as follows:

	Meg	*James*	
Salary	$46,000		
Employment expenses....................................	(2,800)		ITA: 8
Business income	—	$18,000	
Interest income	800	1,500	
Net income	$44,000	$19,500	
Earned income	$46,000	$18,000	ITA: 63

Since James has the lower net income ($19,500), he must claim the deduction, which is the least of:

(a)	Eligible child care expenses: $15,000 + ($100 × 2 weeks)	$15,200
(b)	Eligible children:	
	$4,000 × 1 = $4,000	
	$7,000 × 2 = 14,000	$18,000
(c)	⅔ × James' earned income: ⅔ × $18,000	$12,000

Since Joanne is age 17, she is not an eligible child. The deduction for the overnight camp for Susie   ITA: 63(3)
is restricted to $100 per week.

(B) is incorrect, because Meg cannot claim the deduction, since she has the higher net income.

(C) and (D) are incorrect because they are not the least amount calculated in (A) above.

Question 4

(B) is correct and is calculated as follows:

Moving van to transport household effects....................		$ 5,000
Travelling cost — self, spouse and two children		
Meals — flat rate ($51 × 4 persons × 5 days)..............	$ 1,020	
Car — flat rate (4,430 kms × $0.555)....................	2,459	
Hotel ($100 × 5 nights)	500	3,979
Legal fees — Vancouver house............................		900
Legal fees — Toronto house		1,100
Hotel costs while waiting for Vancouver house — $100 per day		
for 15 days (max.).....................................		1,500
		$12,479

(A) incorrectly excludes the legal fees on the houses and uses $3,000 as travel costs: $12,479 − $2,000 − $3,979 + $3,000 = $9,500.

(C) incorrectly includes all the hotel costs: $12,479 + 1,500 = $13,979.

(D) incorrectly includes all the hotel costs and the house hunting trip and uses $3,000 as travel costs: $12,479 + $1,500 + $800 − $3,979 + $3,000 = $13,800.

Question 5

(D) is correct. The earned income that should be used to calculate her RRSP deduction for 2009 is her 2008 earned income, which is: ITA: 146(1)

	2008	
Salary...	$100,000	
Taxable benefits	8,000	ITA: 6, 7
Travel expenses	(3,000)	ITA: 8
Business losses	(1,000)	
Rental income (net of expenses and CCA).............	3,200	
Spousal support paid................................	(12,600)	
2008 Earned income	$ 94,600	ITA: 146(1)

(A) and (C) are incorrect. The earned income that should be used to calculate her child care expense deduction for 2009 is $118,000:   ITA: 63(3)

	2009	
Salary...	$110,000	
Taxable benefits	8,000	ITA: 6, 7
Earned income	$118,000	ITA: 63(3)

(A) incorrectly includes 2009 salary only ($110,000).

(C) is the 2009 net income under Division B which includes amounts for travel expenses, RPP contributions, business losses, rental income and spousal support which are not part of the earned income calculation for the child care expense deduction.   ITA: 63(3)

(B) is Sahar's 2009 earned income for computing her 2010 RRSP deduction: ITA: 146(1)

	2009	
Salary...	$110,000	
Taxable benefits	8,000	ITA: 6, 7
Travel expenses	(2,000)	ITA: 8
Business losses	(1,200)	
Rental income (net of expenses and CCA).............	3,600	
Spousal support paid................................	(12,000)	
Net income under Division B	$106,400	

Question 6

(D) is correct. Deductible moving costs are: ITA: 62(3)

Moving van		$2,600
Travelling costs to move Natalie and family		
Meals — flat rate ($51 × 4 persons × 3 days)	$ 612	
Car — flat rate (1,000 kms × $0.505)	505	
Hotel ($100 × 2 nights)	200	1,317
Cost of maintaining vacant former residence (maximum amount)		5,000
Cost of changing address on legal documents		100
		$9,017

(A) which totals $25,700 incorrectly includes all expenses listed, including only $900 for travelling costs.

(B) which totals $16,017 incorrectly includes the actual cost of maintaining the former residence (an additional $4,000) plus the $3,000 house hunting trip.

(C) which totals $12,600 incorrectly includes all actual cost of maintaining the former residence (an additional $4,000) and uses only $900 for travel.

Chapter 9 — Solutions to Exercises

Exercise 1

The $200 monthly payments made for Ursalla's support prior to November 1st are income to Ursalla and deductions to Uriah as long as the agreement provides for their being considered as part of the agreement and the agreement makes a specific reference to subsection 56.1(3). The payments of $200 for November and December are income to Ursalla and deductions to Uriah.

ITA: 56(1)(*b*), 60(*b*)

The mortgage payments of $400 would qualify as income to Ursalla and deductions for Uriah since they are considered to be an allowance as referred to in the legislation, as long as the conditions of these provisions are met. Conceivably, if the payments are recognized in the agreement, then the conditions would be met.

ITA: 56.1(2), 56(1)(*b*), 60(*b*), 60.1(2)

The $700 monthly support payments for the children and the medical expense payments are neither income to Ursalla nor deductions for Uriah, since they are child support amounts.

ITA: 56.1(4)

Exercise 2

The definition of "earned income" is found in two places in the Act, subsections 146(1) and 63(3). The definition found in subsection 63(3) relates to child care expenses. The definition of earned income contained in subsection 146(1) is used in the calculation of the RRSP contribution limit and is quite different from the definition contained in subsection 63(3). You will note that section 146, entitled "Registered Retirement Savings Plans", appears in Division G — Deferred and Other Special Income Arrangements.

ITA: 63(3), 146(1)

The definition of "earned income" pertaining to the child care expense deduction can be seen to reflect the economic activity that the government is encouraging when taxpayers incur child care expenses. These are limited to: employment, carrying on business (in an unincorporated form), or studying where student income like a net research grant is obtained.

The definition of "earned income" pertaining to an RRSP can be seen to reflect, conceptually, a source of income that requires some amount of active involvement in the earning process, rather than a passive source, like a passive investment in stocks or bonds earning dividends or interest.

Exercise 3

The maximum amount that Don is able to deduct in respect of a spousal RRSP is his annual contribution limit, less any contributions made to his own RRSP in respect of the year.

Don's annual contribution limit for 2009 is calculated as the lesser of 18% of his 2008 earned income (i.e., $11,916 as calculated below) and the RRSP dollar limit for 2009, which is $21,000, less the PA reported by his employer in respect of 2008 of $6,084.

Don's earned income for 2008 is calculated as:

ITA: 146(1)

Employment income — Subdivision a	$68,400	
Add: RPP contribution	2,800	$71,200
Rental loss		(5,000)
Earned income		$66,200
18% thereof		$11,916

Therefore, Don is able to deduct $5,832 (i.e., $11,916 – $6,084) of RRSP contributions in 2009. Since he has already contributed $5,000 to a spousal RRSP, he can either contribute $832 to his own RRSP, or an additional $832 to the spousal RRSP for 2009.

Exercise 4

To calculate the after-tax rate of return for the first investment alternative — the bond held outside of an RRSP — you must multiply the pre-tax rate of return by $(1 - t)$. Therefore, the after-tax rate of return will be 4.4% (8% $(1 - 0.45)$), or $660. As the annual after-tax yield is reinvested at the same pre-tax 8%, the compounded yield is $8,073 (i.e., $15,000 $(1.044)^{10}$ – $150,000$).

Inside the RRSP, the 8% interest compounds unhindered by tax, and in 10 years the RRSP amount grows to $17,384 (i.e., $15,000 (1.08)^{10} – $15,000); however, income taxes must be paid on withdrawal from the RRSP at 45% equalling $7,823 and yielding $9,561.

The RRSP approach produces the best after-tax yield, $9,561 versus $8,073 outside the RRSP.

Exercise 5

As this was a spousal RRSP, it is subject to the three-year rule. Douglas will be required to report all of the $6,000 as his income. Under the three-year rule, Donna's income is the lesser of (A) and (B). *(ITA: 146(1))*

(A) Spousal RRSP contributions, current year $0; preceding two taxation years $6,000.

(B) RRSP withdrawn $10,000.

While the income is reported by Douglas, the income tax withholding of $2,000 remains as a credit in Donna's tax return.

Exercise 6

Mr. Retired is able to contribute $20,300 to an RRSP for 2009 [(lesser of 18% of his earned income from 2008 (i.e., 18% of $120,000) and $21,000) less his 2008 PA of $700]. He may make this annual contribution to either his own or a spousal RRSP, as long as the total of the contributions does not exceed $20,300. These contributions may be made in the year or within 60 days of December 31, 2009.

He does not have to include the lump-sum transfer from his RPP in his income nor does he get an offsetting deduction, as long as it is eligible to be transferred. *(ITA: 147.3(4), 147.3(9))*

Mr. Retired is able to transfer $44,000 to his RRSPs in respect of his retiring allowance. Since all of his employer's contributions have vested, he is able to contribute $2,000 for each of the 22 pre-'96 years of employment, including the part year for 1974. Since he is able to make such a transfer in the year or within 60 days of the year, he may make an additional contribution of $4,000 ($44,000 less his initial contribution of $40,000) in the first 60 days of 2010 and he will be able to deduct the full $44,000 in his 2009 return. *(ITA: 60(j.1))*

Mr. Retired may also make a one-time additional $2,000 contribution to his RRSP for 2009 without incurring penalties. He will not receive a deduction for this additional contribution, but as long as he has enough earned income in 2010 to deduct at least $2,000 in respect of 2011, the year prior to the year in which he must remove the funds from the plan (i.e., at the end of the year in which he turns 71, which is 2014), he will not be double-taxed on the funds when they are withdrawn from the plan. This will be the case if, instead of making a $2,000 contribution in 2011, he uses the carryforward rules to deduct the $2,000. It may also be worthwhile for Mr. Retired to contribute the additional $2,000 in 2009 if he expects to have enough earned income in 2011 to make a $2,000 contribution in 2012. Although he is not able to make a contribution to his RRSP in 2013, since his RRSP matured at the end of 2012, he is able to take an RRSP deduction in 2012 using the carryforward rules.

Exercise 7

Allowable moving expense deduction

(A) 2009

Travelling cost — air fare	$ 1,300	*ITA: 62(3)(a)*
Household effects — transporting	1,000	*ITA: 62(3)(b)*
Selling costs of Vancouver residence		*ITA: 62(3)(e)*
— legal fees	500	
— real estate commission	10,000	
Allowable purchase cost of Montreal residence		*ITA: 62(3)(f)*
— legal fees	1,000	
— Quebec transfer tax	300	
Total potential deductions	$14,100	
Less		
Amount paid by the employer not included income	$ 5,000	*ITA: 62(1)(c)*
	$ 9,100	
Deduction restricted to income from new work location — 2009	$ 7,000	*ITA: 62(1)(f)*

(B) 2010

Balance deductible from income from the new
location only in 2010   2,100   ITA: 62(1)

$ 9,100

Exercise 8

This problem situation does not involve a single parent attending a qualifying education program or   ITA: 63(2.2)
both parents attending a qualifying education program at the same time, as the legislation requires.   ITA: 63(2.3)
Therefore, the limits for these situations are not applicable.

Cathy Childcare's maximum deduction is the lesser of: ITA: 63

(A) the least of:
(i) amount paid in the year
($200 × 52) $10,400

(ii) 1 × $4,000 = $ 4,000

2 × $7,000 = $14,000 . . . . . $18,000

(iii) ²/₃ × earned income
(²/₃ × ($47,000
+ $4,000)) $34,000

least amount . . . . $ 10,400

(B) the sum of:
(i) $175 × 2 = $350

(ii) $100 × 1 = 100

$450 × 30 weeks = $13,500

Lesser amount $10,400

Charles Childcare's maximum deduction is the least of: ITA: 63

(a) $200 × 52 weeks = $10,400⎤

(b) 1 child × $4,000 = $ 4,000   ⎥
                                                                  ⎥ $10,400
2 children × $7,000 = $14,000 $18,000   ⎥

(c) ²/₃ × earned income ($23,850)[1] = $15,900⎦

minus amount deducted by Cathy   10,400

Nil

— NOTE TO SOLUTION

[1] Earned income
Gross salary $23,000
Taxable benefits   850
Scholarship (fully exempt)   Nil
$23,850

Note that earned income for child care expenses is defined differently than earned income for a   ITA: 63(3), 146(1)
registered retirement savings plan.

Exercise 9

Net employment income in new location . . . . $ 5,600   ITA: 62(3)(f)
Moving Expenses:
Transportation . . . . $ 3,100
Travelling   3,000

Hotel and Meals ($2,500 × 15/20)	1,875	
Storage fees	1,250	
Lease cancellation fee	1,200	
Legal fees + taxes for new residence	N/A	
	$10,425	
Moving allowance	4,000	(6,425)
Carryforward of moving expenses to following year		$ 825

Eligible moving expenses incurred in the year are $6,425. However, the maximum deduction is limited to net employment income of $5,600 and $825 is carried forward and available for a deduction in the following year.

Note that the legal fees incurred on the purchase of the new residence are not deductible because a former residence was not sold as a result of the move.   ITA: 62(3)(*f*)

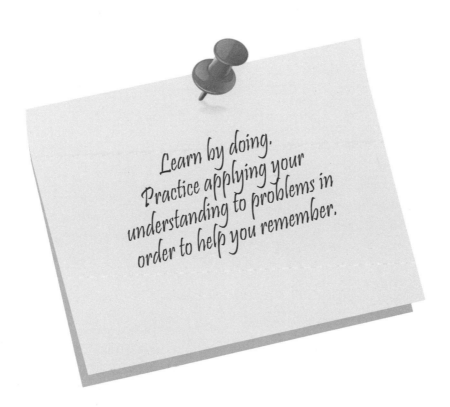

Learn by doing.
Practice applying your
understanding to problems in
order to help you remember.

Chapter 10
Computation of Taxable Income and Taxes Payable for Individuals

LEARNING GOALS

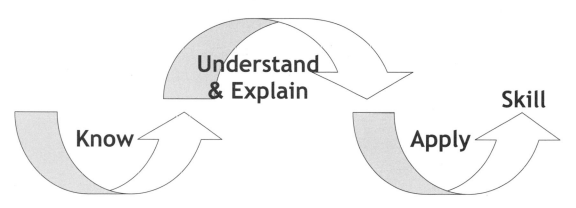

Know

By the end of this chapter you should know the basic provisions of the *Income Tax Act* that relate to the calculation of taxable income and taxes payable for individuals. Completing the Review Questions (¶10,800) and Multiple Choice Questions (¶10,825) is a good way to learn the technical provisions.

Understand and Explain

You should understand and be able to explain how taxable income is computed. With this base you should then understand and be able to explain how federal tax is calculated and how the many refundable and non-refundable tax credits are determined. Completing the Exercises (¶10,850) is a good way to deepen your understanding of the material.

Apply

You should be able to apply your knowledge and understanding of the determination of taxable income and tax liability in a way that accomplishes a client's goals. Completing the Assignment Problems (¶10,875) is an excellent way to develop your ability to apply the material in increasingly complex situations.

Chapter 10 — Learning Chart

Topic	Example Problem (✓)	Review Questions (¶10,800)	Multiple Choice (¶10,825)	Exercises (¶10,850)	Assignment Problems (¶10,875)
¶10,000 COMPUTATION OF TAXABLE INCOME FOR AN INDIVIDUAL					
¶10,005 Calculation of Taxable Income				1, 15	1, 2
¶10,010 Miscellaneous Division C Deductions and Additions			1, 4		
¶10,015 Employee stock options	✓				3
¶10,020 Deduction for certain receipts					
¶10,025 Home relocation loan	✓				3
¶10,030 Loss Carryovers		1		2, 3	2, 3, 4, 5
¶10,032 Legislative intent and government policy					
¶10,035 Non-capital loss carryovers					
¶10,040 Net capital loss carryovers	✓				
¶10,045 Farm loss					
¶10,060 Capital Gains Deduction					
¶10,061 Historical Overview					
¶10,065 The qualified farm property CGD					
¶10,066 The qualified fishing property CGD					
¶10,070 Ordering of Division C Deductions					
¶10,075 General ordering rules for Division C					
¶10,080 Ordering of section 111 loss carryovers	✓				
¶10,090 Taxable Income of Non-Residents					
¶10,100 COMPUTATION OF TAX FOR INDIVIDUALS					
¶10,110 Basic Computation of Tax					
¶10,115 Tax rates					
¶10,120 Annual indexing adjustment					
¶10,125 Overview of tax credit and tax calculation system					
¶10,130 Provincial and territorial tax					
¶10,135 Marginal tax rates		2, 3, 4		11, 12	
¶10,140 Section 118 Tax Credits			2, 4	4, 5, 6, 15	6, 8, 14
¶10,145 Married status credit					
¶10,150 Equivalent-to-married status for wholly dependent person credit					7
¶10,155 Child amount					
¶10,160 Single status — Basic personal tax credit					
¶10,165 Caregiver credit for in-home care of relative					
¶10,170 Dependants credit					
¶10,175 Additional amount					
¶10,180 Age credit					
¶10,185 Pension income amount					
¶10,190 Canada employment credit					
¶10,195 Summary of personal tax credits	✓				

Topic	Example Problem (✓)	Review Questions (¶10,800)	Multiple Choice (¶10,825)	Exercises (¶10,850)	Assignment Problems (¶10,875)
¶10,200 Adoption Expense Tax Credit					
¶10,210 Public Transit Passes Credit					
¶10,220 Children's Fitness Credit					
¶10,230 Charitable Gifts Credit					
¶10,235 Basic rules					
¶10,240 Income limit and carryforward					
¶10,245 Total charitable gifts		5			
¶10,250 Gifts of publicly traded securities					
¶10,255 Total cultural gifts					
¶10,260 Tickets to events					
¶10,265 Total Crown gifts					
¶10,270 Total ecological gifts					
¶10,280 Medical Expense Credit					8, 9
¶10,285 Calculation of the credit					
¶10,290 Medical expenses	✓				
¶10,295 Notch provision for dependants	✓				
¶10,300 Credit for Mental or Physical Impairment (Disability Tax Credit)					8
¶10,305 Amount of and conditions for impairment credit					
¶10,310 Transfer of impairment credit					
¶10,320 Tuition, Education, and Textbook Credits			3	7	6, 11, 12, 13
¶10,325 Tuition fees					
¶10,330 Education credit					
¶10,335 Textbook credit					
¶10,340 Carryforward					
¶10,345 Transfer of tuition, education, and textbook credits to spouse and parent and grandparent	✓				
¶10,350 Credit for interest on student loans					
¶10,360 Credit for Employment Insurance Premiums and CPP Contributions		6			6
¶10,370 Transfer of Unused Credits to Spouse or Common-law Partner	✓			8	
¶10,380 Dividend Tax Credit and Subsection 82(3) Election					
¶10,385 Dividend tax credit		3	4		
¶10,390 Election to transfer dividends to spouse				9	10
¶10,400 Credits for Part-Year and Non-Residents				14	
¶10,410 Ordering of Credits					
¶10,420 Income Not Earned in a Province					
¶10,430 Credit for Employment Outside Canada		7			
¶10,440 Refundable Goods and Services Tax Credit (GSTC)	✓				13
¶10,450 Refundable Medical Expense Supplement					9

CHAPTER 10

Topic	Example Problem (✓)	Review Questions (¶10,800)	Multiple Choice (¶10,825)	Exercises (¶10,850)	Assignment Problems (¶10,875)
¶10,460 Refundable Canada Child Tax Benefit					13
¶10,465 Home Renovation Tax Credit					
¶10,470 Working Income Tax Benefit (WITB)					
¶10,475 Overview	✓				
¶10,480 WITB supplement for persons with disabilities					
¶10,485 WITB prepayment					
¶10,490 Foreign Tax Credits				10	
¶10,500 Federal Political Contribution Tax Credit					
¶10,510 Tax on Old Age Security Benefits	✓				14
¶10,520 Tax Reduction on Retroactive Lump-Sum Payments					
¶10,530 Application of Rules for Computation of Tax and Credits	✓				
¶10,540 Minimum Tax			5	11, 13	15
¶10,545 Minimum amount					
¶10,550 Adjusted taxable income					
¶10,555 Basic exemption					
¶10,560 Basic minimum tax credit					
¶10,565 Minimum tax carryforward					
¶10,570 Impact of the minimum tax	✓				

CHAPTER 10

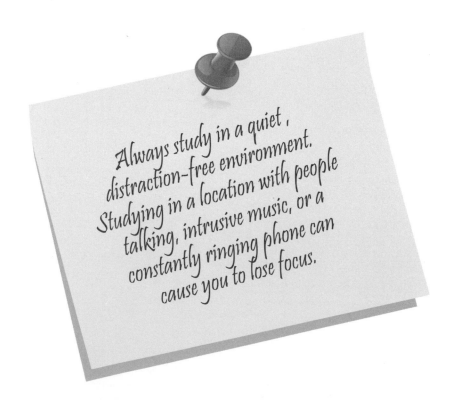

Always study in a quiet, distraction-free environment. Studying in a location with people talking, intrusive music, or a constantly ringing phone can cause you to lose focus.

Study Notes

Chapter 10 —
Discussion Notes for Review Questions

(1) Within section 111 there is no ordering that is required to be followed when choosing among the different kinds of losses, except that the oldest losses are always applied first. Generally, the rule of thumb is that the most restricted losses are claimed first. The factors that would have to be taken into account in making this decision are as follows: ITA: 111(3)(*b*)

(a) Does she have the kind of income needed to offset the losses? She would need net taxable capital gains to offset net capital losses.

(b) Which losses are going to expire first? Net capital losses can be carried back 3 years and forward indefinitely and non-capital losses can be carried back 3 years and forward 10 years for taxation years ending after March 22, 2004, and 20 years for taxation years that end after 2005.

(c) What is the likelihood that she will realize the type of income needed in future years to offset those losses she decides not to claim this year? If she uses up her non-capital losses this year and not her net capital losses, what is the likelihood that she will have a taxable capital gain in the future?

(2) His marginal tax rate on dividend income would be:

Cash dividend	$10,000
Gross-up	4,500
Taxable dividend	$14,500
Federal tax @ 29%	$ 4,205
Dividend tax credit @ 19% of $14,500	(2,755)
Basic federal tax	$ 1,450
Provincial tax @ 17% of $14,500	2,465
Provincial dividend tax credit @ 12% of $14,500	(1,740)
Total tax	$ 2,175

His marginal tax rate on these dividends is $2,175/$10,000 = 21.75%.

(3) His marginal tax rate on interest income would be:

Interest earned	$10,000
Federal tax @ 29%	$ 2,900
Provincial tax @ 17% of $10,000	1,700
Total tax	$ 4,600

His marginal tax rate on this interest is $4,600/$10,000 = 46%.

(4) Her marginal tax rate on capital gains would be:

Capital gain	$10,000
Taxable capital gain (½)	$ 5,000
Federal tax @ 29%	$ 1,450
Provincial tax @ 17% of $5,000	850
Total tax	$ 2,300

Her marginal tax rate on this capital gain is $2,300/$10,000 = 23%.

(5) The Act allows an artist to designate the proceeds of the piece of art that is not established to be cultural property at anywhere between the cost and the fair market value, in this case between $200 and $8,000. Looking at the two alternatives: ITA: 118.1(7)

(a) if she designates $200 she will report no net income since her proceeds equal her cost. However, she will receive a donation receipt for $200 which is worth a federal credit of $200 × 15% = $30;

(b) if she designated $8,000 as the proceeds, she would report an additional $7,800 in income and pay an additional federal tax of $7,800 × 15% = $1,170. However, she will also receive a donation receipt for $8,000 which will generate a federal credit of $200 × 15% + $7,800 × 29% = $2,292.

On a net basis she would have a net federal credit from this alternative of $2,292 – $1,170 = $1,122.

On a net basis, she would be further ahead to designate the full $8,000 as the proceeds. She would receive an incremental benefit of $1,092 (i.e., $1,122 – $30) plus the provincial tax credit.

The Act deems the artist to have received proceeds of disposition equal to the cost of the work of art that is a cultural gift. However, the legislation would entitle the artist to a credit based on the certified fair market value of the work. As a result, no income needs to be reported on the disposition and a credit based on the full value is available.

ITA: 118.1(7.1)
ITA: 118.1(1)

(6) Ms. Hurry will receive a personal credit of 15% times the maximum CPP contribution for the year of $2,119. The excess $2,119 will be refunded to her since it will be an overcontribution. She will not have any liability for CPP on her self-employed earnings since the full amount has been paid by her and the matching employer contributions.

ITA: 118.7

(7) Given the short-term nature of the move, the fact that his family does not move with him, and the fact that he will be moving back to Canada within 15 months indicate that he will continue to be a resident of Canada for income tax purposes and he will be taxable in Canada on his worldwide income. However, since he is a Canadian resident, was employed by a Canadian resident corporation and was working outside Canada on a construction contract for more than six months, Mr. Jones will be entitled to a tax credit. The credit for 2009 will be equal to:

ITA: 122.3

the lesser of:

(a) $80,000 × 365/365 = $80,000
(b) 80% × $120,000 = $96,000 } $80,000

divided by $120,000

times the tax otherwise payable.

As a result, he will receive a credit for $80,000/$120,000 or 66⅔% of his tax otherwise payable on his personal tax return for 2008. In 2009, the same calculation would be made prorating the $80,000 for the 90-day period abroad and another credit would be claimed.

Chapter 10 —
Solutions to Multiple Choice Questions

Question 1

(C) is correct. Since BL is a CCPC and is at arm's length with Brad, the stock option benefit will be included in Brad's income in the year of sale (along with Brad's taxable capital gain). The stock option benefit is $3,000 (($5 – $2) × 1,000). Brad's taxable capital gain is $1,000 (½ × ($7 – $5) × 1,000). Since Brad held the shares for at least two years, he can claim a Division C deduction of $1,500 (½ × his $3,000 option benefit).

ITA: 7(1.1)

ITA: 110(1)(*d*.1)

(A) incorrectly includes the section 7 benefit in 2007 and ignores the deduction.

(B) incorrectly includes the employment benefit and the incorrectly calculated Division C deduction (at ¼ of the $3,000 benefit) in 2007.

ITA: 7, 110(1)(*d*.1)

(D) incorrectly ignores the Division C deduction.

ITA: 110(1)(*d*.1)

Question 2

(C) is correct and is calculated as follows:

Basic	$10,320		
Age: $6,408 – 15% × ($47,500 – $32,312)	4,130		
Pension	2,000		
Employment	1,044		
	$17,494 × 15% =	$2,624	
Dividend tax credit: 19% × $2,500		475	
		$3,099	

ITA: 118(1)(*c*)
ITA: 118(2)
ITA: 118(3)
ITA: 8(10)

ITA: 121

(A) incorrectly ignores the dividend tax credit: ($10,320 + $4,130 + $2,000 + $1,044) × 15% = $2,624.

ITA: 121

(B) incorrectly ignores the pension credit and the employment credit: ($10,320 + $4,130) × 15% + $475 = $2,643.

ITA: 118(3), 118(10)

(D) incorrectly ignores the income restriction on the age credit: ($10,320 + $6,408 + $2,000 + $1,044) × 15% + $475 = $3,441.

ITA: 118(2)

Question 3

(C) is correct. Shabir's net income and taxable income is calculated as follows:

Scholarship income (exempt)	$ Nil	
Employment income	10,000	
Moving expenses:		
to McGill University (limited to scholarship income)	Nil	
to Toronto	(200)	
	$ 9,800	

Since Shabir's income is less than $10,320, his entire tuition fee, education, and textbook credits can be transferred to his parent (up to a maximum of $5,000).

ITA: 118.9

Tuition fee	$3,900
Education credit: 8 × $400	3,200
Textbook credit: 8 × $65	520
	$7,620; max. $5,000 × 15% = $750

(A) incorrectly computes the credit base on tuition only ($3,900 × 15% = $585).

(B) incorrectly includes the scholarship in income and claims the full moving costs to McGill: $1,500 + $10,000 – $500 – $200 = $10,800. Since this income exceeds $10,320 ($10,800 – $10,320 = $480), then $4,520 ($5,000 – $480) can be transferred resulting in a credit of $678 to a parent.

(D) incorrectly ignores the $5,000 limit: $7,620 × .15 = $1,143.

Question 4

(A) is correct.

Salary	$ 60,000
Cdn dividends ($20K × 1.45)	29,000
Stock option benefit	200,000
Taxable capital gain (½ × $200K)	100,000
Net income	$389,000
Stock option deduction (½ × $200K)	(100,000)
Taxable income	$289,000

Tax:

1st $126,264	$ 26,720
balance @ 29% of $162,736	47,193
Basic personal amount ($10,320 × 15%)	(1,548)
Transfer of tuition, education, and textbook credits (15% × $5,000 × 3)	(2,250)
Employment (15% of $1,044)	(157)
Dividend tax credit (19% of $29,000)	(5,510)
Federal tax	$ 64,448

(B) incorrectly omits the gross-up on the dividend and the dividend tax credit: $64,448 − (29% × $9,000) + $5,510 = $67,348

(C) incorrectly omits the dividend tax credit: $64,448 + $5,510 = $69,958

(D) incorrectly omits the stock option deduction: $64,448 + 29% × $100,000 = $93,448

Question 5

(A) is correct.

Taxable income	$289,000
Add:	
30% of capital gain	60,000
⅗ of the stock option deduction	60,000
Deduct:	
Gross-up on dividends	(9,000)
Adjusted taxable income	$400,000
Less: Basic Exemption	(40,000)
Net	$360,000
Minimum tax before minimum tax credit ($360,000 × 15%)	$ 54,000
Basic personal amount ($10,320 × 15%)	(1,548)
Employment ($1,044 × 15%)	(157)
	$ 52,295

(B) incorrectly deducts the $2,250 transfer of tuition and education credits: $52,295 − $2,250 = $50,045.

(C) incorrectly omits the adjustment to add back the stock option deduction: $52,295 − 15% × $60K = $43,295.

(D) incorrectly omits the adjustment to add back the tax-free portion of the capital gain and the stock option deduction: $52,295 − 15% × $120K = $34,295.

CHAPTER 10

Chapter 10 — Solutions to Exercises

Exercise 1

(a) Property income   ITA: 3

(b) Business income

(c) Employment income

(d) Employment income

(e) Business income

(f) Property income

(g) Employment income

(h) Business income

(i) Business income

(j) Other income

(k) Property income

(l) Employment income

Exercise 2

(A)

	2007	2008	2009	
Income from non-capital sources (≥0):				ITA: 3(a)
Property income	$ 1,000	Nil	$ 2,000	
Net taxable capital gains (≥0).				ITA: 3(b)
Taxable capital gains				
(see Schedule 1, Part (A), below)	$18,750	$25,000	$ 5,625	
Allowable capital losses	(7,500)	Nil	(11,250)	
	$11,250	$25,000	Nil	
Total income	$12,250	$25,000	$ 2,000	ITA: 3(b)
Losses from non-capital source and ABIL:				ITA: 3(d)
Property loss	Nil	$ (7,000)	Nil	
ABIL	Nil	(15,000)	Nil	
Division B income	$12,250	$ 3,000	$ 2,000	ITA: 3(e)
(B) Deduct: Net capital losses (see Schedule 1,				
Part (B) below for maximum)	(4,102)	(Nil)	Nil	
Non-capital losses	Nil	Nil	Nil	
Taxable income (max. equal to personal tax credit base)	$ 8,148	$ 3,000	$ 2,000	

SCHEDULE 1

	2007	2008	2009
(A) Net taxable capital gains			
Taxable capital gains (TCG)	$18,750	$ 25,000	$ 5,625
Allowable capital losses (ACL)	(7,500)	—	(11,250)
	$11,250	$ 25,000	$ (5,625)

ITA: 111(1)(b),
111(1.1)(a),
111(8)(a)

(B) Net capital losses

	2007	2008	2009
Lesser of:			
(i) Net TCGs for the			
year	$11,250	$25,000	Nil

(ii) Total of adjusted
net CLs .... $ 7,500 $ 9,023 $9,023

Lesser amount ..... $7,500 $9,023   Nil

(C) Loss continuity schedule

	2005	2009	Total
Net CL	$ 7,500	$5,625	$13,125
Utilized in 2007	(4,102)	N/A	(4,102)
Available in 2010	$ 3,398	$5,625	$ 9,023

Exercise 3

Taxpayer computation of net income for tax purposes	A	B	ITA: 3, 111
Paragraph 3(*a*)			
Section 5 Employment income	$45,000	$15,000	
Section 12 Interest income	2,000		
Section 9 Net income from a business	5,000		
Paragraph (*d*) Current-year business loss		(15,000)	
Net income for tax purposes	$52,000	0	
Non-capital loss carryforward			
Current business loss ($18,000) – loss utilized ($15,000) =		$(3,000)	

Charitable donations are a non-refundable tax credit and reduce taxes payable.

Exercise 4

(A) Personal tax credits   ITA: 118

Basic personal tax credit base	$10,320	ITA: 118(1)(*a*)
Dolly's tax credit base: $10,320 – $3,000	7,320	ITA: 118(1)(*a*)
Child amount ($2,089 × 2)	4,178	ITA: 118(1)(*b*.1)
Don:[1] over 18 years old and not infirm	Nil	ITA: 118(1)(*d*)
Dave: caregiver credit base:[2] $4,198 – ($3,200 – $14,336)	4,198	ITA: 118(1)(*d*)
Mother's tax credit base:[3] $4,198 – ($6,000 – $5,956): claim	Nil	ITA: 118(1)(*d*)
Caregiver credit[3]	4,198	ITA: 118(1)(*c*.1)
Total tax credit base[4]	$30,214	
Total personal tax credits @ 15%	$ 4,532	

— NOTES TO SOLUTION

[1] Don's father may claim the transferred tuition fee, education, and textbook tax credits, since ITA: 118.9(1)
Don's income tax will be completely offset by his basic personal tax credit.

[2] The infirm dependant tax credit would have the same base of $4,198, but a lower threshold of
$5,956.

[3] The infirm dependant tax credit would have a lower base of $4,154 (i.e., $4,198 – ($6,000 –
$5,956)).

[4] An impairment tax credit of $1,079 ($7,196 × 15%) is also available in respect of the mother ITA: 118.3(1)
and son Dave, if their impairment is certified by a medical doctor.

Exercise 5

(A) Optimum personal tax credit:
Jack's tax credit base:

— Jack	$10,320	ITA: 118(1)(*a*)
— Jill: $10,320 – $10,600	Nil[1]	

— ETM	Nil[2]	ITA: 118(1)(*b*)
	$10,320	
Jack's tax credit @ 15%	$ 1,548	

Jill's tax credit base:

— Jill	$10,320	ITA: 118(1)(*b*)(i)
— one of Jill's children[3]	10,320	ITA: 118(1)(*b*)(ii)
— child amount[4]	4,178	ITA: 118(1)(*b*.1)
	$24,818	
Jill's tax credits @ 15%	$ 3,723	

(B) In 2010, Jack and Jill could each claim a basic personal tax credit. Neither is eligible for the equivalent-to-married tax credit.

— *NOTES TO SOLUTION*

(1) All income of a spouse during the year of marriage is used in determining a spousal tax credit.

ITA: 118(1)(*a*)(ii)

(2) Jack does not have the option of claiming either of the children as ETM since they were not related to nor living with him at the time during the year that he was single.

ITA: 118(1)(*b*)

(3) Jill has the option of claiming either Jack (however, his income is too high in this fact situation) or one of her children as ETM since she falls into both paragraphs. It would appear that Jack and Jill cannot both claim each other at the same time according to a court decision which determined that spouses cannot simultaneously support each other. (See *The Queen v. Robichaud.*)

ITA: 118(1)(*a*)
ITA: 118(1)(*b*); IT-513R, par. 27
83 DTC 5265 (F.C.T.D.)

(4) It appears from the legislation that Jill can claim both children for the child amount even though she is claiming one as equivalent-to-married.

Exercise 6

$300 contribution is an employment deduction.

ITA: 8(1)(*m*)

$800 is pension income.

ITA: 56(1)(*a*)

A pension credit is not available since the amount is not from a life annuity, as required in the definition of "qualified pension income".

ITA: 118(3), 118(7)

Exercise 7

(A) Division B and taxable income		$5,000
Federal tax @ 15% of $5,000		$ 750
Less: basic personal tax credit		(1,548)
Federal tax payable		Nil

Credits available for transfer:

Tuition fee tax credit (15% of $1,800)	$ 270
Education tax credit (15% of $400 × 8)	480
Textbook tax credit (15% of $65 × 8)	78
Total	$ 828

Amount deductible by qualified transferee:
Lesser of:
(a) $750
(b) student's tuition fee, education, and textbook tax credits — $828

} $ 750

Less: amount of tax credit required to reduce student's tax payable to nil	Nil
Net amount deductible by transferee	$ 750

Note that the Employment Insurance premium and CPP contribution tax credits cannot be transferred.

(B) If Sammy was married, his wife could deduct the $750 in tuition fee, education, and textbook tax credits, since Sammy's federal tax, after his personal tax credit, is nil. Sammy's parent or grand-parent can deduct all or some part of the $750 as a tax credit, if Sammy so designates.   ITA: 118.7

Exercise 8

Tax payable by Tina:

Division B income and taxable income		$ 9,205
Federal tax 15% of $9,205		$ 1,381
Less: basic personal tax credit	$1,548	
other tax credits (age, pension)	1,014	(2,562)
Federal tax payable		Nil

Transferable tax credits available:

Age credit (15% of $6,408)	$ 961
Pension credit (15% of $350)	53
Total credits available to Tina's husband	$1,014
Less: federal tax payable net of basic personal tax credit ($1,381 – $1,548)	—
	$1,014

Exercise 9

Income increased by grossed-up dividend			$1,305
Increase in federal tax @ 29% of $1,305			$ 378
Less increase in tax credits:			
Married credit with election [15% of ($10,320 – nil]) $ 1,548			
Married credit without election [15% of ($10,320 – $1,305)]	(1,352)	$ 196	
Dividend tax credit (19% of $1,305)	248	444	
Net federal tax reduction		$ 66	

ITA: 82(3)

Therefore, the election should be made in this case.   ITA: 82(3)

Exercise 10

Federal foreign tax credit

lesser of:

(i) $225

(ii) $\dfrac{\$1,500}{\$156,800 - \$6,000} \times (\$33,835 + \$83^*) = \$337$ } $225

* The dividend tax credit is equal to 19% of the grossed-up dividend of $435 (i.e., 1.45 × $300).

Exercise 11

	Regular Part I Tax		Minimum Tax	
(A) $100 interest	($100 × .29) =	$29	($100 × .15) =	$15
(B) $100 cash dividend				
($145 grossed up)	$145 × .29 = $42		($100 × .15)=	$15
	DTC (28)	$14		
(C) $100 capital gains ($50 taxable capital gains)	($50 × .29)	$15	($50 + $30) × .15	$12

Exercise 12

Jacob's marginal tax rate is 41% (26% + 15%) where the provincial marginal tax rate is assumed to be 15%.   ITA: 117(2), 120

Exercise 13

Taxable income	$100,000
Add: CCA loss on resource property shelter	103,500
	$203,500
Less: gross-up of dividends	(13,500)
Adjusted taxable income	$190,000
Less: basic exemption	(40,000)
	$150,000
Minimum tax before minimum tax credit (15% of $150,000)	$ 22,500

Less basic minimum tax credits:

Basic personal (15% × $10,320)	$1,548	
Employment Insurance premiums	110	
CPP contributions	318	
Employment	157	2,133
Minimum amount		$ 20,367

Betty Bucks' Part I tax will be her minimum amount of $20,367 with $10,847 ($20,367 – $9,493) carried forward and applied to reduce tax payable in a subsequent year.

Exercise 14

Since Mr. and Mrs. Ataila were resident in Canada for 245 days, their non-refundable tax credits will be prorated by 245/365. For Mr. Ataila this includes the basic personal tax amount of $10,320 and the spousal amount of $10,320, the Canada Employment credit of $1,044 and the child tax credit of $6,267 ($2,089 × 3 children). Mr. and Mrs. Ataila are considered full-time residents of Canada only for the time since May 1, and will be taxed on their worldwide income. Any income earned during the four months prior to May 1 that they were non-resident will not be subject to tax in Canada.   ITA: 118, 63

The child care expenses are only deductible if Mrs. Ataila has earned income, is in attendance of full-time studies at an educational institution, or is mentally or physically unable to care for the children. If Mrs. Ataila attended full-time studies in order to obtain a job in the workforce, then her husband may claim the child care expenses.

Exercise 15

Pierino's taxable income is: ITA: 118, 63

Salary from Saskatoon Transit	$ 65,000	
Restricted farm loss	(5,250)	($2,500 + .50 ($8,000 – $2,500))
Taxable capital gain	2,000	(50% ($10,000 – $6,000))
Total income	$ 61,750	
RRSP contribution	(10,000)	
Net income	$ 51,750	
Net capital losses forward	(2,000)	(maximum of taxable capital gains)
Taxable income	$ 49,750	

Personal tax credit base amounts	
Basic personal tax credit base	$ 10,320
Canada employment credit	1,044
Eligible dependant	10,320
	$ 21,684

Chapter 11
Computation of Taxable Income and Tax After General Reductions for Corporations

LEARNING GOALS

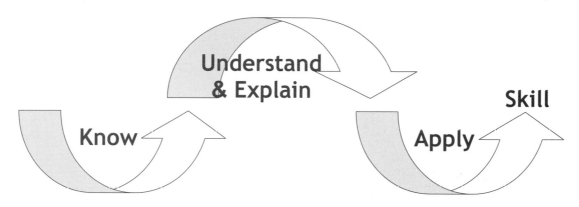

Know

By the end of this chapter you should know the key provisions used in the calculation of the taxable income and the basic tax, net of some general tax credits, for a corporation. Completing the Review Questions (¶11,800) and Multiple Choice Questions (¶11,825) is a good way to learn the technical provisions.

Understand and Explain

You should understand and be able to explain:

- why most Canadian-source inter-corporate dividends are deducted in the calculation of taxable income, after having been included in Division B income for tax purposes;
- how loss carryovers are restricted — particularly, after an acquisition of control;
- how federal corporate taxes are computed with an abatement for provincial taxes; and
- how and why certain tax credits are provided to corporations to reduce basic federal tax.

Apply

You should be able to apply your knowledge and understanding of the key provisions pertaining to the calculation of:

- taxable income for a corporation to evaluate the consequences of an acquisition of control and to decide on the best strategy for dealing with losses in that situation, and
- tax for a corporation to do a basic calculation of corporate tax.

Completing the Assignment Problems (¶11,875) is an excellent way to develop your ability to apply the material in increasingly complex situations

Chapter 11 — Learning Chart

Topic	Example Problem (✓)	Review Questions (¶11,800)	Multiple Choice (¶11,825)	Exercises (¶11,850)	Assignment Problems (¶11,875)
¶11,000 COMPUTATION OF TAXABLE INCOME FOR A CORPORATION					
¶11,010 Overview					
¶11,020 Deduction of Taxable Dividends					1
¶11,025 Purpose					
¶11,030 Dividends paid from untaxed income					
¶11,035 "After-tax financing"					
¶11,040 Dividends paid on shares subsequently sold for a loss					
¶11,050 Charitable Donations		1		1, 2	1
¶11,060 Loss Carryovers					
¶11,065 Non-capital loss	✓	2		1, 2	1
¶11,070 Treatment of allowable business investment loss	✓			4	
¶11,075 Net capital losses					1
¶11,080 Restrictions and ordering of deductions				5	
¶11,085 Choice to deduct net capital losses to preserve non-capital losses	✓			3	
¶11,090 Acquisition of Control of a Corporation and Its Effect on Losses					
¶11,095 Conceptual overview					
¶11,100 Deemed year-end		5	1		
¶11,105 Accrued or unrealized losses on inventory					
¶11,110 Accrued or unrealized losses on accounts receivable					
¶11,115 Accrued or unrealized losses on depreciable capital property			3		
¶11,120 Accrued or unrealized losses on eligible capital property					
¶11,125 Accrued or unrealized losses on non-depreciable capital property			2		
¶11,130 Elective capital gains and recapture		3			
¶11,135 Allowable business investment losses and losses from property					
¶11,140 Unused charitable contributions					
¶11,145 Deductibility of non-capital losses after an acquisition of control		4	4		
¶11,150 Loss carryback rules					
¶11,155 Summary and application	✓			6	2, 3
¶11,160 Taxable Income of a Corporation in General	✓		5	7, 8	4
¶11,200 BASIC COMPUTATION OF TAX FOR ALL CORPORATIONS					
¶11,210 Objectives of Provisions Affecting Taxation of Corporations		6			
¶11,212 Types of Corporations					
¶11,213 Private corporation					

Topic	Example Problem (✓)	Review Questions (¶11,800)	Multiple Choice (¶11,825)	Exercises (¶11,850)	Assignment Problems (¶11,875)
¶11,214 Canadian-controlled private corporation (CCPC)					
¶11,215 Public corporations					
¶11,216 Diagrammatic summary of types of corporations					
¶11,220 General Rates for Corporations					
¶11,225 Overview of rates and credits					
¶11,235 Effect of provincial corporate tax rates					
¶11,240 Effect of corporation type					
¶11,245 General rate reduction			6		8
¶11,250 Abatement from Federal Tax for Income Earned in a Province					
¶11,255 Purpose of the provision					
¶11,260 Applicable income tax regulations		7			
¶11,265 Cases on the meaning of permanent establishment	✓				5
¶11,270 Taxable income earned in a province or territory	✓				6, 9
¶11,300 TAX DEDUCTIONS/CREDITS					
¶11,310 Manufacturing and Processing Profits Deduction				10	8, 9
¶11,320 Foreign Tax Deduction					
¶11,325 Purpose and approach		8			
¶11,330 Non-business income tax deduction		9, 10		10	6, 8, 9
¶11,335 Business income tax deduction	✓			9, 10	6, 9
¶11,337 Federal Political Tax Credit				10	
¶11,340 Investment Tax Credit					
¶11,345 Overview					
¶11,350 Qualified property	✓			11, 12	8, 9
¶11,355 Qualified scientific research expenditure	✓				7
¶11,360 ITC for Apprenticeship Expenditures					
¶11,370 ITC for Child Care Spaces					

CHAPTER 11

Study Notes

Chapter 11 —
Discussion Notes for Review Questions

(1) Charitable donations are tax credits only on personal tax returns. On corporate tax returns they are deductions under Division C. Donations up to 75% of net income plus 25% of the amount of a taxable capital gain and 25% of recapture in respect of gifts of capital property with appreciated value can be deducted in the year. If the charitable donations are in excess of this amount then the excess can be carried forward for 5 years.

ITA: 110.1

(2) Income can be increased in the current year by not claiming some of the optional deductions for tax purposes. For example, the deductions for the allowance for bad debts, CCA, CECA or scientific research and experimental development expenditures can be foregone in order to increase income. These deductions will be available in future years and will not be lost. Also, the CRA will allow the revision of some permissive deductions for prior years. In addition, the company could consider the sale of any redundant assets to generate income through recapture and/or capital gain.

IC 84-1

(3) Where there has been an acquisition of control, the corporation cannot carry over its net capital losses. To the extent that the corporation has *net* taxable capital gains in the year, it may take an optional deduction of net capital losses which may in turn increase the amount of non-capital losses. Accrued capital losses are deemed to be realized in the deemed year-end immediately preceding the acquisition of control. However, there may be some relief because the corporation is allowed to trigger, on an elective basis, enough unrealized accrued capital gains to use up the net losses that are going to expire.

ITA: 111(4), 111(8)

ITA: 111(4)
ITA: 111(8)

(4) The first restriction is on the type of income against which the loss carryover can be deducted, and the second restriction is on the number of years a loss can be carried over.

Net Capital Losses: Applied against taxable capital gains only; carried back 3 years and forward indefinitely.

Non-capital Losses: Applied against all sources of income; carried back 3 years and forward 20 taxation years.

Restricted Farm Losses: Applied only against farm income; carried back 3 years and forward 20 taxation years.

Farm Losses: Applied against all sources of income; carried back 3 years and forward 20 taxation years.

(5) The deemed year-end applies whenever there is an acquisition of control even if the company acquired is not a loss company. Mr. Magoo will not be able to claim a full year of CCA since CCA is prorated for a short fiscal year.

ITR: 1100(3)

(6) The three main objectives are:

(a) alleviate double taxation;

(b) prevent the avoidance of tax through the use of a corporation; and

(c) provide tax incentives to corporations.

See the text in ¶11,210 of Chapter 11 for details.

(7) The gross revenue from that sale will be attributed to Alberta since, even though the sale was handled from Ontario, the order was delivered to a province in which the company had a permanent establishment.

ITR: 402(4)(*a*)

(8) The theory is that the country where the income is earned has the first right to tax the income. Then, in order to prevent double taxation when Canada also taxes this income, a credit is given in Canada for the foreign taxes paid.

(9) Investment income may be taxed in the foreign country even though there is no permanent establishment in that country. Canada assumes that this investment income, other than from real property, is earned through its permanent establishment in Canada and, therefore, considers this income to be earned in a province for purposes of section 124. Foreign business income, on the other hand, is assumed to be earned in a permanent establishment in the foreign country and, therefore, is not eligible for the federal abatement.

(10) Since Lossco does not have any net income or Canadian income tax, it cannot claim a foreign tax credit. No carryover is allowed for non-business income tax. However, the corporation can deduct the foreign taxes which will increase its loss for the year. This deduction will at least provide the benefit of the foreign taxes being carried forward as part of the non-capital losses.

ITA: 126(1)
ITA: 20(12)

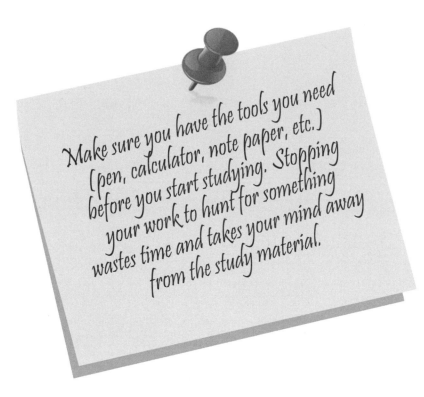

Make sure you have the tools you need (pen, calculator, note paper, etc.) before you start studying. Stopping your work to hunt for something wastes time and takes your mind away from the study material.

Chapter 11 —
Solutions to Multiple Choice Questions

Question 1

(B) is correct. Loss Co may select any date, within the 53-week period commencing February 1, 2009, as its new year-end.

ITA: 249(4)(*b*), 249(4)(*d*)

(A) is incorrect, as the taxation year is deemed to have ended immediately before control was acquired. Since control was acquired on February 1, 2009, the year is usually deemed to have ended January 31, 2009. (Technically, it is possible to have an acquisition of control occur at a specific time, say, 10 am, on February 1, in which case, the taxation year can be deemed to have ended on February 1 at 9:59 am. Usually, a time is not specified, in which case, the taxation year is deemed to end the day before.)

ITA: 249(4)(*a*)

(C) is incorrect because the corporation is deemed not to have established a fiscal period yet. This being the case, the corporation is free to select any year-end, within the 53-week limitation.

ITA: 249(4)(*d*)

(D) is incorrect for the same reason as (C).

Question 2

(C) is correct. The ACB of the land is reduced from $200,000 to $140,000, its FMV. The $60,000 reduction is deemed to be a capital loss for the taxation year ended May 14, 2009.

ITA: 111(4)(*c*), 111(4)(*d*)

(A) is incorrect as it includes the $25,000 accrued loss on the building which is depreciable property. Depreciable property is specifically excluded.

ITA: 111(4)(*c*)

(B) is incorrect as it includes the $20,000 accrued loss on the inventory which is not a capital property.

(D) is incorrect, because the $60,000 accrued loss on the land was reduced by the $10,000 accrued gain on the marketable securities. The recognition of the accrued gain on the marketable securities is not required. An election is available to recognize the accrued gain, if it is desirable.

ITA: 111(4)(*e*)

Question 3

(C) is correct. The UCC of the Class 45 computer equipment is reduced by $5,000, from $38,000 to $33,000. The UCC of the Class 8 office furniture and equipment is reduced by $10,000, from $58,000 to $48,000. The total of the two reductions, $15,000, is deemed to have been claimed as CCA in the year ended March 31, 2009.

ITA: 111(5.1)

(A) is incorrect as this amount adjusts the UCC of all the classes to the FMV of the classes. This amount includes an adjustment of $8,000 to increase the UCC of the Class 10 automobiles and the Class 12 assets to the FMV of the respective classes. The $8,000 is then subtracted from the $15,000 reduction calculated in (C). This is incorrect. The adjustment applies only to the classes where the UCC is higher than the FMV.

ITA: 111(5.1)

(B) is incorrect as it includes only 72% of the adjustment calculated in (C).

(D) is incorrect for the same reason as (A). The difference between (A) and (D) is that in (D) the positive and negative adjustments have been totalled, whereas in (A) they have been netted.

Question 4

(D) is correct. For its year ending December 31, 2009, Loss Co will be able to deduct non-capital losses of $15,000 (maximum), provided the widget retailing business is carried on throughout the taxation year ended December 31, 2009 with a reasonable expectation of profit.

ITA: 111(5)(*a*)

(A) is incorrect as net capital losses incurred prior to the acquisition of control expire on the date control is acquired.

ITA: 111(4)(*a*)

(B) is incorrect. Non-capital losses realized prior to an acquisition of control cannot be deducted against taxable capital gains incurred after the acquisition of control. Non-capital losses are only deductible against income from the business in which the losses were incurred and income from a similar products or services.

ITA: 111(5)(*a*)

(C) is incorrect. The non-capital loss deduction has been limited to the income from a similar products or services net of the loss from the widget business. The netting of the widget business loss is not required.

ITA: 111(5)(*a*)

Question 5

(D) is correct.

Net income for tax purposes	$ 600,000
Canadian dividends	(100,000)
Charitable donations	(200,000) – not exceeding $450,000 (75% of net income)
	$ 300,000

ITA: 112

(A) incorrectly makes no adjustments: $600,000.

(B) incorrectly omits the deduction for charitable donations: $600,000 – $100,000 = $500,000.

(C) incorrectly omits the section 112 deduction for Canadian dividends: $600,000 – $200,000 = $400,000.

Question 6

(B) is correct.

Taxable income as per the answer to Question 5	$300,000
Part I tax on taxable income	
Tax @ 38% on $300,000	$114,000
Deduct: Federal tax abatement (10% × 90% × $300,000)	(27,000)
	$ 87,000
Deduct: M&P deduction (9% of $250,000)	(22,500)
Deduct: 9% rate reduction on income not eligible for the M&P deduction: 9% × [$300K – $250K]	(4,500)
Total federal tax	$ 60,000

(A) incorrectly applies the rate reduction to all income, including that eligible for the manufacturing and processing profits deduction: $60,000 + $4,500 – 9% × $300K = $37,500.

(C) incorrectly omits the 9% rate reduction: $60,000 + 4,500 = $64,500.

(D) incorrectly calculates the rate reduction as 7% × $300K rather than 9% × 300K. $87,000 – 7% of $300,000 = $66,000.

Chapter 11 — Solutions to Exercises

Exercise 1

	2007	*2008*	*2009*
Income under Division B............	$(7,350)	$22,050	$14,700
Deduct: charitable donations limited by 75% of income above			
— carried forward	Nil	$ 2,625	Nil
— current	Nil	Nil	4,700	(7,325)	$11,025[1](11,025)
unlimited charitable donation			
— carried forward	Nil	—	$ 3,675
— current	Nil	Nil	$14,725[2](14,725)	—	(3,675)[3]
non-capital loss from 2007[4]	Nil	Nil	Nil
Taxable income	Nil	Nil	Nil

—NOTES TO SOLUTION

[1] Limited to 75% of $14,700 = $11,025; $975 is available to carry forward five years to 2014.

[2] If the donation of the land gave rise to a capital gain, the taxable portion would be included in the amount of income under Division B.

[3] $1,300 ($19,700 – $14,725 – $3,675) is available to carry forward four more years to 2013.

[4] $7,350 is available to carry forward 20 taxation years to 2027.

Exercise 2

	2007	*2008*	*2009*
Option A: Claiming maximum charitable donations			
Income before CCA	$ 100,000	$115,000	$132,250
CCA...................................	(200,000)	(101,667)[1]	(116,917)
Income (loss) under Division B................	$(100,000)	$ 13,333	$ 15,333
Charitable donations:			
— Carried forward	Nil	(10,000)[1]	(11,500)[1]
— Current	Nil	Nil	Nil
Non-capital loss carried forward from 2007	N/A	(3,333)	(3,833)[2]
Taxable income	Nil	Nil	Nil
Option B: Non-capital loss utilization			
Income before CCA	$100,000	$115,000	$132,250
CCA	(107,167)[3]	(86,333)	(132,250)
Income (loss) under Division B	$ (7,167)	$ 28,667	Nil
Charitable donations:			
— carried forward	Nil	(21,500)	Nil
— current	Nil	Nil	Nil
Non-capital loss carried forward from 2007	N/A	(7,167)[3]	Nil
Taxable income	Nil	Nil	Nil

	2007	2008	2009
Option C: Maximum donation and non-capital loss utilization			
Income before CCA	$100,000	$115,000	$132,250
CCA	(107,166)	(101,667)	(116,917)
Income (loss) under Division B	$ (7,166)	$ 13,333	$ 15,333
Charitable donations:			
— Carried forward	Nil	(10,000)[4]	(11,500)[4]
— Current	Nil	Nil	Nil
Non-capital loss carried forward from 2007	N/A	(3,333)	(3,833)
Taxable income	Nil	Nil	Nil

• *Summary*	*Options*		
	A	B	C
Total donations claimed	$ 21,500	$ 21,500	$ 21,500
Total CCA claimed	418,584	325,750	325,750
Unclaimed non-capital loss	92,834	Nil	Nil

— NOTES TO SOLUTION

[1] CCA amount selected to provide sufficient Division B income for a deduction of charitable donations (maximum of 75% of Division B income). The 2003 charitable donations would, otherwise, expire after 2008.

[2] $92,834 of non-capital loss from 2007 remains.

[3] Determined by looking forward to 2008 and creating the maximum non-capital loss in 2007 that can be fully utilized in 2008.

[4] Uses the five-year carryforward of charitable donations to the maximum — i.e., the $11,500 donations of 2004 may be carried forward to 2009, as in Option A.

Exercise 3

Sum of: loss from business	$129,000
allowable business investment loss	8,000
dividends deductible under sec. 112	10,750
net capital loss deducted [½ × ($46,400 − $12,000)]	17,200[1]
	$164,950

Less: income from property	$32,250	
net taxable capital gains [½ × ($46,400 − $12,000)]	17,200[1]	(49,450)
Non-capital loss for the year		$115,500

— NOTE TO SOLUTION

[1] The corporation may deduct the net capital loss from income even though it has no impact on the taxable income. However, the deduction is restricted to the net taxable capital gain for the year. Once deducted, the net capital loss can be included in the non-capital loss computation.

Exercise 4

Allowable capital loss (excluding ABIL)	$ 51,750
Less: taxable capital gain	(4,700)
Net	$ 47,050
Add: unutilized allowable business investment loss in respect of which the carryover period expires in the year (i.e., the 10th carryforward year)	Nil
Net capital loss for the year	$ 47,050

Exercise 5

	Option A[(1)]	Option B[(1)]
Income from business	$55,500	$55,500
Taxable capital gains	37,000	37,000
Income under Division B	$92,500	$92,500
Less: net capital losses	(37,000)[(2)]	(10,000)[(2)]
non-capital losses	(55,500)	(82,500)
Taxable income	Nil	Nil
Summary:		
Unutilized non-capital losses	$27,000	Nil
Unutilized net capital losses	3,000[(2)]	$30,000[(2)]

NOTES TO SOLUTION

[(1)] In Option A, maximum net capital losses are claimed before non-capital losses. In Option B, maximum non-capital losses are claimed before net capital losses.

		Option A	Option B
[(2)] 1999 Net capital losses available		$60,000	$60,000
Adjusted to 2009 ($60,000 × ½ / ¾)		40,000	40,000
Utilized in 2009 (limited to TCG)		(37,000)	(10,000)
Available to carryforward		$ 3,000	$30,000

Exercise 6

Part (a)

Because of the acquisition of control by Holdco Ltd., Loser Ltd. is deemed to have a taxation year-end on March 9, 2009. This taxation year will be only 69 days long, having commenced on January 1, 2009. The exception does not apply, since the date of the acquisition of control is more than seven days after the last year-end.   ITA: 249(4), 256(9)   ITA: 249(4)(c)

Loser Ltd. will be required to make certain adjustments as of March 9, 2009. The adjustments will increase the company's business losses of $3,000 to $48,000, as follows:

Business losses	$ 3,000
Excess of UCC ($70,000) over fair market value ($40,000) of assets in Class 8	30,000
Accrued inventory losses	Nil
Doubtful accounts receivable deemed to be actual bad debts	15,000
Losses from non-capital sources (all from business)	$48,000

ITA: 111(5.1)

ITA: 111(5.3)

The balance in the CEC account is not affected by the acquisition of control, because there was no unrealized loss at the time of the acquisition of control (i.e., ¾ of the fair market value of $68,000 = $51,000 which is greater than the $50,000 CEC account balance).

Division B income for the deemed taxation year ended March 9, 2009 would be computed as follows:

Par. 3(a):	Income from non-capital sources		Nil
Par. 3(b):	Net taxable capital gains:		
	Election under par. 111(4)(e) on land (½ × $56,000)	$28,000	
	Allowable capital losses	Nil	$28,000
Par. 3(c):	Par. 3(a) + par. 3(b)		$28,000
Par. 3(d):	Losses from non-capital sources (above)		(48,000)
	Division B income and taxable income		Nil

CHAPTER 11

Since the net capital losses of $30,000 will expire on March 10, 2009, if nothing is done, the corporation should deduct the net capital losses of $30,000. Although the taxable income will be unaffected, the non-capital losses can be increased by this amount.

The non-capital loss for the deemed year ending March 10, 2009, would be:

Losses from business sources	$48,000
Add: net capital losses deducted at ½ inclusion rate ($30,000 × ⁴⁄₃ × ½)	20,000
	$68,000
Less: par. 3(c) income determined above	28,000
Non-capital loss for deemed year	$40,000

The adjusted cost base of the land will be increased by the amount of the gain elected to $256,000 (i.e., $200,000 + $56,000) on March 10, 2009. **ITA: 111(4)(e)**

The undepreciated capital cost in Loser's Class 8 will be reduced from $70,000 to $40,000 as at March 10, 2009. Loser Ltd. will be deemed to have deducted the $30,000 as capital cost allowance for taxation years ending before March 10, 2009; thereby, making Loser Ltd. liable for recapture on that amount if the assets are subsequently sold. **ITA: 111(5.1)**

Similarly, the corporation will be deemed to have made a claim for bad debts totalling $15,000. Accordingly, Loser Ltd.'s accounts receivable will be $225,000 as at March 10, 2009, the start of its next taxation year. **ITA: 20(1)(p), 111(5.3)**

Loser Limited will be allowed the deduction of the 2008 $600,000 non-capital losses in any year up to 2028 including the short deemed taxation year (if the corporation reverts to a December 31 year-end) after which they will expire. However, in order to be deducted, the widget manufacturing business must be carried on by Loser Ltd. for profit or with a reasonable expectation of profit throughout each of those taxation years. Similarly, the $40,000 non-capital losses of the March 9, 2009 taxation year will be eligible for carryforward 20 years, under the same conditions, to December 31, 2028 if the company reverts to a December 31 year-end. It appears that this condition will be met, since Holdco Ltd. will provide capital and management to turn Loser's business around. The non-capital losses may be deducted in a carryforward year from the incomes of the widget manufacturing business and a business with similar products in that year. **ITA: 111(5)**

Part (b)

Loser Limited would still have business losses of $3,000 plus the deemed business loss on the Class 8 assets of $30,000 and the loss on the accounts receivable of $15,000, which gives a total of $48,000 of losses from business sources. In addition, Loser Limited has a property loss of $10,000.

The 1999 net capital loss of $30,000 is $20,000 when converted from a ¾ to a ½ inclusion rate.

The minimum designated proceeds or deemed proceeds would be as follows: **ITA: 111(4)(e)**

Deemed proceeds = 2 × ($20,000 net capital losses plus $10,000 property losses)
  plus ACB of the land of $200,000
  = $260,000

Now, the Division B and taxable income for the deemed taxation year ended March 9, 2009 would be:

Par. 3(a)	Income from non-capital sources			Nil
Par. 3(b)	Net taxable capital gains:			
	Election under par. 111(4)(e) —			
	($260,000 − $200,000) × ½		$30,000	
	Less allowable capital losses		Nil	$30,000
Par. 3(c)				$30,000
Par. 3(d)	Losses from non-capital sources:			
	Business losses		$48,000	
	Property losses		10,000	(58,000)
Division B income				Nil
Division C deductions:				
	Net capital losses			$20,000
Taxable income				Nil

Note how just enough paragraph 3(*c*) income was created (i.e., $30,000) to offset the property loss of $10,000 plus the net capital loss of $20,000, both of which are about to expire.

The non-capital loss balance for the deemed year ended March 9, 2009 would be:

Par. 3(*d*) losses	$58,000
Add: net capital losses deducted	20,000
	$78,000
Less: par. 3(*c*) income	(30,000)
Total non-capital loss for the year ended March 9, 2009	$48,000

The non-capital loss of $48,000 for the year ended March 9, 2009 would be added to the 2008 non-capital loss balance to give a total of $648,000 to be deducted in the future. If Loser Limited reverts to a December 31 year-end, these could be deducted in any year that the loss business is carried on against income of the business that generated the loss or against business income from the sale of similar products up to:

2008 non-capital loss	2027
March 2009 non-capital loss	2028

The adjusted cost base of the land will now be increased to $260,000.

Exercise 7

	2008	2009
Net income (loss) per financial accounting statements	$(53,000)	$126,000
Add total of items not deductible for tax purposes	127,700	240,700
	$ 74,700	$366,700
Less CCA ($7,900 less in 2008)	51,700	51,670
Income for tax purposes	$ 23,000	$315,030
Inter-company dividends $23,000		$23,000
Charitable donations (max. 75% of income):		
Carried over . . . . —	15,000	
Current . . . . Nil	15,000	
Non-capital loss carryover . . . . —	23,000 18,000	71,000
Taxable income	Nil	$244,030
Taxable income originally computed	Nil	$245,610

Conclusion:

This calculation produces better results. All of the inter-company dividends are fully deductible in 2008 with the reduction of the capital cost allowance by $7,900. Both options allowed, in total, an equal amount of non-capital losses and donations to be claimed over the two-year period. Although the original calculation enabled $6,320 (i.e., $59,600 + $50,090 − $51,700 − $51,670) more capital cost allowance to be claimed in total over the two years, the original calculation could not utilize $7,900 of the potential dividend deduction. This alternative increases the future CCA write-offs by $6,320 as shown below.

		Building *Class 1: 4%*	Equipment *Class 8: 20%*
Capital cost allowances were computed as follows:			
2009:	UCC, January 1, 2009	$ 356,250	$ 187,100*
	CCA (total deduction: $51,670)	(14,250)	(37,420)
2010:	UCC, January 1, 2010	$ 342,000	$ 149,680
	UCC originally computed	$ 342,000	$ 143,360

---

* $179,200 + $7,900.

Exercise 8

Division B income		$116,850
Less: charitable donations limited to 75% of $116,850		
or $87,638		
— carried forward	$10,250	
— current	77,388[1]	(87,638)
dividends from taxable Canadian corporations		(12,300)
subtotal		$ 16,912
non-capital losses[2]		(16,912)
net capital losses[2] (not to exceed the taxable capital gains		
for the year)		(Nil)
Taxable income		Nil

— *NOTES TO SOLUTION*

[1] The balance of $2,612 in current charitable donations may be carried forward to the next five years.

[2] These carried-over losses may be claimed in a different sequence and in different amounts from that shown. For example, if there is little prospect of future capital gains, the corporation might make the following deductions:

subtotal	$16,912
net capital losses ($41,000 × ½ / ¾)	(27,333)
non-capital losses	Nil
taxable income	Nil

The balance of the net capital losses may be carried forward indefinitely.

Net capital losses claimed are added to the non-capital loss balance carried forward.

Exercise 9

Income from Japan in Canadian dollars (77,515,723 yen × .009793)		$ 759,111
Total income under Division B ($2,500,000 + $759,111)		$3,259,111
Less: Dividends deductible under sec. 112	$100,000	
Net capital losses carried forward		
(adjusted to current year inclusion rate)	25,000	125,000
Taxable income		$3,134,111
Tax @ 38%		$1,190,962
Less: general tax reduction @ 9% of 3,134,111		(282,070)
Net tax		$ 908,892

Foreign Business Tax Deduction

Least of: (a) amount paid (31,006,289 yen × .009793)	$ 303,645

$$\text{(b)} \quad \frac{\text{income from Japan}}{\substack{\text{Div. B income minus s. 112 ded.} \\ \text{and net capital loss ded.}}} \times \substack{\text{tax otherwise} \\ \text{payable before} \\ \text{abatement}}$$

$= \dfrac{\$759,111}{\$3,259,111 - (\$100,000 + 25,000)} \times \$908,892 =$	$ 220,142
(c) Part I tax otherwise payable plus surtax minus foreign	
non-business tax credit ($908,892 – nil)	$ 908,892

Therefore, the foreign tax deduction is $220,142.

* 1.12% of $3,114,500.

Exercise 10

Income under Division B...................................		$2,645,000
Less. Charitable donations.............................	$ 69,000	
Taxable dividends deductible under sec. 112..........	517,500	
Non-capital losses.............................	127,600	714,100
Taxable income		$1,930,900
Tax @ 38%..		$ 733,742
Less: Federal tax abatement (10% of 86% of $1,930,900)		166,057
		$ 567,685
Less: Non-business foreign tax credit (see Schedule 1)	$ 25,875	
Business foreign tax credit (see Schedule 2)..........	36,800	
Manufacturing and processing profits deduction (9% of $1,495,000)	134,550	
Tax reduction (see Schedule 3)	39,231	
Federal political contributions tax credit (max.)	650	237,106
Part I tax payable..		$ 330,579

Schedule 1: Non-business foreign tax credit

Lesser of: (a) amount paid		$ 25,875

$$(b) \frac{\text{foreign non-business income}}{\substack{\text{Div. B income minus s. 112 ded.}\\ \text{and net capital loss ded.}}} \times \substack{\text{tax otherwise payable}\\ \text{after abatement minus}\\ \text{general tax reduction}}$$

$$= \frac{\$172,500}{\$2,645,000 - (\$517,500 + 0)} \times \$528,454^{(1)} \dots\dots \quad \$ \ 42,848$$

Schedule 2: Business foreign tax credit

Least of: (a) amount paid		$ 36,800

$$(b) \frac{\text{foreign business income}}{\substack{\text{Div. B income minus s. 112 ded.}\\ \text{and net capital loss ded.}}} \times \substack{\text{tax otherwise payable}\\ \text{before deductions}\\ \text{minus general tax}\\ \text{reduction}}$$

$$= \frac{\$115,000}{\$2,645,000 - (\$517,500 + 0)} \times (\$733,742 - 39,231) \quad \$ \ 37,541$$

(c) $733,742 − $39,231 − $25,875 .... $668,636

Schedule 3: Tax reduction

Taxable income	$1,930,900
Less M&P profits	1,495,000
Net..	$ 435,900
9% of $435,900	$ 39,231

NOTE TO SOLUTION

(1) $733,742 − $166,057 − $39,231 (Schedule 3)

Exercise 11

The total investment tax credit is 10% of $900,000 = $90,000.

Taxable income before CCA on eligible property........................	$300,000
Less: CCA on qualified property (½ × 6% of $900,000)	27,000
Taxable income	$273,000

CHAPTER 11

Net federal tax: @ 19% of $273,000		$ 51,870
Less: fed. pol. contributions tax credit	$ 500	
investment tax credit (limited to ($51,870 – $500))	51,370	$(51,870)
Part I tax payable		Nil

Note that the $51,870 of investment tax credit will reduce the balance of UCC in Class 1 in the following year. The remainder of $38,130 (i.e., $90,000 – $51,870) of ITC may be carried back three taxation years and forward 20 taxation years. Any amount used to reduce tax in a particular carryover year will reduce the UCC in the year following the year of use or the year following the purchase, whichever is later.

Exercise 12

Earned investment tax credit of 10% of $3,500,000 = <u>$350,000</u>

Income under Division B before CCA on eligible property		$2,645,000
Less: CCA on eligible property ($\frac{1}{2}$ × .50 × $3,500,000)		875,000
Income under Division B.		$1,770,000
Less: charitable donations	$ 69,000	
taxable dividends deductible under sec. 112	517,500	
non-capital losses	127,600	714,100
Taxable income		$1,055,900
Tax @ 38%		$ 401,242
Less: federal tax abatement (10% of 86% of $1,055,900)		90,807
		$ 310,435
Less: manufacturing and processing profits deduction		
(see Schedule 1)	$55,800	
non-business foreign tax credit (see Schedule 2)	25,875	
business foreign tax credit (see Schedule 3)	33,238	
Tax reduction (see Schedule 4)	39,231	
federal political contribution tax credit	500	154,644
Part I tax payable before investment tax credit		$ 155,791
Investment tax credit		(155,791)
Part I tax payable		Nil

The remaining investment tax credit of $194,209 (i.e., $350,000 – $155,791) can be carried forward 20 years.

The UCC balance in Class 29 will be reduced by $155,791 in the following year and by the amount of the $194,209 remainder in subsequent years, if that amount is deducted.

Schedule 1: Manufacturing and processing profits deduction

manufacturing and processing profits before CCA on		
eligible property		$1,495,000
less: CCA on eligible property ($\frac{1}{2}$ × .50 × $3,500,000)		875,000
manufacturing and processing profits		$ 620,000
9% of $620,000		$ 55,800

Schedule 2: Non-business foreign tax credit

Lesser of:

(a) amount paid		$25,875
(b) $\dfrac{\$172,500}{\$1,770,000 - \$517,500}$ × $271,204^{(1)}$		$37,351

Schedule 3: Business foreign tax credit

Least of:

(a) amount paid . . . . $ 36,800

(b) $\dfrac{\$115,000}{\$1,770,000 - \$517,500} \times (\$401,242 - \$39,231)$ $33,238

(c) $401,242 – $39,231 – $25,875 . . . . $336,136

Schedule 4: Tax reduction

Taxable income	$1,055,900
Less M&P profits	620,000
Net	$ 435,900
9% of $435,900	$ 39,231

— *NOTE TO SOLUTION*

[1] $401,242 – $90,807 – $39,231 (Schedule 4).

Chapter 12
Integration for Business and Investment Income of the Private Corporation

LEARNING GOALS

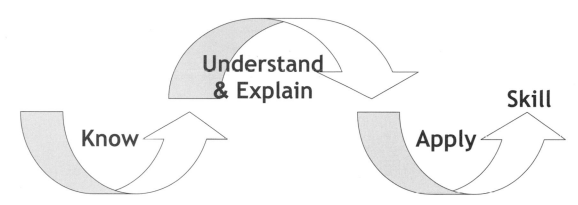

Know

Understand & Explain

Skill

Apply

Know

By the end of this chapter you should know how the income tax system works to integrate the tax on individual shareholders with the tax on private corporations for business and investment income. Completing the Review Questions (¶12,800) and Multiple Choice Questions (¶12,825) is a good way to learn the technical provisions.

Understand and Explain

You should understand and be able to explain:
- the concept of integration;
- how the small business deduction from tax is computed and how it helps to achieve integration of business income;
- the rules for the association of corporations and why they exist;
- the base on which the additional investment tax credit for a Canadian-controlled private corporation is computed and how it is limited for scientific research and experimental development expenditures;
- what investment income of a private corporation is and how it is taxed to achieve integration; and
- the advantages and disadvantages of incorporating sources of business income and sources of investment income.

Apply

You should be able to apply your knowledge and understanding of the key provisions pertaining to:
- associated corporations, where that term is used in the legislation;
- the calculation of:
  - the small business deduction,
  - the additional investment tax credit for scientific research and experimental development expenditures,
  - the income taxes on investment income of a private corporation, including refundable tax, and
- the complete calculation of taxes payable by a private corporation with income from business and investment sources.

Completing the Assignment Problems (¶12,875) is an excellent way to develop your ability to apply the material in increasingly complex situations.

Chapter 12 — Learning Chart

Topic	Example Problem (✓)	Review Questions (¶12,800)	Multiple Choice (¶12,825)	Exercises (¶12,850)	Assignment Problems (¶12,875)
¶12,000 THE CONCEPT OF INTEGRATION					
¶12,010 Problems Addressed by Integration					
¶12,020 Objectives of Integration		1. 2			
¶12,030 The Major Tool for Integration in the Income Tax Act					
¶12,035 The concept		13, 14			
¶12,040 Application of the concept in theory					
¶12,045 Basis for the calculation of the dividend tax credit		3, 12			
¶12,100 INCOME FROM AN ACTIVE BUSINESS OF A CCPC					
¶12,110 Introduction to the Small Business Deduction		4, 5			
¶12,120 Mechanics of Calculation of Small Business Deduction					
¶12,125 The basic limits		6, 7	1	6	7, 9, 10, 11
¶12,130 Elimination of small business deduction for large CCPCs	✓				5
¶12,140 Definition of "Active Business"					
¶12,145 The "default" definition			2	1	1, 12, 13
¶12,150 Specified investment business	✓		2	1	1, 12, 13
¶12,155 Personal services business			2		12, 13
¶12,160 Income incidental to an active business					
¶12,170 Associated Companies					
¶12,175 Overview					
¶12,180 Related persons	✓			2	
¶12,185 Basic association rules	✓		5, 6	3, 4, 10, 13	2, 3, 12, 13
¶12,190 Concept of control					4
¶12,195 Extended meaning of control			6		4
¶12,200 Ownership of shares					3
¶12,205 Association with third corporation	✓		5		2, 3, 12
¶12,210 Deemed association				4, 5	3, 4
¶12,220 Corporate Partnerships					
¶12,230 Manufacturing and Processing Profits and the Small Business Deduction	✓	10	3	6	7, 9
¶12,240 Investment Tax Credit Revisited					
¶12,245 Overview					
¶12,250 The ITC rate for CCPCs					6, 9
¶12,255 Refundable investment tax credit	✓				6
¶12,260 Prescribed proxy amount					6
¶12,265 Capital expenditures	✓				6

Topic	Example Problem (✓)	Review Questions (¶12,800)	Multiple Choice (¶12,825)	Exercises (¶12,850)	Assignment Problems (¶12,875)
¶12,270 Incorporated Business Income and Integration					
¶12,275 Corporate tax rate incentives to incorporate in general					
¶12,280 Specific tax savings (cost) and deferral (prepayment) possibilities					
¶12,285 Summary of advantages and disadvantages of incorporating active business income		8, 9			
¶12,300 INCOME FROM INVESTMENTS OF A CCPC					
¶12,310 Overview of Integration for Income from Investments of a CCPC					
¶12,315 Purpose					
¶12,316 Capital Dividend Account					
¶12,317 Components of the account					
¶12,318 "The period"					
¶12,319 Example of disposition of eligible capital property	✓				
¶12,320 Conceptual illustration of integration		15			
¶12,330 Special Refundable Taxes in Respect of Income from Investments of a CCPC					
¶12,335 Aggregate investment income					9
¶12,340 Additional refundable tax (ART)					5, 7, 9, 11, 13
¶12,345 "Refundable dividend tax on hand" (RDTOH)		12		13	8, 11, 13
¶12,350 "Deeming rules"		16		11, 13	12, 13
¶12,355 Part IV tax on portfolio and other dividends	✓	11, 12, 17, 18	4	7, 10	8, 9, 11, 12
¶12,360 Dividend refund		12			8, 9, 11
¶12,365 Anti-avoidance rule					8, 9
¶12,370 Summary of conditions for Part IV tax					
¶12,375 Application of non-capital losses					
¶12,380 Actual Application of the Scheme	✓			12	14
¶12,390 Imperfections in the Integration System for Income from Investments of a CCPC					
¶12,395 Tax deferral at higher tax rates on personal income					
¶12,400 Permanent tax savings or costs					
¶12,405 Summary of advantages and disadvantages of incorporating investment income eligible for refundable tax					
¶12,500 COMPREHENSIVE SUMMARY OF TYPES OF CORPORATE INCOME AND FEDERAL CORPORATE INCOME TAX RATES	✓			8, 9	9, 10, 11

Study Notes

Chapter 12 —
Discussion Notes for Review Questions

(1) The purpose of integration is to avoid the double taxation of income earned through a corporation. Integration should cause the total tax paid by a corporation and its shareholders to be equal to the total tax paid by an individual who carries on the same economic activity directly and not through a corporation. The system should be neutral as to the form of organization used.

(2) Ideal integration depends on:

(a) When the corporation itself pays tax, the shareholder must include in income and pay tax on the full pre-tax income earned by the corporation and then get a full credit for all the income tax paid by the corporation.

(b) All after-tax income would have to be either paid out as dividends in the year earned or taxed in some manner at the shareholder level in that year to avoid the indefinite deferral of tax that might otherwise be available if the corporate rates were lower than individual tax rates. This would equate the position of the shareholder with the position of the proprietor, partner or owner of investments who must pay tax on income from his or her economic activity whether or not it is distributed.

(3) The gross-up is intended to add to the dividend received by the individual shareholder an amount equal to the total income tax paid by the corporation on the income that gave rise to the dividend. Thus, the grossed-up dividend is intended to represent the corporation's pre-tax income. The shareholder will pay tax on the grossed-up dividend at his or her personal rate. The tax credit is intended to give the shareholder credit for the total tax paid by the corporation on the shareholder's behalf. This procedure is intended to equalize the tax paid on the income that is flowed through the corporation to its shareholders with the tax paid on the same income that is earned directly. When the gross-up is 25% and the total (i.e., federal and provincial) corporate tax rate is 20%, integration is theoretically perfect. When the gross-up is 45% and the total (i.e., federal and provincial) corporate tax rate is 31%, integration is, also, theoretically perfect.

(4) Its purpose is to help small CCPCs retain capital in order to expand their businesses. This is accomplished by using a relatively low corporate tax rate after the small business deduction to defer tax until the income is paid out as a dividend.

(5) There is a deemed year-end on July 15 as a result of the acquisition of control and he is deemed to acquire control at the commencement of that day. Mr. Smith can now choose any year-end he wants and the company should qualify as a CCPC throughout the year. ITA: 249(4), 256(9)

(6) Paragraph 125(1)(*a*) deals with Division B income (net of expenses) while paragraph 125(1)(*b*) starts off with taxable income. Therefore, if there are Division C deductions such as donations or loss carryforwards then paragraph 125(1)(*b*) could be lower.

(7) The concept is that foreign income which is not taxed in Canada because of a foreign tax credit should be removed from the base amount on which the small business deduction is calculated.

A $^{10}/_3 \times$ factor is applied to the non-business foreign tax credit in order to estimate the foreign non-business income. This is based on the theory that the corporate rate is 30%.

A $3 \times$ factor is applied to the business foreign tax credit in order to estimate the foreign business income. This is based on the theory that the corporate rate is 40% less the general tax reduction of 8.5% on foreign business income. The abatement is not applied since it is assumed that the income is attributable to a permanent establishment outside of Canada.

(8) Some advantages of incorporation are:

- limited liability except for personal guarantees;

- tax savings if the combined corporate tax rate is under 20%;

- tax deferral;

- income splitting with family members as employees or shareholders (beware of the attribution rules and the tax on split income);

- estate freezing;

- availability of registered pension plans to the owner;

- separation of business and personal activities;

- greater flexibility as to the timing of income received personally;

- continuity of separate legal entity;

- deferral of accrued capital gains on transfer of shares to a spouse;

- access to financing

- availability of capital gains exemption on QSBCS; and

- availability of deferral of capital gains on shares of a SBC.

(9) Some disadvantages of incorporation are:

- tax cost if combined corporate tax rate is over 20%;

- a prepayment of tax at lower levels of personal income on business income not eligible for the small business deduction;

- additional costs including provincial capital tax; and

- inability to deduct losses against personal income. This disadvantage may be offset somewhat by the availability of the ABIL.

(10) He will not be able to get the M&P profits deduction on income eligible for the small business deduction. In addition, the question does not indicate whether this venture is incorporated. If it is not, then these deductions are not available since they are only available to incorporated businesses. *ITA: 125.1(1)(a)*

(11) Part IV tax of 33⅓% on portfolio dividends prevents a significant deferral of tax.

(12) (a) Refundable Part I tax;

(b) Part IV tax;

(c) Dividend gross-up and tax credit;

(d) Refundable dividend tax on hand; and

(e) Dividend refund.

(13) The gross-up is intended to place the shareholder in an income position equivalent to that of the corporation before it paid corporate taxes. At an assumed corporate tax rate of 20% or 31%, the 25% or 45% gross-up, respectively, represents the underlying corporate tax. This is added to the after-tax dividend to tax, theoretically, the pre-tax corporate profits in the hands of the individual shareholder.

(14) The dividend tax credit is intended to give the shareholder credit against his or her taxes for the taxes paid by the corporation on the income from which the dividend was paid. Since the gross-up theoretically takes the dividend up to the pre-tax corporate income level, the dividend tax credit is needed to reduce the individual tax by the theoretical amount of corporate tax already paid on that income. At a corporate tax rate of 20%, for example, tax of $20 would be paid on corporate income of $100. The gross-up of 25% would take the individual's income on that dividend of $80 back up to the $100 of corporate pre-tax income level. Assuming a provincial dividend tax credit of 6⅔% the total dividend tax credit would be 20% of the grossed-up dividend or $20. Thus the dividend tax credit represents the underlying corporate tax paid on the dividend.

(15) Of the $1,000 capital gain, $500 is not taxable and is allocated to the capital dividend account to be passed out to the shareholders tax-free as a capital dividend. This provides for the tax-free receipt of this $500 whether the capital gain is realized in the corporation or by the individual directly. *ITA: 82(3)*

The remaining $500 is theoretically taxed at an approximate initial rate of Part I tax of 40%. An additional refundable tax of 6⅔% is also levied and added to this account. Then, 26⅔% of the income is classified as refundable Part I tax and added to the refundable dividend tax on hand account. Dividend payments result in a return to the corporation of $1 for every $3 of dividends that are paid. This would leave an effective tax rate in the corporation on taxable capital gains of 20% which is the level at which integration works.

(16) Ordinarily the interest would be taxed at the full rate of 38% plus the 6⅔% additional refundable tax under Part I with part of this being classified as refundable Part I tax and added to the refundable dividend tax on hand account. However, since the two companies are associated and the interest is being deducted against the active business income of Opco, the deeming rules will deem the interest income to be active business income and not eligible for the refundable tax treatment. *ITA: 129(6)*

(17) While A Ltd. does not have more than 10% of the votes and value of B Ltd., A Ltd. does have control, since A Ltd. and the son of the only shareholder are related and do not deal at arm's length. Thus, over 50% of the voting shares belong to a person with whom A Ltd. does not deal at arm's length. *ITA: 186(2)*

(18) The factors to be considered are:

- the same non-capital losses cannot be deducted under both provisions;
- the normal corporate tax rates under Part I are usually higher than the 33⅓% Part IV tax;
- the Part IV tax is a refundable tax and not a permanent tax like Part I tax;
- the non-capital losses would otherwise expire without any value; and
- the corporation is not expected to pay a dividend to claim the refund until years in the future.

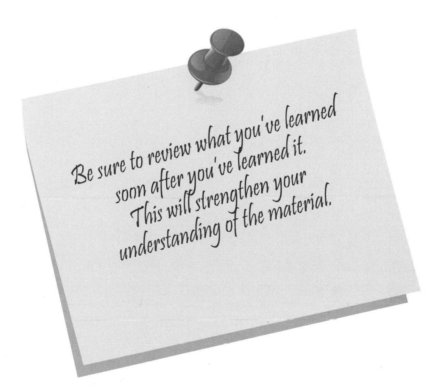

Be sure to review what you've learned soon after you've learned it. This will strengthen your understanding of the material.

Chapter 12 –
Solutions to Multiple Choice Questions

Question 1

(B) $18,400 is correct. It is calculated as follows:

Least of: (a)	income from an active business carried on in Canada	$120,000
	net of loss from an active business carried on in Canada	(0)
		$120,000
(b)	taxable income	$132,000
(c)	business limit: $500,000 – $385,000	$115,000

The least is (c): $115,000 × 17% = $19,550

(A) $17,000 is incorrect. The foreign business loss of $20,000 has been netted against the $120,000 of Canadian business income.

(C) $20,400 is incorrect. This amount is 17% of the Canadian active business income.

(D) $22,440 is incorrect. This amount is 17% of the taxable income.

Question 2

(D) is correct. M Ltd. is carrying on an active business. The business is not a personal services business as the services are provided to an associated corporation. M Ltd. and ACC Ltd. are associated. M Ltd. is not a specified investment business as the principal purpose is not to derive income from property. Thus, by default, it is carrying on an active business.   ITA: 125(7) ITA: 256(1)(*d*)

(A) is incorrect. M Ltd. is not carrying on a personal services business for the reasons outlined above.

(B) is incorrect. M Ltd. is not carrying on a personal services business for the reasons outlined above.

(C) is incorrect. M Ltd. is not carrying on a specified investment business as the principal purpose is not to derive income from property.

Question 3

(A) Nil is correct. Cdn. M&P profits are less than ABI eligible for the SBD.

(B) $1,800 is incorrect. This amount is 9% of taxable income in excess of $500,000.

(C) $36,900 is incorrect. This amount is 9% of Cdn. M&P profits in excess of the SBD of $85,000.

(D) $44,550 is incorrect. This amount is 9% × Cdn. M&P profits.

Question 4

(C) $68,000 is correct.   ITA: 186(1), 186(4)

Dividend received from non-connected corporation, C Ltd.:	
$120,000 × ⅓	$40,000
70% of $40,000 dividend refund received by connected	
corporation, B Ltd.	28,000
	$68,000

B Ltd is connected to A Ltd., because of *de jure* control and because A Ltd. holds more than 10% of the issued share capital in both votes and value.   ITA: 186(2), 186(4)

(A) $60,000 is incorrect. This amount is 70% and 8% of the dividend refunds received by B Ltd. and C Ltd., respectively.

(B) $64,000 is incorrect. This amount applies the Part I tax rate on investment income, 26⅔%, to the total dividends received.

(D) $80,000 is incorrect. This amount is $\frac{1}{3} \times$ the dividends received and ignores the special rules for connected corporations.

Question 5

(D) is correct. Neither J Co. nor D Co. is associated with R Co., since neither Joanne nor David own at least 25% of the shares of R Co. through J Co. and D Co. Their ownership is only 22% (i.e., 55% of 40%). Hence, J Co. and D Co. cannot be associated through R Co.

ITA: 256(2)

(A) and (B) are incorrect because Joanne controls J Co. and her spouse controls D Co. Two corporations are associated under paragraph 256(1)(c), if related persons control each corporation and either person owns at least 25% of the shares of the related persons' corporation. Spouses are related by marriage.

ITA: 251(6)(b)

(C) is incorrect because if a trust for their twin daughters controls a third company, T Co., those shares are deemed to be owned by the beneficiaries. In addition, because those beneficiaries are minors, their shares are deemed to be owned by each of Joanne and Doug. Therefore, J Co. and T Co. are associated because they are deemed to be controlled by the same person (Joanne). The same is true for D Co. and T Co. (each deemed to be controlled by Doug). The two corporations are associated with each other unless an election is made to deem the third corporation (T Co.) to have a business limit of nil.

ITA: 256(1.2)(f)(ii), 256(1.3)
ITA: 256(1)(a)

ITA: 256(2)

Question 6

(C) is correct. X Ltd. and Y Ltd. are not associated because although X Ltd. is controlled by a person who is related to each member of the various groups of persons (i.e., an pair of the two daughters and one son or all three) who controls Y Ltd., there is no cross-ownership of at least 25%. Thus, X Ltd. and Y Ltd. are not associated.

ITA: 256(1)(d)

(A) is not correct. X and Y are associated. The same group (Rod and Patrick) controls both corporations. This group controls X Ltd., despite the fact that Patrick himself controls X Ltd. It does not matter that the individuals are not related.

ITA: 256(1)(b)
ITA: 256(1.2)(b)(i)

(B) is not correct because X Ltd. and Y Ltd. are associated because they are controlled by related persons (a parent and son are related by blood) and one of the persons owns not less than 25% of the shares of both companies.

ITA: 256(1)(c)
ITA: 251(6)(a)

(D) is not correct. Sibco and Parentco are associated. Sibco is controlled by a related group of two, three, or four of its shareholders. Parentco is controlled by the related group of the mother and father. Each member of any related group that controls Sibco is related to each member of the related group that controls Parentco. The mother and father, together, own at least 25% of the shares of both corporations.

ITA: 256(1)(e)

Chapter 12 — Solutions to Exercises

Exercise 1

[Note: The facts of this case are those of *The Queen v. Rochmore Investments Ltd.* However, the legislation under which the case was decided did not contain a definition of "active business" or "specified investment business".]

76 DTC 6156 (F.C.A.)

Under the current legislation, "active business" is defined to exclude "a specified investment business" in such a way that if a business is not a specified investment business (and is not a personal service business), it is an active business. Note that the definition includes an adventure in the nature of trade and is only applicable in respect of the small business deduction.

ITA: 125(7), 248(1)

In this particular case, the facts indicate that it is carrying on a specified investment business. It would appear that the principal purpose of the corporation's business is to derive income from interest on mortgage loans. It does not appear to be carrying on the business of a credit union and it is not in the business of leasing movable property. If it did, the corporation would be considered to be carrying on an active business. Since the corporation had no full-time employees, it cannot escape the definition of a specified investment business, to be treated as an active business, through paragraph (*a*) of the definition, which requires more than five full-time employees.

ITA: 125(7)

The only possibility for escape is in paragraph (*b*) of the definition of "specified investment business". If the taxpayer company did not have more than five full-time employees because another corporation associated with it provided the services to the taxpayer corporation that would otherwise be performed by its own full-time employees, then the taxpayer corporation could be considered as carrying on an active business. In this case, the two principal operators of the taxpayer corporation own and manage a number of other companies. Further facts are required to determine if any of these other corporations are associated with the taxpayer corporation and if such an associated corporation provides services that would otherwise be provided by more than five full-time employees of the taxpayer corporation. This seems unlikely given the facts outlined in the case.

ITA: 125(7)

The taxpayer corporation, therefore, is likely carrying on a specified investment business. It is not carrying on a personal services business because it is not likely that the principals of the taxpayer corporation would reasonably be regarded as employees of the persons to whom the mortgage loans were made.

Exercise 2

(A) (i)　Mr. Beta is at arm's length with the corporation because his 25% ownership does not give him control. However, paragraph 251(1)(*b*) could always apply if the facts indicate that the non-related persons are not dealing at arm's length at a particular moment in time.

ITA: 251(2)(b)

(ii)　Mr. Beta and his brother are not at arm's length with the corporation. Mr. Beta and his brother form a related group; since they are siblings, each is related by blood.

ITA: 251(2)(b)(ii), 251(6)(a)

(iii)　Mr. Delta is not at arm's length with the corporation because of the share purchase option. This provision deems Mr. Delta to control Alpha Corp. unless the exceptions in this subparagraph are met.

ITA: 251(5)(b)(i)

(iv)　Mr. Epsilon is at arm's length with the corporation because of the exception, which is contingent on the death of Mr. Beta, unless paragraph 251(1)(*b*) applies, as described in (i), above.

ITA: 251(5)(b)(i)

(B) (i)　The corporations are not at arm's length. This subparagraph applies where Lambda Corp. is controlled by a person (i.e., A) and Tau Corp. is controlled by a related group (i.e., A and B). A is related to himself for purposes of share ownership and to his brother.

ITA: 251(2)(c)(iii), 251(5)(c), 251(6)(a)

(ii)　The corporations are at arm's length because subparagraph 251(2)(*c*)(iv) does not apply where there is an unrelated group of persons controlling one corporation, unless the person controlling the other corporation is related to each member of the unrelated group. For example, if two first cousins control one corporation and their grandfather controls the other, the two corporations would be related. Of course, factual non-arm's length can always apply as described in (A)(i), above.

(iii)　The corporations are related and, hence, they are not at arm's length. This provision deems two corporations to be related where each corporation is related to another common corporation.

ITA: 251(3)

Exercise 3

(A) Jay-one Ltd. and Jay-two Ltd. are associated, both being controlled by the same person. Jay-one Ltd. and Jay-three Ltd., are associated. Since Janna has voting control of Jay-one Ltd. and Jay-one Ltd. in turn has voting control of Jay-three Ltd., then Janna controls Jay-three Ltd. Therefore, all three corporations are controlled by the same person. As a result of this application of the association rule in paragraph 256(1)(*b*), the election under subsection 256(2) is not available to Jay-one Ltd., because Jay-three Ltd. and Jay-two Ltd. are associated without subsection 256(2).

ITA: 251(1)(*b*), 256(1)(*a*), 256(1)(*b*)

(B) Benco Ltd. and Rayco Ltd. are associated. Benco Ltd. is controlled by Rayna's mother and Rayco Ltd. is controlled by Rayna. Rayna and her mother are related. Rayna owns at least 25% of the shares, which are not of a specified class, of both corporations.

ITA: 256(1)(*a*), 256(1)(*c*)

(C) Adamco Ltd. and Kidco Ltd. are associated. Adamco Ltd. is controlled by Adam. Kidco Ltd. is controlled by the group consisting of Adam, his daughter and his son-in-law. Adam is related to himself, to his daughter and to his son-in-law. Adam owns at least 25% of the shares which are not of a specified class of Kidco Ltd.

ITA: 252(1)(*e*), 256(1)(*d*), 256(1.5), 251(6)(*a*), 251(6)(*b*)

(D) Since both corporations are controlled by a group, paragraph 256(1)(*e*) is the only possibility for association. However, while Sisco Ltd. is controlled by a related group of sisters, Cousco Ltd. is not controlled by a related group. The two sisters as a group do not control Cousco Ltd. One sister and her daughter do not control the company. Finally, cousins and aunts and nieces are not related by the rules. Therefore, the condition in paragraph 256(1)(*e*) fails and the two corporations are not associated unless subsection 256(5.1) can be used with the argument that control in fact is exercised by Sister One and Sister Two through direct or indirect influence on their daughters or unless subsection 256(2.1) is invoked on the basis that one of the main reasons for the separate existence of the two corporations is to reduce taxes.

ITA: 251(6)(*a*)

ITA: 251, 252

Exercise 4

Taxit and Sibling are associated:

ITA: 256(1)(*c*)

— each corporation is controlled by one person;

— the person who controlled one was related to the person who controlled the other;

— one of these persons owned not less than 25% of the shares which are not of a specified class of each corporation.

Since the two corporations are associated, they must share the small business deduction on a maximum of $500,000 of active business income. The Act requires that the corporations file an agreement, in prescribed form, allocating the $500,000 business limit. If an agreement is not filed within the time period indicated in subsection 125(4), that subsection empowers the Minister to make an allocation.

ITA: 125(3)

They could each gain their eligibility for the small business deduction on a full $500,000 by having Beta reduce her holdings in Taxit to below 25% or by having Beta convert her holdings in Taxit to shares of a specified class (i.e., in essence, non-voting preferred shares). However, this strategy would work only as long as there are no factors present of the kind that would enable the deeming provisions to apply.

ITA: 256(2.1)

Exercise 5

Since neither corporation is controlled by one person, and both corporations are not controlled by the same group of persons, the only provision in subsection 256(1) that can potentially apply is paragraph 256(1)(*e*). That paragraph sets out three conditions, each of which must be met by the facts of the case for association.

(1) Each corporation must be controlled by a related group. — The group of brothers controlling Chutzpah Enterprises Limited is related. The group consisting of Bett and Dalled Chutzpah controlling Schlock Sales Limited are related as brother-in-law and sister-in-law or by paragraph 251(6)(*a*) and paragraphs 252(2)(*b*) and (*c*). Therefore, the condition is met.

ITA: 251(2)(*a*), 251(6)(*a*)
ITA: 251(6)(*b*)

(2) Each of the members of one of the related groups was related to all of the members of the other related group. — Consider the group consisting of Aleph and Bett Chutzpah which is a related group controlling Chutzpah Enterprises Limited and the group Bett and Dalled Chutzpah which is a related group controlling Schlock Sales Limited. Aleph is related to his brother Bett, as discussed above, and to Dalled. Bett is related to himself and his sister-in-law, Dalled, as discussed above. Therefore, the condition is met.

ITA: 251(2)(*a*), 251(6)(*a*), 256(1.5)

(3) One or more members of both related groups must own, either alone or together, not less than 25% of the issued shares of any class, other than a specified class, of shares of the capital stock of the other corporation. — Bett, who is a member of both related groups, owns alone the minimum 25% of the shares necessary to meet this condition. Common shares are not shares of a specified class.

ITA: 256(1.1)

Exercise 6

Part I tax payable

Part I Tax on Taxable Income

Taxable income	$ 79,700
Tax @ 38% on $79,700	$ 30,286
Deduct: Federal tax abatement (10% of $79,700)	7,970
Net	$ 22,316

Additional refundable tax (ART) — 6⅔% × lesser of:

(a) AII	$ 7,000	
(b) TI – SBD amount (Schedule 1)	$ 3,500	
6⅔% of $3,500 (i.e., $79,700 – $76,200)		233
Total		$ 22,549

Deduct: Non-business foreign tax credit (assumed)	$ 1,050	
Small business deduction (see Schedule 1)	12,954	
Manufacturing and processing profits deduction (M&P profits less than inc. eligible from SBD)	Nil	
General reduction (see Schedule 2)	Nil	14,004
Part I federal tax payable		$ 8,545
Provincial tax @ 5.5% of $79,700		4,384
Total tax payable		$ 12,929

Schedule 1: *Small Business Deduction*

17% of the least of:

Income from an active business		$110,000(I)
Taxable income	$79,700	
Less: ¹⁰⁄₃ × foreign non-business tax credit (see above) (¹⁰⁄₃ × $1,050)	3,500	$ 76,200(II)
Business limit		$500,000(III)

Small business deduction — 17% of $76,200 = $12,954

Schedule 2: *General Reduction*

taxable income		$ 79,700
less: M&P profits	$ Nil	
¹⁰⁰⁄₁₇ of the small business deduction	76,200	
AII	7,000	(83,200)
net		Nil
8.5% of Nil		Nil
Total		$ Nil

Exercise 7

Paragraph 186(1)(*b*) requires that Part IV tax be calculated as follows:

$$\frac{\$90,000}{\$120,000} \times \$18,000 = \$13,500$$

Exercise 8

(A) *Computation of Taxable Income*

Net income for income tax purposes		$186,250
Deduct: taxable dividends	$18,750	
non-capital losses	37,500	
net capital losses ($68,750 × ½ / ¾; limited to TCG)	37,500	93,750
Taxable income		$ 92,500

Part I Tax on Taxable Income

Tax @ 38% of $92,500		$ 35,150
Deduct: federal tax abatement (10% of $92,500)		9,250
Net		$ 25,900
Additional refundable tax (ART) — 6⅔% of lesser of:		
(a) AII ($37,500 + $45,000 + $18,750 − $37,500 − $18,750) = $45,000		
(b) TI − SBD amount ($92,500 − $85,000) = $7,500		500
		$ 26,400
Deduct: small business deduction (see Schedule 1)	$14,450	
General reduction	Nil	$ 14,450
Part I tax payable (federal)		$ 11,950
Provincial tax @ 8% of $92,500		7,400
Total tax payable		$ 19,350

Schedule 1: Small Business Deduction

Income from active business	$ 85,000(I)
Taxable income (no foreign tax credits)	$ 92,500(II)
Business limit	$500,000(III)
17% of the least of amounts (I), (II), and (III)	$ 14,450

(B) *Refundable Portion of Part I Tax*

Least of:

(a) 26⅔% × aggregate investment income (26⅔% × ($45,000 + $37,500 + $18,750 − $37,500 $18,750))		$ 12,000
(b) Taxable income	$ 92,500	
Less: Amount eligible for the SBD	(85,000)	
26⅔% × $7,500 =		$ 2,000
(c) Part I tax		$ 11,950
Refundable portion of Part I tax — the least amount		$ 2,000

Part IV Tax on Taxable Dividends Received

Taxable dividends subject to Part IV tax × ⅓ ($18,750 × ⅓)	$ 6,250
Deduct: non-capital loss claimed for Part IV × ⅓ (all claimed under Part I)	Nil
Tax	$ 6,250

Refundable Dividend Tax on Hand

Refundable dividend tax on hand at end of last year	Nil	
Deduct: dividend refund for last year	Nil	
	Nil	
Add: refundable portion of Part I tax	$ 2,000	
Part IV tax	6,250	$ 8,250

Dividend Refund

Taxable dividends paid in the taxation year ($112,500 × ⅓)	$ 37,500(VI)
Refundable dividend tax on hand	$ 8,250(VII)
Dividend refund — lesser of (VI) and (VII)	$ 8,250

Exercise 9

(A) *Part I Tax on Taxable Income*

Tax @ 38% of $130,000	$ 49,400
Deduct: federal tax abatement (10% of 95% of $130,000)	12,350
Net	$ 37,050

Additional refundable tax (ART) — $6\frac{2}{3}$% of lesser of:
   (a) AII ($50K + $30K + $20K + $50K − $20K − $50K) = $80,000
   (b) TI − SBD amount ($130K − $90K) = $40,000   2,667

Total		$ 39,717
Deduct: non-business foreign tax credit (given)	$ 4,000	
business foreign tax credit (given)	1,000	
small business deduction (see Schedule 1)	15,300	
General reduction	Nil	20,300
Part I tax payable (federal)		$ 19,417
Provincial tax @ 7% of 95% of $130,000		8,645
Total tax		$ 28,062

Schedule 1: *Small Business Deduction*

17% of least of:

Income from active business		$ 90,000(I)
Taxable income $130,000		
Deduct: non-business foreign tax credit × $\frac{10}{3}$ $13,333		
business foreign tax credit × 3 3,000	16,333	$113,667(II)
Business limit		$500,000(III)
Small business deduction — 17% of $90,000		$ 15,300

(B) *Refundable Portion of Part I Tax*

Least of:

(a) $26\frac{2}{3}$% × aggregate investment income ($26\frac{2}{3}$% ×			
$80,000)	$ 21,333		
Less: non-business foreign tax credit $4,000			
minus: $9\frac{1}{3}$% × foreign investment			
income ($9\frac{1}{3}$% × $30,000) . . . . (2,800)	(1,200)	$ 20,133	
(b) Taxable income $130,000			
Less: amount eligible for SBD . . . . (90,000)			
$\frac{25}{9}$ × non-business FTC ($4,000) . . . . (11,111)			
3 × business FTC ($1,000) . . . . (3,000)			
$26\frac{2}{3}$% × $25,889 =		$ 6,904	
(c) Part I tax		$ 19,417	
Refundable portion of Part I tax — The least		$ 6,904	

Part IV Tax on Taxable Dividends Received

Taxable dividends subject to Part IV tax:

Non-connected corporations × $\frac{1}{3}$ ($30,000 × $\frac{1}{3}$)	$ 10,000
Connected corporations to the extent of share of dividend refund to	
payer	4,000
Total Part IV tax payable	$ 14,000

Refundable Dividend Tax on Hand

RDTOH at end of last year	Nil	
Deduct: Dividend refund for last year	Nil	Nil

Add: Refundable portion of Part I tax	$ 6,904
Part IV tax	14,000
RDTOH at end of year	$ 20,904

Dividend Refund

Taxable dividends paid in year ($70,000 × ⅓)	$ 23,333(VI)
RDTOH at end of year	$ 20,904(VII)
Dividend refund — lesser of (VI) and (VII)	$ 20,904

Exercise 10

(A) Splitinc Limited and Husband Ltd. are associated. Husband Ltd. is controlled by one person, Mr. Split. He is related to each member of the group, Husband Ltd. and Wife Ltd. that controls Splitinc Limited, because he is related to Husband Ltd. which he controls and he is related to Wife Ltd., which is controlled by his wife. Also, he owns not less than 25% of the shares of Splitinc Limited through his ownership of shares in Husband Ltd. These shares are not specified shares. By a similar analysis, Splitinc Limited and Wife Ltd. are associated.

ITA: 256(1)(d)
ITA: 251(2)(b)(i),
251(2)(b)(iii)

ITA: 256(1.2)(d)

Since the rental income would be deductible as an expense from the income of an active business of an associated payer, it will not be income from property of the recipient. It will be deemed to be income from an active business of the recipient, Husband Ltd. Since Husband Ltd. has only dividend income it will be eligible for the small business deduction in respect of the rental income as long as it is allocated a part of the business limit of the associated corporations.

ITA: 129(6)(a)(i)

ITA: 129(6)(b)(i)
ITA: 125(1)

(B) Since Splitinc is connected with both holding companies there will be no Part IV tax liability unless Splitinc gets a dividend refund as a result of the dividends it pays. However, Splitinc earns only active business income which is not subject to refundable taxes and dividend refunds.

Exercise 11

(A) Rent from RCSL:

  (i) RCSL is associated with JML;

ITA: 256(1)(b)

  (ii) RCSL deducts the rent from its active business.

Therefore, the rent is deemed to be income of JML from an active business, eligible for the small business deduction.

ITA: 125(1), 129(6)(b)(i)

(B) Services fee from Dr. Adam:

  (i) JML's income from providing services would be considered income from an active business unless further facts indicate that it is carrying on a personal services business;

  (ii) the business of providing services would be a personal services business if one or both of the shareholders of JML, who are specified shareholders (because they own at least 10% of the shares of JML), performed the services and would be regarded as an employee of the professional practice of Dr. Adam.

Therefore, if the services fee is considered income from an active business, it would qualify for the small business deduction.

Exercise 12

Interest income		$ 7,000
Dividends grossed up (⁵⁄₄ × $15,000)		18,750
Taxable capital gains (½ × $6,000)		3,000
Incremental taxable income		$28,750
Federal tax on total taxable income of $48,750		
(i.e., $28,750 incremental + $20,000 other income):		
Tax on first $40,726	$ 6,109	
Tax on next $8,024 @ 22%	1,765	$ 7,874
Less: dividend tax credit (13⅓% of $18,750)	$ 2,500	
other personal tax credits	1,800	(4,300)
Basic federal tax		$ 3,574
Provincial tax		
Tax on first $40,726	$ 4,073	
Tax on next $8,024 @ 12%	963	
		$ 5,036
Less: dividend tax credit (6⅔% of $18,750)	$ 1,250	
other personal tax credits	1,200	(2,450)
Total tax on taxable income of $48,750		$ 6,160

Taxation of Income from Investment Portfolio through a Corporation

		Available cash
Corporation		
Interest income	$ 7,000	
Dividends	15,000	
Taxable capital gains	3,000	
Income	$25,000	$25,000[1]
Less: dividends [sec. 112]	15,000	
Taxable income	$10,000	
Tax under Part I @ 43.5% (38% – 10% + 15.5%)	$ 4,350	
Additional refundable tax at 6⅔% of $10,000 ($7K + $15K + $3K – $15K)	667	
Tax under Part IV @ 33⅓% of $15,000	5,000	10,017
Retained in corporation[1]		$14,983
Refundable tax:		
Part I (26⅔% of ($7K + $15K + $3K – $15K))	$ 2,667	
Part IV (33⅓% × $15,000)	5,000	7,667
Available for distribution to shareholders as taxable dividend		$22,650[2]

Shareholder		
Taxable dividend (per requirements)		$15,000
Gross-up (¼ × $15,000)		3,750
Incremental taxable income		$18,750
Federal tax on total taxable income of $38,750		
(i.e., $18,750 incremental + $20,000 other income):		
Tax @ 15%		$ 5,813
Less: dividend tax credit (13⅓% of $18,750)	$2,500	
other personal tax credits	1,800	(4,300)
Basic federal tax		$ 1,513
Provincial tax		
Tax @ 10%		$ 3,875
Less: dividend tax credit (6⅔% of $18,750)	$1,250	
other personal tax credits	1,200	(2,450)

Total tax on taxable income of $38,750 .... $ 2,938

Total Taxes Paid

Through corporation:

Corporation after refund on $15,000 of dividends paid
($10,017 − ⅓ × $15,000) .... $ 5,017

Shareholder 2,938

Total[3] .... $ 7,955

Received directly .... $ 6,160

—*NOTES TO SOLUTION*

[1] Ignores the non-taxable portion of capital gain which can be distributed tax free.

[2] Note that a dividend of $22,650 will result in a dividend refund of only $7,550 (i.e., $22,650 × ⅓), not the $7,667 that was added to the RDTOH for the year. This deficiency results from imperfections in the tax rates. A larger dividend of $23,000 (i.e., 3 × $7,667) would have to be paid, using other sources of funds, to clear the RDTOH. Alternatively, the maximum dividend that can be paid in this case is $22,475, determined algebraically, as follows:

$$R = \tfrac{1}{3} D$$
$$D = N - T + R$$
$$\quad = N - T + \tfrac{1}{3} D$$
$$\quad = (N - T) \times \tfrac{3}{2}$$
$$\quad = (\$25,000 - \$10,017) \times \tfrac{3}{2}$$
$$\quad = \$22,475$$
$$R = \$7,492$$

where: R = dividend refund
D = dividend
N = Division B net income
T = total tax

Note that if the combined federal and provincial corporate tax rate had been 40%, before the additional refundable tax and the dividend refund, the amount available for dividends would be sufficient to clear the RDTOH.

[3] This amount is higher because not all of the corporate tax has been refunded as yet, and because the provincial corporate tax is 5.5% higher than the theoretical rate of 10%.

Exercise 13

The two corporations are considered associated for Canadian tax purposes. Generally, interest income received from an associated corporation that is deductible in computing that corporation's active business income would be considered active business income. However, as the interest is U.S.-sourced, and not from a "source in Canada", and is not deductible in computing active business income in Canada, it will be considered investment income to the Canadian corporation and not income from an active business. Hence, the small business deduction will not apply. ITA: 256   ITA: 129(6)

The interest will be subject to the full corporate tax rate, including the 6⅔% additional refundable tax on investment income. The addition to RDTOH (26⅔%) will also apply. ITA: 123.3, 129(1)

Chapter 13
Planning the Use of a Corporation and Shareholder-Manager Remuneration

LEARNING GOALS

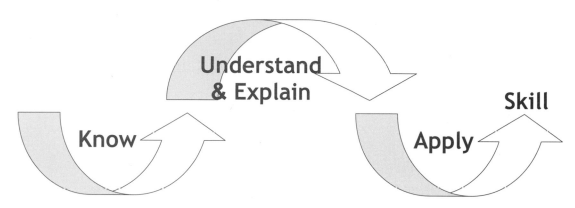

Know

By the end of this chapter, you should know the basic provisions of the *Income Tax Act* that relate to the compensation of a corporation's owner-manager and that relate to the general anti-avoidance rule. Completing the Review Questions (¶13,800) and Multiple Choice Questions (¶13,825) is a good way to learn the technical provisions.

Understand and Explain

You should understand and be able to explain:

- the more common elements in the remuneration of a shareholder-manager, including salary, bonus, dividend, and loan and the considerations needed to make a choice;
- the salary versus dividend trade-off, including the amount of dividends that can be distributed tax free;
- the reasons for the use of a holding corporation, the benefits of the capital gains deduction, and rules that inhibit family income splitting through a corporation; and
- why the general anti-avoidance rule exists and how it has been interpreted and used.

Apply

You should be able to apply your knowledge and understanding of the key elements of compensation to:

- choose the optimal compensation components to minimize remuneration costs in a particular owner-manager situation;
- maintain the eligibility of shares for the capital gains exemption;
- avoid the adverse income tax effects of using a corporation to split family income; and
- generally determine whether the general anti-avoidance rule might apply in a particular planning situation.

Completing the Assignment Problems (¶13,875) is an excellent way to develop your ability to apply the material in increasingly complex situations

Chapter 13 — Learning Chart

Topic	Example Problem (✓)	Review Questions (¶13,800)	Multiple Choice (¶13,825)	Exercises (¶13,850)	Assignment Problems (¶13,875)
¶13,000 EMPLOYMENT REMUNERATION					
¶13,010 Considerations in Choosing Elements of Shareholder-Manager Remuneration					
¶13,015 Cash needs					
¶13,020 Individual's tax bracket					
¶13,025 25% dividend gross-up and credit					
¶13,030 45% dividend gross-up and credit					
¶13,035 Availability of tax deferral					
¶13,040 Avoid exceeding the business limit for the small business deduction					
¶13,050 Salaries, Bonuses, and Other Payments to the Shareholder-Manager					
¶13,055 General guidelines		7			
¶13,060 Salaries and bonuses		2			
¶13,065 Accrued bonuses and other amounts		1, 3, 4	3	1	3
¶13,070 Shareholder Benefits and Loans					
¶13,075 Shareholder benefits	✓				1
¶13,080 Shareholder loans	✓	5, 6	1, 2	2, 3, 4	2, 3, 4
¶13,090 Other Planning Considerations for Shareholder-Manager Remuneration					
¶13,095 Income splitting					
¶13,100 Fringe benefits				5	
¶13,200 SALARY VERSUS DIVIDENDS					
¶13,210 The Basic Trade-Off					
¶13,220 Approximate Amounts of Taxable Dividends That Can Be Distributed Tax-Free					
¶13,230 Distribution Out of Income Taxed at Small Business Rate	✓	8		6, 7	5, 6, 7
¶13,240 Distributions Out of Income Not Eligible for the Small Business Deduction					
¶13,250 Summary of the Salary Versus Dividends Issue					
¶13,300 OTHER PLANNING ASPECTS OF USING CORPORATIONS					
¶13,310 Use of Holding Companies					
¶13,315 An extension of integration					
¶13,320 Compensation					
¶13,325 Deferral of tax on dividends					
¶13,330 Implementing an estate freeze					
¶13,340 Qualified Small Business Corporation Share (QSBCS)					
¶13,345 Small business corporation (SBC)	✓	10, 11	7	8	
¶13,350 Basic QSBCS rules applied to a single corporation	✓				8

Topic	Example Problem (✓)	Review Questions (¶13,800)	Multiple Choice (¶13,825)	Exercises (¶13,850)	Assignment Problems (¶13,875)
¶13,355 Modification of the asset test (stacking rule)	✓				9
¶13,360 Capital Gains Deduction					
¶13,365 Overview					
¶13,370 Computation of deduction				9	10
¶13,375 Allowable business investment losses		9			
¶13,380 Cumulative net investment loss (CNIL)					
¶13,385 Other related provisions	✓				
¶13,390 Attribution Through a Corporation	✓	12	6	10	11
¶13,400 Income-Splitting Tax ("Kiddie Tax")					
¶13,500 GENERAL ANTI-AVOIDANCE RULE UNDER THE INCOME TAX ACT					
¶13,510 The Statutory Provision			4	11, 12	
¶13,515 Purpose					
¶13,520 Defined terms					
¶13,525 Limitation					
¶13,530 Examples in the technical notes					
¶13,535 Administration and application			5		12, 13
¶13,540 Federal Court of Appeal — OSFC Holdings Ltd.					
¶13,545 The findings					
¶13,550 Application of OSFC case analytical framework					
¶13,560 Supreme Court of Canada — Canada Trustco and Mathew et al.					
¶13,565 The transactions					
¶13,570 Application of the OSFC tests and interpretations					
¶13,580 The Saga Continues — Decisions Since Canada Trustco					
¶13,585 L. Mark Evans (2005 DTC 1762 (T.C.C.))					
¶13,590 Michael Overs (2006 DTC 2192 (T.C.C.))					
¶13,595 Jordan B. Lipson and Earl Lipson (2006 DTC 2687 (T.C.C.)/2007 DTC 5172 (F.C.A.)/2009 DTC 5015 (S.C.C.))					

Study Notes

Chapter 13 —
Discussion Notes for Review Questions

(1) Mr. Smith can pay the bonus within the 179-day limit and loan the net after-tax amount back to the company. If he actually does this, he should consider charging interest to the company in order to reduce payroll taxes by converting his salary into interest income. This will also protect his ability to claim a capital loss or an ABIL in the event the company was unable to repay the loan. He should also consider securing the loan.

ITA: 78(4)

(2) (a) If he leaves the money in the company, the income over $500,000 will not be eligible for the small business deduction, but it will be eligible for the general rate reduction. The marginal tax rate will be 31% (i.e., 38% − 10% − 9% + 12%).

(b) If he declares and pays the bonus the personal marginal tax rate will be 46% (i.e., 29% + 17%).

(c) He can defer approximately 15% (see calculation below) of tax by leaving the income in the company to be taxed.

(d) If he leaves the income in the company to be taxed, he will have to pay tax on the dividend when he eventually pays it out. The combined tax rate at that point, assuming the 45% dividend tax credit, will be approximately 46.4% which is slightly above the 46% personal tax cost of paying out the bonus now.

(e) Calculation:

Corporate income	$1,000
Corporate tax	(310)
After-tax income	$ 690
Dividend paid	$ 690
Gross-up (45%)	311
Taxable dividend	$1,001
Tax @ 46%	$ 460
Dividend tax credit	(311)
Net personal tax	$ 149
Net cash after tax	$ 541
Total tax ($310 + $149)	$ 459

(3) If he or she chooses a fiscal year-end on or after July 6, but no later than December 31, then the bonus can be paid within the 179 days in either this calendar year or on January 1 of the next calendar year.

ITA: 78(4)

(4) The following are the five criteria for the deductibility of bonus accruals as decided in the *Totem Disposal* case:

- reasonableness of the bonus in relation to profit and services rendered;

- payment for real and identifiable service;

- some justification for expecting a bonus over regular salary (e.g., a company policy);

- reasonableness of the time between determining profit and establishing the bonus; and

- a legal obligation to pay the accrued bonus.

(5) Mr. Crunchy is related to his brother-in-law. Therefore, they are deemed not to deal with each other at arm's length and the brother-in-law is connected with Mr. Crunchy. As a result, the conditions in the shareholder loan rule are met and none of the exceptions are met. Therefore, the brother-in-law will be required to take the full amount of the loan into income in 2009 since none of it was repaid by December 31, 2010. In 2011 and 2012, the brother-in-law will be able to deduct the principal repayments. The imputed interest benefit included in his 2009 tax return can be removed through an amended return to eliminate the benefit.

ITA: 15(2.1), 251(2)
ITA: 15(2), 15(2.4)
ITA: 20(1)(*j*)

ITA: 80.4(3)(*b*)

(6) Since Ms. Jones is a shareholder and received a loan, the shareholder loan rules apply. Although Ms. Jones is an employee, the boat does not fit into one of the exceptions. Therefore, Ms. Jones will have to take the $25,000 into income unless she repays it within one year from the end of the taxation year in which she received the loan. If she has to include the principal in income then the imputed interest rules will not apply.

ITA: 15(2)

ITA: 15(2.4)(*b*)–(*d*), 15(2.6)

ITA: 80.4, 80.4(3)(*b*)

(7) This provincial tax holiday would bring the combined corporate tax rate on income eligible for the small business deduction down below 20% and would provide a tax incentive to flowing active business income through a corporation, paying corporate tax and then paying dividends. Thus, there would then be an advantage to paying dividends instead of salary to the owner due to the fact that the dividend tax credit is greater than the underlying corporate tax.

(8) With the dividend gross-up his taxable income would be $37,500. The federal tax would be $5,625 less the dividend tax credit of $5,000 and the personal credit of $1,548 (in 2009) leaving basic federal tax of nil. Provincial tax on $37,500 would be $3,750, less the provincial dividend tax credit of $2,500 (i.e., 6⅔ % of $37,500) and the provincial personal tax credit of $960 (i.e., ($1,440/.15) × .10), leaving provincial tax of $290.

(9) It is true that in order to claim an ABIL the shares need to be shares in a small business corporation. However, the definition of small business corporation allows the status as a small business corporation to continue for 12 months for purposes of the ABIL provisions. Since she sold the shares within six months she should be able to claim the loss as an ABIL.

ITA: 248(1)

ITA: 39(1)(*c*)

(10) In several Interpretation Bulletins, the CRA states that the phrase means at least 90%. It should be noted that this phrase has not been specifically determined by the courts and it is unclear whether the courts would allow 85% or require 95% as the percentage necessary to meet this test. Practitioners generally use 90%.

IT-151R5, par. 31 (for example)

(11) This corporation is neither, since in order to meet the definition of "small business corporation" it has to meet the 90% test at the determination time. Since the corporation does not meet this test it is neither an SBC nor a QSBC.

(12) The preamble to the corporate attribution rule refers only to situations where "individuals have transferred or loaned property." In this case his corporation has loaned the funds to her corporation. It could not even be said that he did it indirectly since he has not loaned or transferred any money to his own corporation. Therefore, even though her corporation is not an SBC, the corporate attribution rules should not apply. However, GAAR should be considered.

ITA: 74.4(2)

Chapter 13 —
Solutions to Multiple Choice Questions

Question 1

(A) is correct. The entire loan will be included in Stan's income in 2009, the year he received the loan. He does not meet the criterion for exclusion, as the loan will not be repaid within one year after the end of the taxation year of the lender in which the loan was made. He does not meet the other criteria for exclusion. Since such a loan is not available to other employees, it is not reasonable to conclude that he received the loan because of his employment.

ITA: 15(2)
ITA: 15(2.6)
ITA: 15(2.4)

(B) is incorrect. If the loan is not repaid within one year of the end of the year of S Ltd. in which the loan was made, then $200,000 must be included in the year of the loan. Repayments are deductible in the year of the repayment.

(C) is incorrect. There is no imputed interest benefit when the loan is included in income. If there was an imputed interest benefit the prescribed rate protection rule would not apply as the loan was not received because of his employment.

ITA: 80.4(1), 80.4(3)(*b*), 80.4(4)

(D) is incorrect. One year after the end of the calendar year in which the loan is received has no significance. The shareholder loan rule includes the loan in income in the year it is *received* unless it is repaid by one year after the end of the taxation year of the *lender* in which the loan was made, or the loan meets one of the specific exclusions.

ITA: 15(2)

Question 2

(C) is the correct answer. The shareholder loan rule would include the principal amount of the loan in Mrs. C's income in 2009 because none of the exception tests are met.

ITA: 15(2.2), 15(2.3), 15(2.4), 15(2.6)

(1) The exception test in subsection 15(2.2) does not apply because Mrs. C is resident in Canada.

(2) The exception in subsection 15(2.3) does not apply since the money is not lent in the ordinary course of money lending business.

(3) None of the exceptions for employees in subsection 15(2.4) are met, because it is not reasonable to conclude that the loan is received because of employment since no other employees have received similar loans.

(4) The exception in subsection 15(2.6) does not apply since the debt was repaid on April 1, 2011, which is more than one year from the end of S Ltd.'s December 31, 2009 fiscal year.

The loan in (A) would not be included in Mrs. A's income because the one-year repayment exception test applies: the debt is repaid on April 1, 2010, which is within one year from the end of S Ltd.'s December 31, 2009 fiscal year. Note, however, that the imputed interest benefit rule would apply to compute a deemed interest benefit on the loan.

ITA: 15(2.6)

ITA: 80.4(2)

The loan in (B) would not be included in B Ltd's income because the shareholder loan rule does not apply to corporate shareholders resident in Canada.

ITA: 15(2)

The loan in (D) would not be included in Mr. D's income because one of the exceptions for employees is met: Mr. D is not a specified employee and it is reasonable to conclude that the loan is received because of employment, since the computer is for employment use and other employees currently working at home have received similar loans. Since Mr. D is not a specified employee, the loan does not have to be for any specified purpose. A specified employee is an employee who is either a specified shareholder (i.e., generally, a person who owns at least 10% of the shares of any class of the corporation) or a person who does not deal at arm's length with the corporation. Since Mr. D owns only 5% of the shares of S Ltd. and deals at arm's length with the corporation, he is not a specified employee.

ITA: 15(2.4), 248(1)

Question 3

(D) is correct. Since the $300,000 bonus is unpaid on the 180th day after the end of the taxation year of Fortelli Inc. in which the expense was incurred, it is not deductible until 2010, the taxation year in which it is actually paid.

ITA: 78(4)

(A) is incorrect. This amount refers to the rules in subsection 78(1) for unpaid amounts due to related persons, other than pension benefits, retiring allowances, salary, wages, or other remuneration.

(B) is incorrect. Subsection 78(4) does not distinguish between amounts owed to related and unrelated persons.

(C) is incorrect for the same reason as (A).

Question 4

The correct answer is (B). There is no penalty. The tax benefit that would otherwise have been enjoyed is denied.   ITA: 245(2)

(A) is incorrect as it is true in accordance with subsection 245(2).

(C) is incorrect as it is true in accordance with subsection 245(3).

(D) is incorrect as it is true in accordance with subsection 245(4).

Question 5

(C) is correct. The purpose of the transaction seems to be the reduction or avoidance of tax on the income earned on the $10,000 gift. This transaction goes against the spirit of the Act, read as a whole, and falls within the definition of an avoidance transaction. Note that an attribution rule would apply if it was a loan instead of a gift.   ITA: 245(3)
ITA: 56(4.1)

(A) is incorrect. The transaction is an estate freeze which can reasonably be considered to have been undertaken for *bona fide* purposes other than to obtain the tax benefit. This transaction does not result in a misuse or abuse of the Act, read as a whole.   IC 88-2, par. 10

(B) is incorrect. The incorporation of a business and the claiming of a small business deduction by a CCPC is specifically provided for in the Act. This transaction does not result in a misuse or abuse of the Act, read as a whole.   IC 88-2, par. 11

(D) is incorrect. The Act will deny the deduction of the bonus to the extent it is in excess of a reasonable amount. To the extent the transaction is reasonable, it does not result in a benefit. Corporate tax will be reduced by the accrual, but Mary will pay tax on the income personally.   ITA: 67; IC 88-2, par. 18

Question 6

(D) is correct. All the conditions for corporate attribution are met. As a result, Mr. Investor is deemed to have income of 6% × $1 million = $60,000.   ITA: 74.4

(A) incorrectly attributes the cash dividend received by Mrs. Investor to Mr. Investor: $10,000.

(B) incorrectly attributes the grossed up dividend received by Mrs. Investor to Mr. Investor: $12,500.

(C) incorrectly computes the attributed amount to Mr. Investor based on $500,000:   ITA: 74.4
6% × $500,000 = $30,000.

Question 7

(C) is correct. In order to be a small business corporation, the percentage of assets used in an active business by the corporation and the corporation controlled by Ms. Prentice's brother must be at least 90%. It is now 80% (60% + 20%) or $3.2 million.   ITA: 248(1) "small business corporation"

Therefore total assets must be $3.2 million/90% or $3,555,555.

Therefore $444,445 ($4 million − $3,555,555) of the non-active business assets must be sold.

(A) is incorrect because the corporation does not currently meet the 90% test.

(B) incorrectly assumes that 10% of the assets must be sold: 10% × 4 million = $400,000.

(D) incorrectly ignores the assets used by the related corporation and calculates that since active business assets are $2.4 million (60% × $4M), total assets must be $2.4 million/90% or $2,666,666 to meet the 90% test. As a result, $1,333,333 ($4 million − $2,666,666) of the non-active business assets must be sold.

Chapter 13 — Solutions to Exercises

Exercise 1

(A) The bonus must be paid on or before 179 days from the end of the year in which it was deducted. In this case, it must be paid on or before March 28, 2010. (Administrative practice would allow payment on the 180th day).

IT-109R2, par. 10

(B) If the bonus is not paid on or before March 28, 2010, the corporation may not deduct the bonus in its 2009 taxation year. The bonus may only be deducted when it is paid.

(C) (i) The rent must be paid within two years from the end of the year in which it was deducted. In this case, it must be paid by September 30, 2011.

(ii) If the rent is not paid by September 30, 2011, the corporation must add the $10,000 to its income for its 2012 taxation year beginning October 1, 2011. This does not cancel the payable, such that if the rent is ever paid, the shareholder will declare the rental income, but there will be no deduction for the corporation.

(iii) An election can be filed before the date on which the corporation must file its tax return for 2012. In this case, that date is March 31, 2013. If such an election is filed, Mr. Slip will be deemed to have income of $10,000 and to have loaned that amount back to the corporation on October 1, 2011. When the loan is repaid to Mr. Slip, there are no tax consequences since the amount of the loan has already been taxed. The election can be filed late. However, $2,500 (effectively, a late-filing penalty) will be added back to the income of the corporation for its 2012 fiscal year. Mr. Slip's tax position is not affected by this late-filed election.

ITA: 78(1)(b)

ITA: 78(3)

Exercise 2

(A) *Employee*

Principal-Amount

— Note that the shareholder loan rule applies in this case because he is a shareholder.

ITA: 15(2)

(a) House Loan

The Act would exempt the principal amount of this loan from income since Mr. Leverage received the loan in his capacity as an employee (i.e., by virtue of his employment), the purpose of the loan was to purchase a house and *bona fide* arrangements were made for repayment of the loan within a reasonable time;

ITA: 15(2.4)(b)

— however, an interest benefit on a "home purchase loan" would be included in income as shown in the calculation below.

ITA: 80.4

(b) Furniture Loan

There is no exemption from income for this loan because it was not repaid within one year of the 2009 taxation year of the corporation;

ITA: 15(2.3), 15(2.4), 15(2.6)

— since the loan is included in income in 2009, it is an exception for the purposes of the imputed interest benefit and, hence, there is no interest benefit.

ITA: 15(2), 80.4(3)(b)

(c) Share Purchase Loan

This loan is exempt from income because Mr. Leverage received the loan in his capacity as an employee and *bona fide* arrangements were made to repay the loan within a reasonable time;

ITA: 15(2.4)(c)

— since this type of loan is not an exception to the imputed interest rules, there is an interest benefit as shown in the calculation below.

ITA: 80.4

Interest Benefit

(a) interest on "home purchase loan" made to an officer or employee computed, at lesser of: (i) the prescribed rate in effect during the period in the year that the loan was outstanding, and (ii) the prescribed rate in effect at the time the loan was made. This "lesser of" choice can be made on a quarter-by-quarter comparison of tax rates. In this case, the 3% prescribed rate in June 2009, when the loan was received, is less than the rate for the other two quarters of 2009 in which the loan was outstanding. Therefore, the benefit would be based on the following calculation:

ITA: 80.4(1)(a), 80.4(4)

June–Dec. 2009: 3% of $75,000 $\times$ $^{214}/_{365}$ $1,319

(b) interest on share purchase loan computed at prescribed rates in effect
   during the period in the year that the loan was outstanding   ITA: 80.4(1)(*a*)

$$\text{June 2009: 3\% of \$10,000} \times 30/365 = \$\ 25$$
$$\text{July–Sept. 2009: 4\% of \$10,000} \times 92/365 =\ \ 101$$
$$\text{Oct.–Dec. 2009: 4\% of \$10,000} \times 92/365 = \underline{\ \ 101}\qquad \underline{\ \ \ \ 227}$$

Subtotal $1,546

(c) Less: interest paid on above loans (2% of $75,000 × 214/365) . . . .   <u>879</u>

Benefit calculated under ssec. 80.4(1) and included in employment income $ 667   ITA: 61(1)(*a*), 6(9)

Less: deduction for imputed interest on loan to buy shares . . . .   <u>227</u>   ITA: 20(1)(*c*), 80.5

Net benefit under Division B . . . . $ 440

Since the loan to purchase the house is a "home relocation loan", the Act provides for a deduction   ITA: 248(1). 110(1)(*j*)
from taxable income in Division C, calculated as the least of:

(a) the net imputed interest on the home purchase loan computed
     under paragraph 80.4(1)(*a*) as the lesser amount above $1,319
     less: interest paid in respect of the year, ...   <u>879</u> $ 440

(b) interest on $25,000 computed under paragraph 80.4(1)(*a*) as
     the lesser amount above ($25,000/$75,000 × $1,319) . . . . $ 440

(c) benefit deemed received under section 80.4 for the year . . . . . . $ 667

Therefore, the deduction would be $440.   ITA: 110(1)(*j*)

(B) *Shareholder*

If Mr. Leverage received the loans by virtue of being a shareholder, then all the loans would be
included in income in the year that the loans were received, unless the loans were repaid by the end of
the fiscal year in which the loans were made. Where a loan is outstanding in the year in which the loan   ITA: 80.4(2)
was made, there would be an imputed interest inclusion. However, the inclusion would be reversed on   ITA: 15(2)
the filing of the amended return for the loan inclusion.

For imputed interest, the main difference is that the benefit on the loan to purchase the house
would be based only on the prescribed rate in effect during the period in the year that the loan was
outstanding and reduced by the amount of interest paid on the loan by the shareholder in the period not
later than 30 days after the corporation's year-end. This is because the calculation of the imputed   ITA: 80.4(2), 80.4(7),
interest benefit by virtue of shareholdings does not take into account the special rules for a "home   248(1)
purchase loan" or a "home relocation loan". Therefore, there would also not be a deduction available.   ITA: 110(1)(*j*)

Exercise 3

(A) The Department indicates that it examines the balance in the account at the end of each year   IT-119R4, par. 34-35
of the lender considering a net increase as a loan to be included in the income of the borrower and a net
decrease as a repayment to be deducted from the income of the borrower. This approach would result in
the following:

Lender's year end	*Change from previous year*	*Income [ssec. 15(2.6)] or repayment [par. 20(1)(j)]*
Year 2	$45,000	income
Year 3	(32,000)	repayment
Year 4	(2,000)	repayment
Year 5	12,000	income
Year 6	(14,000)	repayment

(B) If there is no series of loans and repayments, then repayments are considered to apply first to   IT-119R4, par. 27
the oldest loan out-standing unless the facts clearly indicate otherwise. Applying this approach would
result in the following:

Lender's year end	Net inclusion (or deduction)	Explanation
Year 2	$25,000	— only the $20,000 borrowed in year 2 is repaid within one year of year 2; the $25,000 loan was not fully repaid within one year, so it must be taken into income in year 2
Year 3	(12,000)	— repayment of $12,000 of the $25,000 year 2 loan previously included
Year 4	(12,000)	— repayment of part of balance of year 2 loan
	Nil	— Nov. 30/year 4 loan repaid within one year of year 4
Year 5	(1,000)	— repayment of remainder of April 30/year 2 loan
	23,000	— full amount of Nov. 30/year 5 loan, since not fully repaid within one year of year 5
Year 6	(14,000)	— repayment of $14,000 of year 5 loan

Note that these methods of calculation are based on administrative practice and are not stipulated by the Act. Note that based on these methods, while total inclusions net of deductions over the period amount to $9,000 under each alternative, the time pattern of net inclusion is more favourable in this case if there is no series of loans and repayments considered.

If the loans are all part of a single running loan account, they are likely a series of loans and repayments. However, if the loans are for separate purposes, with differing repayment or other terms, and the repayments relate to specific loans, the facts might suggest there was no series of loans and repayments.

Exercise 4

Since he is a shareholder of the corporation, the shareholder loan rule applies and the loan that was received by the taxpayer should be included in income. However, the Act provides an exclusion for the $35,000 principal amount of the loan because: ITA: 15(2)
ITA: 15(2.4)(*d*)

— the taxpayer is an employee of the lender;

— the loan is to enable him to acquire a motor vehicle to be used by him in the performance of his employment duties;

— the taxpayer received the loan because of his employment, not because of his share-holdings, since other employees were eligible for a loan; and

— *bona fide* arrangements were made, at the time the loan was made, for repayment within a reasonable time.

Since the loan is a low-interest loan, the imputed interest benefit rule applies to impute an interest benefit calculated as follows: ITA: 80.4(1)

April 1 to June 30: $^{91}/_{365} \times 4\%$ of $35,000 = ...	$ 349
July 1 to Sept. 30: $^{92}/_{365} \times 5\%$ of $35,000 = ...	441
Oct. 1 to Dec. 31: $^{92}/_{365} \times 6\%$ of $35,000 = ...	529
Total	$1,319
Less: interest *paid* (not payable) ($^{214}/_{365} \times 3\%$ of $35,000)	616
Net interest benefit	$ 703

The Act deems the imputed interest benefit of $703 to have been paid in the year. As a result, a part of the interest will qualify as a deduction of interest *paid* limited as follows: ITA: 80.5
ITA: 8(1)(*j*), 67.2

Lesser of:

(a) interest deemed paid	$703	
interest *paid* ($^{214}/_{365} \times 3\%$ of $35,000)	616	$1,319

(b) $\dfrac{\$300}{30}$ × 214 days of interest paid $2,140

Lesser amount × 60% business usage (60% of $1,319) . . . . $ 791

Exercise 5

Shareholder-Manager Pays Tax on Benefit

Benefit from use of car:

     standby charge[1] (10,000km/20,004km ×⅔ × $6,000)   2,000

     value of operating costs of personal use[2]   1,000   ITA: 6(1)(*e*)

Incremental taxable income . . . . $ 3,000

Tax @ 46% on $3,000 of incremental taxable income . . . . $ 1,380

Shareholder-Manager Leases Car Personally

Incremental taxable income ($2,880 + $6,000) . . . . $ 8,880

Less: deduction for business use of car [66⅔% of ($6,000 + $2,880)] . . . .   (5,920)

Add: GST rebate (5/105 × $5,920)[3]   282

Incremental taxable income . . . . $ 3,242

Tax @ 46% on $3,242 of incremental taxable income . . . . $ 1,491

Tax net of GST rebate . . . . $ 1,209

Notice that the second alternative is the better by $171.

— *NOTES TO SOLUTION*

[1] This calculation assumes that business usage of 80% meets the test that the primary distance   ITA: 6(2)
travelled was for business. Generally, the term "primarily" has been interpreted by the CRA to mean
more than 50%.

[2] The election includes a benefit of 50% of the standby charge of $2,000 (i.e., $1,000) which is less   ITA: 6(1)(*k*)
than 24¢ × 10,000km or $2,400.

[3] In reality, the GST rebate would have to be taken into income in the following year. Note that
the present value considerations on the rebate have been ignored. Also, ignored is the effect of the input
tax credit (ITC) received by the corporation if it incurs the annual lease and operating costs. If the
corporation pays additional salary equal to its net costs for these items after ITC and, hence, if the
shareholder manager must pay the GST from other sources, it can be shown that the shareholder-
manager's after-tax retention is reduced by the after-tax equivalent of the GST costs. This would reduce
the advantage of the second alternative.

Exercise 6

	Remuneration alternatives		
Corporation	*Salary*	*Dividends*	*Combination*
Income before salary and taxes	$ 20,000	$20,000	$ 20,000
Salary	(20,000)	—	(11,000)
Taxable income	Nil	$20,000	$ 9,000
Tax @ 16% (i.e., 38% − 10% − 17% + 5%)	—	(3,200)	(1,440)
Available for dividends	Nil	$16,800	$ 7,560
Shareholder			
Employment income (ssec. 8(1) deduc- tions not considered)	$ 20,000	—	$ 11,000
Grossed-up dividends (⁵/₄ × dividend) . . .	—	$21,000	9,450
Taxable income	$ 20,000	$21,000	$ 20,450
Federal tax before dividend tax credit . . .	$ 3,000	$ 3,150	$ 3,068
Dividend tax credit (13⅓% of grossed-up dividend)	—	(2,800)	(1,260)

| | Remuneration alternatives | | |
	Salary	Dividends	Combination
Personal tax credits	(2,000)	(2,000)	(2,000)
Basic federal tax*	$ 1,000	$ Nil	$ Nil
Provincial tax	2,000	2,100	2,045
Provincial dividend tax credit (6⅔% of grossed-up dividend)	—	(1,400)	(630)
Provincial personal tax credits	(1,290)	(1,290)	(1,290)
Total tax*	$ 1,710	Nil	$ 125

Summary

Income before salary and taxes	$ 20,000	$20,000	$ 20,000
Less: tax paid by corporation	Nil	(3,200)	(1,440)
tax paid by shareholder	(1,710)	Nil	(125)
Net cash to shareholder	$ 18,290	$16,800	$ 18,435
Excess federal dividend and personal tax credits ($3,150 − $2,800 − $2,000)		$ 1,650	

* Cannot be negative.

Effect of additional $100 of salary on all-dividend alternative at the corporate level when all of the income is distributed:

Increase in salary expense	$ 100.00
Decrease in corporate tax @ 16%	(16.00)
Decrease in amount available for dividend	$ 84.00

Effect of additional $100 in salary on all-dividend alternative at shareholder level:

Increase in salary	$ 100.00
Decrease in dividend	(84.00)
Decrease in gross-up	(21.00)
Decrease in taxable income	$ (5.00)
Decrease in federal tax @ 15% of $5.00	$ (.75)
Decrease in federal dividend tax credit (13⅓% of ⁵⁄₄ × $84.00)	14.00
Increase in tax	$ 13.25
Additional salary to eliminate $1,650 in excess tax credit ($1,650/.1325)	$ 12,453

Corporation:

Income before salary	$ 20,000
Salary	(12,453)
Taxable income	$ 7,547
Corporate tax @ 16%	(1,208)
Available for dividend	$ 6,339

Shareholder:

Income from salary	$ 12,453
Income from dividend	6,339
Gross-up	1,585
Taxable income	$ 20,377
Federal tax	$ 3,057
Dividend tax credit (13⅓% of ⁵⁄₄ × $6,339)	(1,057)
Personal tax credits	(2,000)
Net federal tax (cannot be negative)	Nil
Provincial tax	2,038
Provincial dividend tax credit	(528)
Provincial personal tax credits	(1,290)

Total tax		$ 220
Net cash to shareholder ($20,000 − $1,208 − $220)		$ 18,572
Improvement ($18,572 − $18,435)		$ 137

Exercise 7

(A) *Taxation of Income from Sole Proprietorship*

Income from business and taxable income		$80,000
Federal tax		
Tax on first $40,726	$ 6,109	
Tax on next $39,274 @ 22%	8,640	$14,749
Personal tax credits		(2,100)
Basic federal tax		$12,649
Provincial tax (12% of ($80,000 − $40,726) + $4,073)		8,786
Provincial personal tax credits		(1,400)
Total tax paid		$20,035

(B) *Taxation of Income through a Corporation*

	All salary	All dividends	Combination
Corporation			
Income before salary and taxes	$ 80,000	$ 80,000	$ 80,000
Salary	(28,667)	—	(10,331)[3]
Taxable income	$ 51,333	$ 80,000	$ 69,669
Tax @ 17% (i.e., 38% − 10% − 17% + 6%)	(8,727)	(13,600)	(11,844)
Available for dividend	$ 42,606	$ 66,400	$ 57,825
Shareholder			
Salary[1] . . . . (A)	$ 28,667	—	$ 10,331
Dividend . . . . (B)	—	$ 25,000	14,669
Gross-up @ ¼ of dividend	—	6,250	3,667
Income	$ 28,667	$ 31,250	$ 28,667
Federal tax	$ 4,300	$ 4,688	$ 4,300
Dividend tax credit (13⅓% of grossed-up dividend)	—	(4,167)	(2,445)
Personal tax credits	(2,100)	(2,100)	(2,100)
Basic federal tax	$ 2,200	Nil	(245)[4]
Provincial tax	2,867	3,125	2,867
Provincial dividend tax credit	Nil	(2,083)	(1,222)
Provincial personal tax credits	(1,400)	(1,400)	(1,400)
Total tax . . . . (C)	$ 3,667	Nil	Nil
Disposable income (A + B − C)	$ 25,000	$ 25,000	$ 25,000
Total Taxes paid			
Through corporation:			
Corporation	$ 8,727	$ 13,600	$ 11,844
Shareholder	3,667	Nil	Nil
Total	$ 12,394	$ 13,600	$ 11,844
Paid directly by proprietor	$ 20,035	$ 20,035	$ 20,035
Tax Saving (maximum[2])	$ 7,641	$ 6,435	$ 8,191

— *NOTES TO SOLUTION*

(1) Assumes no deductions available to employee.

(2) Assumes amount retained in the corporation can be distributed as taxable dividends in amounts that will not attract tax after personal tax credits.

(3) Note that the marginal analysis used in Example Problem 2 in ¶13,230 of the book can be used to derive this amount. The excess tax credits in the all-dividend alternative amount to $1,937 (i.e., $4,688 − $4,167 − $2,100 + $3,125 − $2,083 − $1,400), assuming that all excess federal credits can be used on other income, as required in this problem. Since only part of the corporate income is being distributed, the focus is on the shareholder-manager. If salary is increased by $100, the following would occur:

Increase in salary	$ 100.00
Decrease in dividend	(100.00)
Decrease in gross-up	(25.00)
Decrease in taxable income	$ (25.00)
Decrease in tax @ 25% (i.e., 15% federal and 10% provincial) of $25.00	$ (6.25)
Decrease in dividend tax credit (20% of 5/4 × $100.00)	25.00
Increase in tax	$ 18.75
Increase in salary to eliminate $1,937 of excess tax credits ($1,937/.1875)	$ 10,331

(4) Negative allowed only due to assumption in the required.

Exercise 8

In each of the cases, the test to be applied to the facts is whether all or substantially all (i.e., at least 90%) of the fair market value of the assets are:

(a) used principally in an active business carried on primarily in Canada by the corporation (or a related corporation);

(b) shares or debt of a connected SBC; or

(c) a combination of (a) and (b).

(A) This situation depends on whether the marketable securities are used in the active business or are passive investments not necessary to the active business. If the marketable securities are used in the active business, then the 90% test is met. This would be the case, for example, if the marketable securities represented a short-term investment of cash surpluses, awaiting the purchase of inventory for the next season.

(B) In this situation, the 90% test is met with a combination of active business assets and shares in a connected SBC.

(C) In this case, the marketable securities cannot be considered to be used in an active business, because the corporation has no other active business assets to carry on such a business. Since the shares of a connected SBC represent only 80% of the total fair market value of the corporation's assets, the 90% test is not met.

(D) Again, this case fits the definition of an SBC if the marketable securities are considered to be used in an active business. If the facts of this case so indicate, then the 90% test is met by a combination of active business assets (including the marketable securities) and the shares of a connected SBC.

Exercise 9

(A) Unused lifetime deduction in 2009:

Lifetime cumulative deduction limit	$ 375,000
Less: prior years' deductions:	
Capital gains deduction claimed in 2007	75,000
Capital gains deduction available for 2009	$ 300,000

(B) Annual gains limit for 2009:

Net taxable capital gains for 2009[1]	$ 225,000

Minus:

Net capital losses deducted in 2009	Nil	
ABILs realized in 2009[1]	5,000	5,000
Annual gains limit for 2009		$ 220,000

(C) Cumulative gains limit for 2009:

Cumulative net taxable capital gains ($75,000 + $225,000)			$ 300,000
Minus:			
Cumulative net capital losses deducted		Nil	
Cumulative ABILs realized	$	5,000	
Cumulative capital gains deductions		75,000	
Cumulative net investment loss:			

Investment expenses —				
Cumulative carrying charges	$ 1,075			
Cumulative net rental losses				
($1,100 + $220)	1,320			
	$ 2,395			
Investment income —				
Cumulative interest income				
($600 + $1,200)		(1,800)		
Cumulative grossed-up dividends		(140)	455	80,455
Cumulative gains limit for 2009				$ 219,545

(D) Least of (A), (B), (C) . . . . $ 219,545

— *NOTE TO SOLUTION*

[1] Allowable business investment loss (ABIL):

BIL before ssec. 39(9) reduction			$ 160,000
Disallowed portion — Lesser of:			
(a) BIL		$ 160,000	
(b) Adjustment factor × cumulative			
CG deductions of previous			
years (2 × $75,000)	$150,000		
Minus: Cumulative disallowed			
BIL of prior years	Nil	$ 150,000	
Lesser of (a) and (b)			(150,000)
BIL after adjustment			$ 10,000
ABIL (½ × $10,000)			$ 5,000
Allowable capital loss (ACL):			
Disallowed portion of BIL			$ 150,000
ACL (½ × $150,000)			$ 75,000
Net TCG for 2009:			
TCG			$ 300,000
Less: ACL			75,000
Net TCG			$ 225,000

Exercise 10

The disposition of the real estate is a transfer for tax purposes in 2009. The facts do not provide enough details on the cost base to determine the tax effect of the disposition.

In this case it can likely be established that one of the main purposes of the transfer of the building may reasonably be considered to be to reduce the income of Mr. Albert and to benefit Mrs. Albert who is a designated person and a specified shareholder. Had Mr. Albert kept the building himself he would have earned $20,000 of rental income on which he would have been taxable. Instead, he will receive $1,000 of interest and $2,000 of dividends. Mrs. Albert benefited from the rental income since this will accrue to the common shares of the corporation. Therefore, it may be argued that the purpose test will have been met.

Furthermore, the corporation will no longer be a "small business corporation", since the fair market value of the assets of the corporation will be as follows:

ITA: 248(1)

Retail assets, 75%	$600,000
Building, 25%	200,000
Total	$800,000

Even if 20% of the building (FMV $40,000) is classified as an active business asset, the corporation will still not be a small business corporation since all or substantially all of the fair market value of the assets are not used principally in an active business carried on primarily in Canada.

Mr. Albert's attributed amount	
FMV of the building transferred	$200,000
Less: cash received	(80,000)
Outstanding amount	$120,000
Interest imputed at 4%	$4,800
Less: interest received (5% of $20,000)	(1,000)
$^5/_4$ of dividends received	(2,500)
Attributed amount	$1,300
Mr. Albert would also have	
Interest income	1,000
Taxable dividends ($2,000 × 1.25)	2,500
Total income	$4,800

Exercise 11

The following comments are based on the application of the logic presented in Exhibit 13-11 to the facts of this situation.

(1) Does any other provision of the Act or other rule of law apply to stop the taxpayer from achieving the intended advantage? No, the amount paid is considered to be reasonable and, hence, is not prohibited. Remuneration is considered to be an expense incurred to produce income from business and, thus, is not prohibited.

ITA: 67
ITA: 18(1)(*a*)

(2) Does the transaction result, directly or indirectly, in a tax benefit, i.e., a reduction, avoidance or deferral of tax or an increase in a refund? On the one hand, corporate tax is reduced, but on the other hand the individual receives income subject to tax at approximately the same rate. However, the reduction of income to the corporation reduces the potential for double taxation on income taxed at more than a 20% rate in the corporation which may be considered to be a tax benefit. If it is concluded that there is no tax benefit, GAAR should not apply.

ITA: 245(1)

(3) Is the transaction part of a series of transactions, which would result, directly or indirectly, in a tax benefit? If the answer to question 2 is yes, then proceed directly to question 4.

(4) Can the transaction reasonably be considered to have been undertaken or arranged primarily for *bona fide* purposes other than to obtain the tax benefit? No, a tax reduction for the corporation was probably the primary purpose. On the other hand, it might be argued that, since the amount paid was reasonable, it is necessary remuneration.

(5) Can it reasonably be considered that the transaction would result directly or indirectly in a misuse of the provisions of the Act or an abuse having regard to the provisions of the Act read as a whole? No, "the Act recognizes the deductibility of reasonable business expenses."

IC 88-2, par. 18

Exercise 12

The general anti-avoidance rule allows for transactions or a series of transactions to be disregarded if they are without a *bona fide* purpose. If your client's spouse and children are not providing any services to her business, it is obvious that the transactions were arranged primarily to obtain a tax benefit with no bona fide purpose, and they will be disregarded by the CRA. Any tax benefit derived from the transactions will be eliminated. If there is some service being provided to justify a salary, the amount of salary must be reasonable in the circumstance or the deduction by your client can be disallowed without the need to apply the GAAR. In fact, if the unreasonable salaries are still taxed in the hands of the spouse and children, after the expense is disallowed, the result is worse than the application of the GAAR that disregards the payment.

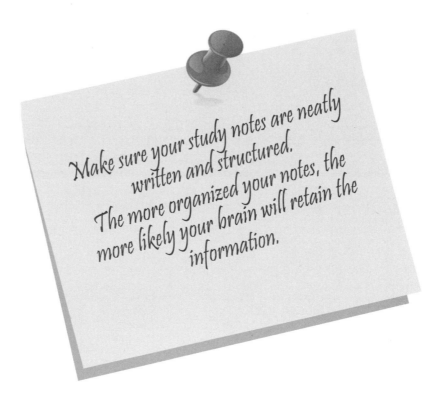

Make sure your study notes are neatly written and structured. The more organized your notes, the more likely your brain will retain the information.

Chapter 14
Rights and Obligations Under the Income Tax Act

LEARNING GOALS

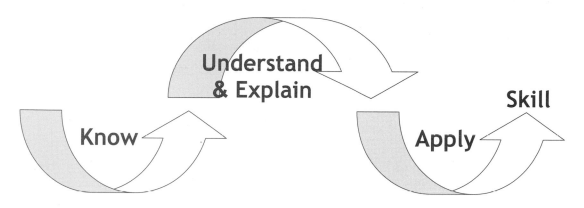

Know

By the end of this chapter you should know the basic provisions of the *Income Tax Act* and the *Excise Tax Act* that relate to the taxpayer compliance rules, the powers of the Canada Revenue Agency (CRA), and a taxpayer's rights and requirements on appeals. Completing the Review Questions (¶14,800) and Multiple Choice Questions (¶14,825) is a good way to learn the technical provisions.

Understand and Explain

You should understand and be able to explain:

- The requirements for taxpayers of income tax and registrants for GST to make payments, file returns, and, possibly, incur penalties and interest, if the taxpayer does not comply with the legislation on an accurate and timely basis;
- The powers and obligations of the CRA to assess and reassess a taxpayer's or registrant's filings;
- The rights of taxpayers and registrants to appeal within deadlines; and
- The compliance rules applicable to employers, other payers of tax, and representatives of deceased taxpayers.

Apply

You should be able to apply your knowledge and understanding of the key elements of compliance pertaining to payment of tax and filing returns and appeals to achieve a client's goals of minimizing interest and penalties in the early stages of the process. Completing the Assignment Problems (¶14,875) is an excellent way to develop your ability to apply the material in increasingly complex situations.

Chapter 14 — Learning Chart

Topic	Example Problem (✓)	Review Questions (¶14,800)	Multiple Choice (¶14,825)	Exercises (¶14,850)	Assignment Problems (¶14,875)
¶14,000 OBLIGATIONS OF THE TAXPAYER UNDER THE INCOME TAX ACT					
¶14,010 Returns, Penalties, and Criminal Offences		1		1	
¶14,015 Returns					
¶14,018 Functional currency tax reporting					
¶14,020 Penalties			1	8,9,10,12	3, 4
¶14,025 Criminal offences				8, 10	
¶14,030 Payments and Interest				11	
¶14,035 Individuals	✓	1, 2	6	5	1
¶14,040 Corporations	✓		5	6	2, 3
¶14,050 Books and Records					
¶14,100 POWERS AND OBLIGATIONS OF THE CRA					
¶14,110 Assessments and Reassessments	✓	5	2, 3	2, 4, 7	
¶14,120 Refunds and Interest		3		11, 15	
¶14,200 RIGHTS OF THE TAXPAYER					
¶14,210 Objections and Appeals		4		13	
¶14,220 Amended Returns					
¶14,300 OBLIGATIONS OF PAYERS AND OTHER PERSONS					
¶14,310 Employers	✓			3	
¶14,320 Obligations of Other Payers, Trustees, etc.					
¶14,325 Payments to residents of Canada				3	
¶14,330 Payments to non-residents				14	5, 6, 7
¶14,335 Foreign reporting requirements	✓				7
¶14,340 Deceased Taxpayers		6			
¶14,345 Tax returns			4	17	8
¶14,350 Rights or things				16, 17	8
¶14,355 Other return				16	
¶14,360 Personal tax credits				10	
¶14,400 OBLIGATIONS OF THE REGISTRANT UNDER THE EXCISE TAX ACT					
¶14,410 Collection and Remittance of Tax					9
¶14,420 Disclosure of Tax					
¶14,430 Returns and Reporting Periods					9
¶14,440 Remittance of Tax					
¶14,450 Books and Records					9
¶14,500 POWERS AND OBLIGATIONS OF THE CRA IN RESPECT OF THE EXCISE TAX ACT					
¶14,510 Assessments and Reassessments					
¶14,520 Refunds and Interest					
¶14,600 RIGHTS OF THE REGISTRANT					
¶14,610 Objections and Appeals					
¶14,620 Amended Returns and GST Adjustments					
¶14,700 SIMPLIFIED METHOD AND QUICK METHOD					

Study Notes

Chapter 14 —
Discussion Notes for Review Questions

(1) (a) False. All corporations resident in Canada have to file tax returns within six months of the end of the year.   ITA: 150(1)(*a*)

(b) True. An individual is required to file a tax return if he or she "has disposed of a capital property". Even if there is no taxable income or tax liability a return must be filed. In addition, Mr. Lucky may lose his capital gains deduction in respect of this transaction, if he does not file the return.   ITA: 110.6(6), 150(1)

(c) False. Instalments must be paid on the 15th of each of those months.   ITA: 156(1)

(2) An instalment interest offset is available on prepaid or overpaid instalments. However, this credit offset can only be applied against instalment interest owing; it is not refundable and may not be applied against any other debt. To benefit, he would have to pay the December 15 instalment on September 15 which would offset the fact that the June 15 instalment was three months late. In addition, the prescribed interest rate for the last quarter would have to be equal to or greater than the prescribed interest rate for the second quarter.   ITA: 161(2.2)

(3) They will not be able to collect interest for the last three years. Interest will not be paid for the period prior to the filing of the tax return for the year in which the request is made to carry the loss back.   ITA: 164(5)

(4) Since the accountant sent a letter to the CRA, it may take some time before a reply is received. If the reply is received late and there is disagreement, it may be too late to file a Notice of Objection. Therefore, it may be prudent to file the Notice of Objection in the first place unless the matter is a minor one.   ITA: 165(1)

(5) In order to amend the tax returns for the third preceding year the company would have had to file form T2A by the time the corporate tax returns are due for the loss year which is six months after the fiscal year-end. However, Bad Luck did not meet this deadline since it did not file until seven months after the year-end. Therefore, the CRA will not have to let the corporation carry the loss back at all. However, the loss will still be available to be carried forward.   ITA: 152(6)

(6) The following are the three returns that can be filed:

(a) Terminal return — This return reports the income for the period in the year before the date of death and includes any gain or loss on the deemed disposition on death. Full personal credits may be claimed.   ITA: 70(1)

(b) Rights or things — "Rights or things" can be reported on a separate return to take advantage of the lower marginal tax brackets. Also, the full personal tax credits allowed can be claimed again.   ITA: 70(2), 118(1), 118(2)

(c) Trust return — Similar rules to those in (c) above apply to those situations that have more than one trust year-end in the same calendar year. This would only apply in the case of a testamentary trust since they are the only ones that can have an off-calendar year-end. Again, the lower marginal tax rates and the personal tax credits are available.   ITA: 104(23)(*d*)

Chapter 14 –
Solutions to Multiple Choice Questions

Question 1

(B) is correct. The penalty is $900. The initial penalty rate of 5% is increased by 1% for each *complete* month after April 30, 2009 that the return was not filed to a maximum penalty of 5% + 4% = 9%.

ITA: 162(1)

(A) is incorrect as it includes only the initial penalty of 5% of the unpaid tax.

(C) is incorrect as it includes ½% for the half month of September. Only complete months should be counted for purposes of the penalty.

(D) is incorrect as it includes 1% for the month of September. Only complete months should be counted for purposes of the penalty.

Question 2

(B) August 15, 2012 is correct. The normal reassessment period for a CCPC ends three years after the day of mailing of a notice of assessment for the year.

ITA: 152(3.1)

(A) December 31, 2011, three years after the end of the taxation year, is incorrect. The three-year period commences with the date of mailing of the notice of assessment, not the last day of the fiscal year.

(C) December 31, 2012, four years after the end of the taxation year, is incorrect.

(D) August 15, 2013, four years after the day of mailing of a notice of assessment for the year, is incorrect. It would be correct if the taxpayer were a corporation other than a CCPC.

ITA: 152(3.1)

Question 3

(D) June 15, 2010 is correct. The notice of objection filing due date is one year after Darol's filing-due date for 2008.

ITA: 165(1)

(A) December 31, 2009, being one year after the end of the taxation year, is incorrect.

(B) January 14, 2010, being 90 days after the date of mailing of the notice of assessment, is incorrect in this case. For an individual and a testamentary trust, the due date is the later of this date and one year after the filing-due date for the tax return.

(C) April 30, 2010, being one year after the filing-due date for 2008 for an individual *not* carrying on a business, is incorrect. Darol's filing-due date for 2008 was June 15, 2009, as he carried on business in 2008.

Question 4

The correct answer is (D) September 30, 2009, being six months after the date of death.

ITA: 150(1)(*b*)

(A) is incorrect. It is the most common due date for 2008 personal tax returns. This date is not correct for two reasons: first, he has income from carrying on business, and second, he died after October 2008.

ITA: 150(1)(*a*)(i)

(B) is incorrect. It is the date the return would have been due if he had not died.

ITA: 150(1)(*a*)(ii)

(C) is incorrect as it is six months after the end of the year for which the return is being filed.

Question 5

(A) is correct. The minimum monthly instalment is the least of:

– ¹/₁₂ of the estimated taxes payable: ¹/₁₂ × $200,000 = $16,667

– ¹/₁₂ of the prior year's taxes payable: ¹/₁₂ of $140,000 = $11,667

– ¹/₁₂ of the second prior year's taxable payable (¹/₁₂ of $180,000 = $15,000) for two months and 10 payments of $11,000 (¹/₁₀ × [$140K – 2 × $15,000]).

The least of these is either the prior year method or the second prior year method. Only the prior year method ($11,667 per month) is listed as a choice in this question. Because X Ltd. had taxable income in the prior year of more than the small business deduction limit, it must pay its final balance due within two months of year end (February 28, 2010).

(B) and (C) incorrectly base the instalments on estimated taxes payable. (B) has the correct final due date. (C) incorrectly uses the balance-due day that is three months after the end of the year which is applicable only for Canadian-controlled private corporations that have taxable income that is less than the small business deduction limit in the prior year.

(D) incorrectly uses the amount for the first two payments of the second prior year method for all 12 payments but has the correct final due date for the balance due. (D) would have been a correct answer had it indicated that the payments for the last 10 months would be $11,000 per month.

Question 6

(D) is correct (two payments of $3,825 and two payments of $4,375). The minimum monthly instalment is the least of:

– $\frac{1}{4}$ of the estimated taxes payable: $\frac{1}{4} \times \$25,000 = \$6,250$

– $\frac{1}{4}$ of the prior year's taxes payable: $\frac{1}{4}$ of $16,400 = \$4,100$

– $\frac{1}{4}$ of the second prior year's taxable payable ($\frac{1}{4}$ of $15,300 = \$3,825$) for two months and two payments of $4,375 ($\frac{1}{2} \times [\$16,400 - 2 \times \$3,825]$).

(A) is incorrect because four payments of $6,250 is not the minimum payment.

(B) is incorrect because two payments of $4,100 and two payments of $6,250 is not the minimum amount. Four payments of $4,100 would result in the minimum amount.

(C) is incorrect because two payments of $3,825 and two payments of $4,100 is not the minimum amount. If the first two payments are $3,825, the last two payments must be $4,375. Alternatively, four payments of $4,100 can be made.

Chapter 14 — Solutions to Exercises

Exercise 1

Subsection 150(1):

(a) corporations — within 6 months from the end of the taxation year;

(b) deceased persons — for a tax return of a given year where the individual died after October 31 of the given year and before the normal filing due date for that year, on or before the later of 6 months after the day of death and the day the return would otherwise be due; in all other cases by April 30 (or June 15, if the deceased individual or his or her spouse carried on a business in the year of death) following the year of death (i.e., if the death occurs in the first 10 months of a year, the return is due by April 30 or June 15 of the next year);

(c) trust — within 90 days from the end of the taxation year;

(d) individual — on or before April 30 of the next calendar year unless the individual or his or her spouse carried on a business, in which case the deadline is June 15 of the next year.

Exercise 2

Subsection 152(4):

— No limit if fraud or misrepresentation in the 2008 return can be established or on a matter for which the taxpayer has filed a waiver of the limit by May 27, 2012;

— Otherwise, the reassessment must be made within three years of May 27, 2009.

Exercise 3

Subsection 153(1):

(a) salary or wages or other remuneration from employment;

(b) a superannuation or pension benefit;

(c) a retiring allowance;

(d) a death benefit for long service from an employer;

(e) an Employment Insurance benefit;

(f) a benefit under a supplementary unemployment benefit plan;

(g) an annuity payment;

(h) a benefit from a deferred profit sharing plan;

(i) fees, commissions and other amounts for services;

(j) a payment under a registered retirement savings plan;

(k) certain amounts resulting from an income averaging annuity;

(l) a payment from a registered retirement income fund.

Exercise 4

Inheritance, gambling winnings, lottery prize, etc.

Exercise 5

As his net tax owing in the current year and one of the two preceding years is in excess of $3,000, he is required to make instalments.

Instalments of $750 ($\frac{1}{4} \times$ $3,000) must be paid by March 15 and June 15 and instalments of $1,250 (i.e., ($4,000 – 2 $\times$ $750) $\times$ $\frac{1}{2}$) must be paid by September 15 and December 15. The balance of the tax liability must be remitted by the balance-due date of April 30, 2012.

Exercise 6

As the corporation's estimated taxes payable for the current year and the taxes paid for the preceding year exceed $3,000, instalments are required.

The Act would allow the following: ITA: 157(1)(*a*)(iii)

January 31 and February 29, 2011 — ¹/₁₂ of $158,400 or $13,200;

Last day of March to December 2011 — ¹/₁₀ of ($237,600 − 2 × $13,200) or $21,120;

Balance on the last day of the third month after the taxation year-end, where a small business deduction was taken by virtue of section 125 in the current or preceding year and the corporation and associated corporations' aggregate taxable incomes for the preceding year did not exceed the small business deduction limit, or, in this particular case, the last day of February 2012, as applicable to any other case.

Exercise 7   ITA: 165, 169

Rachel should ensure that the required forms are filled out correctly and that they are signed by her employer. If all the forms are in order, she has the right under section 165 to object to an assessment made by the CRA by filing a notice of objection within one year of the April 30 filing due date, or within 90 days after the day of mailing of the assessment notice, whichever is later. If Rachel is not satisfied with the reassessment, she can appeal to the courts as outlined under section 169.

Exercise 8

Subsection 150(1):

Y and Z will incur no penalties; furthermore, Y is not required to file since no tax is payable, unless he disposed of capital property.

Subsection 162(1):

Failure to file when required — 5% of unpaid tax plus 1% of unpaid tax per complete month past due for a first offence:

X — 5% of $4,700 or $235 plus 1% of $4,700 × nil = $235.

Y — 5% of nil or nil.

Z — no penalty as the return is not due until June 15. Interest charges on the unpaid tax from April 30 will, however, apply.

Subsection 238(1):

Failure to file as or when required — liable on summary conviction to a fine of $1,000 to $25,000 or a fine and imprisonment for up to 12 months;

— Y could be fined if there has been a demand to file under subsection 150(2).

Exercise 9

(A) Facts to be determined:

(i) Date of mailing of 2005 original assessment in order to determine the three-year limit (i.e., the   ITA: 152(4)
normal reassessment period for an individual).

(ii) Obtain date of mailing of notice of reassessment.

(iii) Assuming Mr. Dishonest is correct as to the date of the reassessment, determine if the date of the original assessment was prior to June 15, 2006 and if so, whether or not Mr. Dishonest has filed a waiver of the three-year limit.

(iv) If the date of the original assessment was prior to June 15, 2006, you should determine whether Mr. Dishonest is alleged to have made any misrepresentation due to neglect, gross carelessness, wilful default, or has committed a fraud in filing his 2005 return.

(B) Steps to be taken:

(i) Procure an engagement letter or a signed consent form which gives permission to discuss   Form T1013
Mr. Dishonest's case with officials of the CRA.

(ii) Start discussions with the CRA.

(iii) File a Notice of Objection prior to the expiry of the 90-day period based upon the date of mailing determined above (i.e., September 12, 2009, if mailed on June 15, 2009).

(iv) Warn Mr. Dishonest that certain second-time offences may carry heavier penalties than the first-time offence.

(C) A penalty of 10% of unreported income could be imposed on Mr. Dishonest, if the current reassessment is his second offence within three years of the first offence. Under the CRA's voluntary disclosure program, a valid voluntary disclosure may result in a waiver of penalties.

ITA: 163(1), IC 00-1R

Exercise 10

The backdating of the document would be considered to be participating in the making of a false statement or omission in a return. As a result, a penalty is imposed equal to the greater of $100 and 50% of the difference in tax liability.

ITA: 163(1)

In addition, a fine of not less than 50% and not more than 200% of the amount of the tax that was evaded, or the fine plus imprisonment for a term not exceeding two years, would be imposed.

ITA: 238(1)

Both Mr. Trouble and Ms. Back Date would be subject to the above fines and penalties.

Ms. Back Date may also be subject to disciplinary measures by her professional accounting association.

Ms. Back Date could be liable for the civil penalty imposed on third parties for a false statement.

ITA: 163.2

Exercise 11

The Act computes interest at a basic prescribed rate plus 4% on amounts owing to the CRA from the earliest date the amount was due until the date it was paid;

ITA: 161

— the interest is not tax deductible.

Interest is computed at the same basic prescribed rate plus 2% on refunds by the CRA;

ITA: 164(3)

— the interest is taxable;

— if the interest relates to instalments, an interest offset is computed using the 4% addition, against interest owing on late instalments for interest earned on early instalments.

ITA: 161(2.2)

Both interest calculations are based on daily compounding.

Interest on the overpayment of taxes for individuals will start to accrue 30 days after the later of the balance due day for the return (i.e., April 30, 2010 for 2009 returns) or the date the return is filed.

An individual's refund interest accruing over a period can be offset by any arrears interest that accrues over the same period, to which the refund interest relates. Hence, only the excess refund interest is taxed to the individual.

Exercise 12

The following comment on this situation is provided by the CRA:

IC 01-1

There was nothing in the income statement that would have made the accountant question the validity of the information provided to him. Therefore, he could rely on the good faith defence and would not be subject to the preparer penalty.

CHAPTER 14

Use of the flowchart presented in the chapter may be helpful in analyzing this situation and reaching this conclusion.

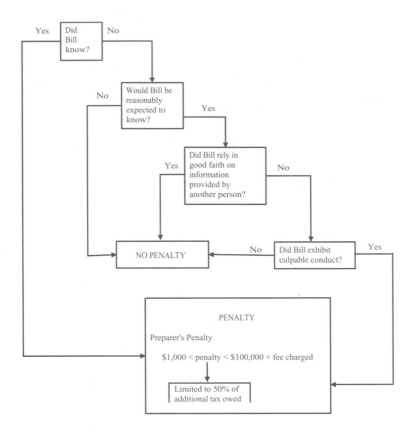

Exercise 13

(a) Notice of objection: ITA: 165(1)

— to be filed by *individual* taxpayers by the later of:

  (i) one year after the filing-due date, which is normally April 30 or June 15 except for trusts   ITA: 248(1)
  and deceased persons, and

  (ii) the 90th day after the mailing date of the notice of assessment;

— to be filed within 90 days of mailing of notice of assessment for all other taxpayers;

— a prescribed form is not required.

(b) Appeal to the Tax Court of Canada: ITA: 169

— after 90 days of date of decision on notice of objection or 90 days after the mailing of the notice of objection if there has been no response to it;

— may be able to elect informal procedure under subsection 18(1) of the *Tax Court of Canada Act*.

(c) Appeal to the Federal Court of Appeal (section 17.6 of the *Tax Court of Canada Act*):

— within 30 days from date of mailing of decision of the Tax Court of Canada only if that taxpayer chose the general procedure in the Tax Court of Canada.

(d) Appeal to Supreme Court of Canada:

— on recommendation of Federal Court of Appeal;

— with permission of Supreme Court of Canada.

Exercise 14

A tax return may be filed by a non-resident within two years after the end of the year that rents were paid;. In that return, rental income for the year, net of expenses, would be reported and any withholding tax paid in the year in respect of rental revenue would be considered taxes paid for the year.

ITA: 216

This individual is eligible to file this return for 2007, 2008, and 2009. The 2004, 2005, and 2006 rents do not fall into the eligible filing period. However, the Minister may extend the time for filing a return. The individual may consider requesting such an extension.

ITA: 216
ITA: 220(3.2)

Exercise 15

Sol will receive interest on the $9,000 only from 30 days after June 15, 2009 (i.e., July 15, 2009) to the date the cheque was mailed. When he determined he had paid excess instalments, he could consider requesting that the instalments be transferred to his employer remittance account, if he has employees from whom he withholds tax.

Exercise 16

(A) The accrued interest is a periodic payment to be reported on the terminal T1 return, due April 30, 2010.

ITA: 70(1)

(B) Since the dividend is not payable until declared, it does not have to be accrued. Because it was declared after death, it is not a right or thing. Therefore, it is income of his estate.

ITA: 70(1), 70(2)

(C) The $800 of CPP would be reported on the terminal T1 return, since no amount was unpaid at the date of death that related to a *completed* pay period. Hence, CPP earned from September 1 to the date of death on September 10 is not considered to be a right or thing, since it is not legally receivable for a completed pay period on the date of death.

(D) The donations are creditable, to the extent of 100% of net income reported, on all the year of death returns combined or in the preceding year's return. Only personal tax credits may be deducted on each of the separate returns for the year of death.

ITA: 118(1), 118(2)
ITA: 118.93

(E) Net capital losses are deductible from any source of income in the year of death and the preceding year.

ITA: 111(2)

(F) Trust income of $900 for the year ended May 31, 2009 must be reported on the terminal return. An election is permitted to report the trust income payable to Sam for the stub period, June 1, 2009 to September 10, 2009 on a separate return, also due April 30, 2010. The personal tax credits can be deducted on this return.

ITA: 104(23)(*d*)

ITA: 118(1), 118(2)

(G) Life insurance proceeds received on death are not taxable.

Exercise 17

Ms. Kaye's 2009 terminal personal tax return is required to be filed by April 30, 2010. In Ms. Kaye's 2009 return all accrued income earned on a periodic basis during the period January 1 to May 1, 2009 should be included. In addition, all capital property (such as her Flying High shares) is deemed to have been disposed of at the fair market value. A claim for the full personal tax credits can be made on the terminal return even though Ms. Kaye died on May 2, 2009. The RRSP contribution of $9,000 is deductible on her 2009 terminal return, since it is less than the maximum amount (i.e., lesser of $19,000 and 18% of $80,000).

ITA: 150(1)(*d*)
ITA: 70(1)
ITA. 70(5)

Ms. Kaye's 2009 terminal return will include the following:

Salary	$22,000
Bond interest	950
Savings account interest	150
GIC interest	140
Dividend income	250
Taxable capital gain [½ ($25 − $10) × 100]	750
RRSP accumulation	34,000
RRSP contribution	(9,000)
Taxable income	$49,240

Ms. Kaye's legal representative can report amounts which were receivable but not received at the date of death, on a separate tax return, called a "rights or things" return, instead of on the terminal return.

ITA: 70(2)

The unpaid salary of $2,000, interest payable of $950 and $250 of grossed-up dividend income would qualify as income from "rights or things." Personal tax credits equal to the amounts claimed in the terminal return may be claimed again on the "rights or things" return. This return is due on the date that is the later of one year after death and 90 days after assessment of any return for the year of death.

Alternatively, the legal representative can assign the income from "rights or things" to a particular beneficiary.

ITA: 70(3)

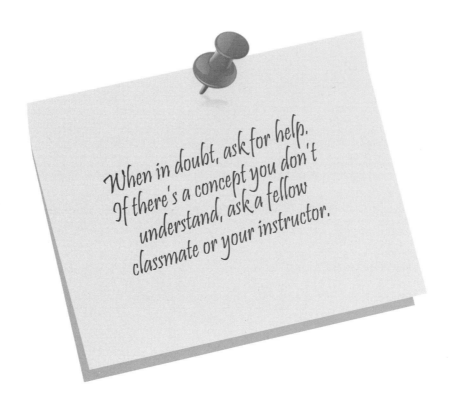

When in doubt, ask for help. If there's a concept you don't understand, ask a fellow classmate or your instructor.

Appendix I
International Taxation in Canada

LEARNING GOALS

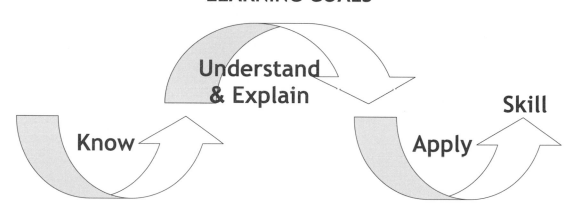

Know → Understand & Explain → Apply → Skill

Know

By the end of this chapter you should know the basics of Canadian taxation of non-residents, the basics of Canadian tax law applicable to international transactions, and Canadian taxation of residents with foreign investments. Completing the Review Questions (¶19,800) and Multiple Choice Questions (¶19,825) is a good way to learn the technical provisions.

Understand and Explain

You should have a basic understanding and be able to explain:

- The taxation of non-residents with Canadian investments or business dealings.
- The tax treatment of international transactions with Canadian residents.
- The taxation of Canadian residents with foreign investments.
- The basic application of tax treaties.

Completing the Exercises (¶19,850) is a good way to deepen your understanding of the material.

Apply

You should be able to apply your knowledge and understanding of the key provisions in the Act applicable to non-residents and international transactions to determine:

- Tax compliance requirements for a non-resident with Canadian investments or business dealings.
- The application and impact of a tax treaty on the taxation of various sources of income earned by non-residents in Canada.
- The Canadian taxation of international transactions and foreign investment by Canadian residents.

Completing the Assignment Problems (¶19,875) is an excellent way to develop your ability to apply the material in increasingly complex situations.

Appendix I – Learning Chart

Topic	Example Problem (✓)	Review Questions (¶19,800)	Multiple Choice (¶19,825)	Exercises (¶19,850)	Assignment Problems (¶19,875)
¶19,000 LIABILITY FOR CANADIAN TAX					
¶19,010 Residents			3		
¶19,020 Non-Residents				2, 5	4
¶19,100 PART-YEAR RESIDENTS		2			
¶19,110 Income, Deductions, and Credits	✓	6,14	2	6	
¶19,120 Deemed Acquisition on Entering Canada	✓	7,12			
¶19,130 Deemed Disposition on Leaving Canada	✓	7		1	5
¶19,200 NON-RESIDENTS					
¶19,210 Income Earned in Canada by Non-Residents					
¶19,215 Employment income					1
¶19,220 Business income	✓			3	3
¶19,225 Branch tax	✓				3
¶19,230 Disposing of taxable Canadian property	✓	5,13	1		2, 4
¶19,240 Deductions and Credits Allowed a Non-Resident					1
¶19,245 Tax credits available to non-residents					
¶19,250 Provincial/Territorial Income Tax Obligation					
¶19,260 Withholding Taxes on Canadian-Source Income — Part XIII Tax	✓	8,9	4		4
¶19,265 Rental income alternative — Section 216 elections	✓				2
¶19,270 Canadian benefits alternative — Section 217 election		10			
¶19,280 Impact of Canada-Foreign Country Tax Treaties					
¶19,285 Application of the treaties		1			
¶19,300 CROSS-BORDER TRANSACTIONS AND LOANS					
¶19,310 Transfer Pricing		3			6, 7
¶19,320 Thin Capitalization — Inbound Loans	✓	4			8
¶19,330 Corporate Debt Owed by a Non-Resident — Outbound Loans	✓	11		4	9
¶19,340 Information Reporting			5		
¶19,400 TAXATION OF CANADIAN RESIDENTS WITH FOREIGN INVESTMENTS					
¶19,410 Active Business Income Earned in a Foreign Jurisdiction		15		7	10
¶19,415 Unincorporated foreign branch operations					
¶19,420 Individuals receiving dividends from foreign corporations					
¶19,425 Corporations receiving dividends from non-foreign affiliates					
¶19,430 Corporations receiving dividends from foreign affiliates					
¶19,440 Passive Income Earned in a Foreign Jurisdiction		16	6	7	10
¶19,445 Controlled foreign affiliates					
¶19,450 Foreign investment entities					

Study Notes

Appendix I —
Discussion Notes for Review Questions

(1) One objective of international tax treaties is to eliminate double taxation. This is accomplished by ensuring that income is not taxed in more than one country or by providing a foreign tax credit for the taxes paid in the other country. The second objective of the treaties is to prevent tax evasion. This is accomplished through "sharing of information" provisions in the treaties.

(2) A part-year resident is a taxpayer who either enters or leaves Canada as a permanent resident at some point in the year. This taxpayer is taxable in Canada on their worldwide income only during their period of residency. Their non-Canadian source pre/post-residency income is not taxable in Canada. A non-resident is a person who is resident somewhere other than Canada. They are taxable in Canada only on Canadian employment or business income, or gains on taxable Canadian property, or by Part XIII withholding taxes on certain other Canadian-source income.   ITA: 2(3)

(3) The transfer pricing rules are intended to ensure that purchases/sales to a related non-resident entity occur at the arm's length price that applies to goods and services between unrelated persons. In that way, profits cannot be exported beyond the Canadian tax authorities.   ITA: 247(1)

(4) The thin capitalization rules are designed to prevent the erosion of Canada's tax base through the withdrawal of profits by deductible interest payments rather than through dividends. By under-capitalizing a Canadian subsidiary, a foreign parent could "force" the subsidiary to pay interest that would otherwise be taxable profits in the subsidiary.   ITA: 18(4)

(5) A non-resident is taxable on the disposition of taxable Canadian property (TCP). TCP is defined in the Act and includes shares of an unlisted corporation resident in Canada. Listed shares of a Canadian resident corporation are TCP only if the non-resident and non-arm's length persons owned not less than 25% of the shares of the corporation. The relevant tax treaty would need to be considered to determine whether a treaty article overrides the domestic law. Unless the shares are treaty-protected property, the purchaser of the shares is required to withhold and remit 25% of the purchase price unless the non-resident obtains a certificate of compliance and remits a tax payment of 25% of the gain on the property to the CRA no later than 10 days after the disposition.   ITA: 248(1)

(6) Some personal tax credits are prorated for the portion of the year the individual is resident in Canada, for example, basic personal tax credit, age credit, etc. Other credits can be claimed in full, for example, donation credit, medical expense credit, etc.

(7) The individual would be taxable only on the gain from the time he or she moved to Canada. The cost base used to calculate the gain would be the fair market value of the property at the date of the move to Canada.   ITA: 128.1(1)(*c*)

(8) A non-resident employer is required to withhold and remit tax from remuneration paid to an employee related to duties performed in Canada. The employee will file a Canadian tax return to include the Canadian employment income unless the income is exempt from tax under the relevant Canadian tax treaty. The tax withholdings will be applied against any taxes payable.   ITA: 153(1); ITR: 102

(9) The withholding tax rate is 25%. However, under the Canada–U.S. Income Tax Convention this rate is reduced to 5% if the shareholder owns at least 10% of the voting stock of the corporation.   ITA: 212(1)

(10) There would only be a benefit to a section 217 election where the individual's tax calculated under Part I on those benefits would be less than 25% (or the reduced rate under the relevant tax treaty).

(11) If the loan is not repaid within one year of the end of the taxation year in which the loan was made, Part XIII tax will apply to a deemed dividend to the shareholder equal to the loan balance. Subsection 17(1) will not apply where Part XIII tax is paid (and not refunded on a repayment of the balance). A refund of the Part XIII tax may be requested within two years of the calendar year in which a repayment of the balance occurs (in which case, subsection 17(1) could apply).   ITA: 15(2), 214(3)(*a*)

(12) The purpose of the deemed disposition/acquisition rule is to provide a tax cost base from which future income/gains are determined for Canadian income tax purposes.   ITA: 128.1(1)

(13) No, public company shares are not taxable Canadian property unless the shareholder holds 25% or more of the issued share capital.

(14) Non-residents who are filing a Canadian income tax return for employment income, business income, or because they have disposed of taxable Canadian property, are entitled to claim the same personal tax credits available to a resident where their Canadian-source income represents 90% or more of their world income.   ITA: 118.94

APPENDIX I

(15) A Canadian resident individual may reduce Part I taxes payable by a non-business income tax deduction for tax withholdings up to a rate of 15%. A Canadian resident corporation may claim a non-business income tax deduction for withholdings (without limit) unless the dividends are received from a foreign affiliate.

ITA: 126(1)

(16) The FAPI rules prevent a Canadian resident from deferring tax on investment income by holding investments offshore in controlled foreign affiliates. The rules require the Canadian investor to pay tax on the foreign investment income as it is earned each year instead of when it is received as a dividend.

ITA: 91(1)

It's all about posture. Always study sitting upright in a comfortable chair. Slouching or hunching over decreases your energy and makes your muscles tired and sore.

Appendix I –
Solutions to Multiple Choice Questions

Question 1

(B) is correct. Jari is taxed as a non-resident on the disposition of taxable Canadian property.   ITA: 2(3), 115

(A) is not correct. Income earned in a particular province for a non-resident includes only employment income and income from carrying on business.   ITR: 2602(1)

(C) and (D) are not correct. Non-residents are taxable on gains from the disposition of taxable Canadian property under Part I of the ITA. Withholding tax is eligible under Part XIII.   ITA: 2(3), 115(1)

Question 2

(B) is correct. The interest was earned while Mai was a non-resident, before she became a resident of Canada.   ITA: 2(3), 212(1)

(A) is incorrect. Only interest that is not fully exempt interest paid to a non-arm's length person and participating debt interest are subject to 25% withholding tax.   ITA: 212(1)(*b*)

(C) and (D) are incorrect. The interest was not earned during her period of residency.

Question 3

(D) is correct. As a resident of Canada, Antonio is taxed in Canada on his worldwide income. Canada provides a foreign tax credit to alleviate potential double taxation of the income.   ITA: 126(2)

(A) is incorrect. As a resident of Canada, Antonio is subject to tax on his world-wide income.

(B) is incorrect. Deductions for business foreign tax credits are not available in Division B of the ITA.

(C) is incorrect. Business income is sourced to the country in which the business activities are carried on (or where a permanent establishment is located under treaty). Brazil has jurisdiction to tax the income.

Question 4

(C) is correct. There are no tax consequences until Betty receives payments from her RRSP/RRIF, at which time, the payer will withhold tax on each payment.

(A) is not correct. Taxable Canadian property, as defined, does not include RRSPs.   ITA: 248(1)

(B) is not correct. Excluded rights or interests are exempt from deemed disposition at the time of emigration.   ITA: 128.1(10)

(D) is not correct. Only payments out of an RRSP are subject to withholding tax.   ITA: 212(1)(*e*)

Question 5

(B) is correct, for the reason stated in the question.

(A) and (C) are incorrect for the reason stated in (B).

(D) is incorrect. Bob would only need to file a U.S. form 1040NR in relation to an income producing property.

Question 6

(D) is correct. The company will be a controlled foreign affiliate of each of the Canadian shareholders because (i) it is a foreign affiliate (each shareholder owns not less than 1% of the shares and not less than 10% of the shares with related persons) of the company, and (ii) it is a controlled foreign affiliate because it is controlled by less than five unrelated Canadian residents. The income of the corporation will be FAPI because it will be considered income from property. The shareholder's participating percentage of the income as of the end of the affiliate's taxation year will be included in Division B income. A deduction for the related U.S. tax paid on the income calculated using the relevant tax factor will also be available.   ITA: 91(1)

(A) is incorrect. The income will be taxed annually. Dividends paid to the Canadian shareholders will be included in Division B income. Foreign tax credits will be available against Part I tax for U.S. tax withholdings. An offsetting deduction will be available for the lesser of the amount of the dividend and the cumulative total of prior year's net income inclusions for FAPI.

ITA: 12(1)

ITA: 126(1)

(B) is incorrect. The U.S. entity is a foreign investment entity. However, the foreign investment entity income inclusions do not apply because the investment is an exempt interest. An exempt interest includes a controlled foreign affiliate of the taxpayer.

ITA: 94.1(1)

(C) is incorrect. The income will be taxed annually. An offsetting deduction for a dividend is not available under Division C because the dividend is not received by a corporation and the dividend is not paid from exempt surplus.

ITA: 113(1)

Appendix I — Solutions to Exercises

Exercise 1

Alan is deemed to have disposed of the shares on emigration at their fair market value of $40,000. Given his ACB of $28,000, he will have a capital gain of $12,000, and a taxable capital gain of $6,000.

Alan can elect to defer paying the tax that results from the deemed disposition rule. The election must be made on or before the balance due date for the year in which emigration takes place. If the election is made, the payment of the tax can be deferred without interest until the properties are actually sold. Since security is not required for up to $100,000 of capital gains resulting from the deemed disposition rule, Alan will not be required to post security with the CRA.

Exercise 2

No, a foreign tax credit is not claimed in both countries. To do so would eliminate the taxes on the income altogether. The country where the income is sourced has the first right of taxation and consequently, a foreign tax credit is allowed only in the other country (the residence country).

A non-resident will pay the Canadian income taxes on income from duties of offices and employment performed in Canada, income from business carried on in Canada, and on capital gains. These taxes will then be used as a foreign tax credit in the country of residence. Note that some countries will recognize CPP/QPP contributions as taxes, in addition to any income taxes paid to Canada. Note that treaties can limit or eliminate a country's jurisdiction to tax source income. The country of residence will provide a tax credit only if taxes are paid.

Exercise 3

Canada levies tax on non-residents who carry on business in Canada. Carrying on business in Canada is distinguishable from carrying on business with Canada. While Sam-son solicits sales from Canadians, it does not solicit sales in Canada through an agent or servant. Given these facts, Sam-son is not carrying on business in Canada and is not liable for Canadian income taxes on the $76,000 profit originating from within Canada.

ITA: 2(3)

Exercise 4

The two corporations are considered associated (section 256) for Canadian tax purposes. Generally, under subsection 129(6), interest income received from an associated corporation that is deductible in computing that corporation's active business income would be considered active business income. However, as the interest is U.S.-sourced, and not from a "source in Canada", and is not deductible in computing active business income in Canada, it will be considered investment income to the Canadian corporation and not income from an active business. Hence, the small business deduction will not apply.

The interest will be subject to the full corporate tax rate, including the 6⅔% refundable tax on investment income. The addition to RDTOH (26⅔%) will also apply.

The second issue is whether any imputed interest income arises under subsection 17(1). That subsection allows that where interest is paid at less than the prescribed rate, the difference is income to the Canadian corporation. There is an exception if the interest paid is at a reasonable rate. As the 2% rate being paid is comparable to the U.S. borrowing rate, it is unlikely that any imputed income arises.

Exercise 5

The Act identifies the types of income a non-resident must declare in Canada, which include:

ITA: 115(1)

- income from an office or employment in Canada;

ITA: 115(1)(*a*)(i)

- income from a business carried on in Canada;

ITA: 115(1)(*a*)(ii)

- recapture of CCA on the disposition of property;

ITA: 115(1)(*a*)(iii.2)

- amounts arising from the sale of an income interest in a partnership in Canada;

ITA: 115(1)(*a*)(iv.1)

- taxable capital gain on the disposition of a life insurance policy;

ITA: 115(1)(*a*)(vi)

- taxable capital gains from disposition of taxable Canadian property (other than treaty protected properties);

ITA: 115(1)(*a*)(iii)

- exercised stock options;

ITA: 115(1)(*a*)(i)

- grants, scholarships.

ITA: 115(1)(*a*)(v)

Exercise 6

The Act defines "moving expenses" as including any expenses incurred as, or on account of, travel costs in the course of moving the taxpayer from the old residence to the new residence, cost of transporting or storing household effects, cost of meals and lodging, etc. It appears Mary Jane's expenses would qualify under this definition; however, the move must be an eligible relocation as defined by the Act. The definition of "eligible relocation" only includes relocations that are both from and to a residence in Canada.

ITA: 62(3)

ITA: 62(1); 248(1)

Exercise 7

Dutchco is a foreign affiliate of Canco as Canco owns not less than 10% of the shares of the company. Dutchco is a controlled foreign affiliate of Canco as it is controlled by a Canadian resident.

Dutchco is earning income from an active business in a country with which Canada has a tax convention. This income would be treated as exempt surplus. The company is also earning income from property. This income would be treated as FAPI and would become part of Dutchco's taxable surplus.

For 2008 and 2009, Canco must include, in respect of each share it owns in Dutchco, the share's participating percentage of FAPI less a deduction for the foreign accrual tax applicable to the FAPI income inclusion.

Income Inclusion	$ 9,600	80% of $12,000	*ITA: 91(1)*
Deduction	$(6,508)	20% of $9,600 multiplied by the relevant tax factor of $1/(38\% - 8.5\%)$	*ITA: 91(4)*
2008 Income Inclusion	$ 3,092		

Income Inclusion	$ 9,600	80% of $12,000	*ITA: 91(1)*
Deduction	$(6,620)	20% of $9,600 multiplied by the relevant tax factor of $1/(38\% - 9\%)$	*ITA: 91(4)*
2009 Income Inclusion	$ 2,980		

When the dividend is paid in 2009, it will be included in Canco's Division B income. A deduction is available for the portion of the dividend prescribed to have been paid from exempt surplus. Exempt surplus includes exempt earnings for any taxation year ending in the period that starts with the first day of the taxation year in which Dutchco became a foreign affiliate and ends at the time the dividend is paid. FAPI is included in taxable surplus in a similar manner. The exempt surplus and taxable surplus balances of Dutchco at the time of the dividend would be as follows:

ITA: 12(1)

	Exempt Surplus	Taxable Surplus	
Income for December 31, 2008 taxation year end of the affiliate	$30,000	$12,000	*ITR: 5907(1)*
Income/profits tax paid to Netherlands tax authorities	($ 6,000)	($ 2,400)	
Balance February 2009	$24,000	$ 9,600	

The portion of the whole dividend of $50,000 deemed to have been paid out of exempt surplus would be $24,000. The portion of the whole dividend deemed to have been paid out of taxable surplus would be $9,600. The remainder, of $16,400, would be considered to have been paid from pre-acquisition surplus.

The 2009 income inclusions less deductions for Canco related to the dividend would be as follows:

Dividend Income	$ 40,000	$50,000 × 80%	*ITA: 12(1)*
Deduction	$(19,200)	$24,000 × 80%	*ITA: 113(1)(a)*
Deduction	$ (3,133)	Lesser of: (1) $9,600 × 80%, and (2) $3,133 [$2,400 × 80% × (1/38% – 1)]	*ITA: 113(1)(b)*
	$ (1,324)	Lesser of: (1) $1,324 [$9,600 × 80% × 5% × 1/29%], and (2) $4,547 [$9,600 × 80% less: 113(1)(b) deduction of $3,133]	*ITA: 113(1)(c)*
	$ (3,092)	Lesser of: (1) $4,547 [$9,600 × 80% – 113(1)(b) of $3,133], and (2) 2008 net FAPI inclusion of $3,092	*ITA: 91(5)*
	$(13,120)	$16,400 × 80%	*ITA: 113(1)(d)*
Net Inclusion	$ 131		

The net inclusion represents the portion of the dividend considered to have been paid from taxable surplus, net the amount of the dividend that has already been taxed in the foreign jurisdiction: $3,223 [$9,600 × 80% less $3,133 (for underlying corporate tax) and less $1,324 (for withholding tax)], less a further $3,092 reduction to reverse the net FAPI inclusion from 2008 (preventing double taxation of the passive income earned in the CFA).

APPENDIX I